MEISTER ECKHART: MYSTIC

MEISTER ECKHART: MYSTICAL THEOLOGIAN

Oliver Davies

First published in Great Britain in 1991

Society for Promoting Christian Knowledge
36 Causton Street
London SW1P 4ST
www.spckpublishing.co.uk

Reissued 2011

British Library Cataloguing-in-Publication Data
A catalogue record for this book is available from the British Library

ISBN 978-0-281-06410-6

10 9 8 7 6 5 4 3 2 1

Typeset by Pioneer Associates, Perthshire
Printed in Great Britain by Ashford Colour Press

In memoriam Magistri Ekhardi

When genuine friends of God – such as was Eckhart to my way of thinking – repeat words they have heard in secret amidst the silence of the union of love, and these words are in disagreement with the teaching of the Church, it is simply that the language of the market place is not that of the nuptial chamber.

Simone Weil

CONTENTS

Acknowledgements   xi

Abbreviations   xiii

Introduction   1

PART I: MEISTER ECKHART'S BACKGROUND
1.   Ways of reading Meister Eckhart   11
2.   Meister Eckhart: the man   22
3.   Meister Eckhart and the religious women of the age   51
4.   Meister Eckhart and the German Dominican school   85

PART II: MEISTER ECKHART'S THOUGHT
5.   The Theology of Union   99
6.   The Imagery of Union   126
7.   The Spirituality of Union   160

PART III: UNDERSTANDING MEISTER ECKHART
8.   Meister Eckhart's Language   179
9.   Meister Eckhart and Christian Orthodoxy   195
10. The Influence of Meister Eckhart   215

Epilogue   235

Appendix I: Establishing the texts of Eckhart's   239
              German sermons

Appendix II: Eckhart as biblical exegete   242

Appendix III: A register of Eckhart's German sermons   244

Select Bibliography   247

Index   254

ACKNOWLEDGEMENTS

This book is the product of a life-long fascination with the person and work of Meister Eckhart. Along the way certain voices have cast particular light, and I should like to express my sincere gratitude to Cyprian Smith OSB, Richard Woods OP, Professor Bernard McGinn and Professor Alois Haas for much wisdom and encouragement. My thanks are due also, as ever, to the staff of SPCK for their help in the production of this book, especially to Judith Longman and Brendan Walsh.

Oliver Davies
March 1991

ABBREVIATIONS

B   Blakney, R. B., *Meister Eckhart.* New York, Harper and Row, 1941.

CL   Clark, J. M., *Meister Eckhart: an Introduction to the Study of his Works with an Anthology of his Sermons.* Edinburgh, Nelson, 1957.

CPTMA *Corpus philosophorum teutonicorum medii aevi.*

CS   Clark, J. M. and Skinner, J. V., *Treatises and Sermons of Meister Eckhart.* New York, Harper and Row, 1958.

DO   *Liber divinorum operum* (The Book of Divine Works) in Migne, Patrologia Latina 147.

DP   Quint, J., ed., *Meister Eckhart: deutsche Predigten und Traktate*, Munich 1963.

DS   *Dictionnaire de spiritualité.* Paris 1932ff.

DW   German works. *Meister Eckhart: Die deutschen und lateinischen Werke*, hrsg., im Auftrage der deutschen Forschungsgemeinschaft. Stuttgart and Berlin, Kohlhammer Verlag, 1936ff.

EE   Colledge, E. and McGinn, B., *Meister Eckhart: the Essential Sermons, Commentaries, Treatises and Defence.* New York, Paulist Press, 1981.

EV   Evans, C. de B., *Meister Eckhart by Franz Pfeiffer.* 2 vols., London 1924 and 1931.

LTK   *Lexikon für Theologie und Kirche.* Freiburg 1957.

LW   Latin works. *Meister Eckhart: Die deutschen und lateinischen Werke,* hrsg., im Auftrage der deutschen Forschungsgemeinschaft. Stuttgart and Berlin, Kohlhammer Verlag, 1936ff.

M   Maurer, A., *Master Eckhart: Parisian Questions and Prologues.* Toronto, Pontifical Institute of Medieval Studies, 1974.

PEPP   *Princeton Encyclopedia of Poetry and Poetics.* Princeton 1965.

PF   Pfeiffer, F., ed., *Meister Eckhart* (Deutsche
            Mystiker des Mittelalters Bd. 2). Leipzig 1987
            (repr. Scientia Verlag Aalen 1962).
PL   Patrologia Latina, Migne (ed.).
RS   *Rechtfertigungsschrift* (Defence).
SCH   Schürmann, R., *Meister Eckhart: mystic and
            philosopher*. Bloomington and London, 1978.
TI   Talks of Instruction.
TP   McGinn, B. with Tobin, F. and Borgstadt, E.,
            Meister Eckhart: Teacher and Preacher. Classics
            of Western Spirituality. London, SPCK; New
            York, Paulist Press, 1986.
VL   *Deutsche Literatur des Mittelalters: Verfasser-
            lexikon*. Berlin 1978ff.
W   Walshe, M. O'C., *Meister Eckhart: German
            Sermons and Treatises*. 3 vols., London and
            Dulverton, Element Books, 1979, 1981 and
            1985.

INTRODUCTION

One of the first things to strike someone who is anxious to deepen their knowledge of Meister Eckhart is the bewildering array of theories that surround him. There can have been few non-fictional figures who have played so diverse and fertile a role within the cultural imagination. He is both heretic and the 'man from whom God nothing hid'. He is Christian pastor and Buddhist sage. He is a Neoplatonist and an Aristotelian, prophet of feminism and ecological saint. He is a Protestant and a Catholic, the founder of an Aryan philosophical dynasty, a humanist inspiration to the modern writers of the erstwhile German Democratic Republic and the object of some considerable interest to modern philosophers and students of literary theory alike.[1] Meister Eckhart, it seems, is all things to all people. An appropriate way to begin this study therefore is by asking why it is that Eckhart has been interpreted in such different and often contradictory ways.

Firstly, and largely at the popular level, it must be admitted that the charm for some lies in the *marginality* of Eckhart within the Christian world, paramountly the condemnation by Pope John XXII of twenty-eight propositions taken from his work. Those interpreters who are keen to tease 'mysticism' away from its setting within dogmatic religion are quick to perceive in Eckhart a congenial spirit. Moreover, Eckhart's widespread use of rhetorical language (e.g. 'other masters tell you this . . . but I say to you') can only contribute to this trend and encourage the impression that Eckhart is a virtuosic spiritual master who stands in some critical sense outside the Church. Thus this highly complex and thoroughly scholastic theologian, whose thinking is deeply embedded in the conceptual structures of the Christian fourteenth century, can all too easily be swathed in ideas and attitudes which belong to conceptual and political worlds which are actually quite remote from his own.

But the academic world, too, has been strikingly divided in its assessment of Eckhart, although this is far less the case today. This has in part been the inevitable result of the unavailability of much of his Latin work, the difficulties in establishing a critical edition of his German sermons (a process which is still under way), together with a belated discovery of the importance and the character of the German Dominican school of theologians of which he was a part. But radical differences in opinion have been the result also of the rhetorical élan of much of what Eckhart wrote, which can at times contain starkly contradictory meanings.[2] And finally, of course, the sheer complexity of Meister Eckhart's thinking should not be underestimated.

In order to establish a reliable reading of Eckhart, one which is founded upon Eckhart's own meaning and not just our own concerns, we must first reconstruct the world which created him. This is not to undermine his originality, rather it is a vital stage in order to establish it, for until we know what comes from others, we cannot know what is his. Chapters 2, 3 and 4 will discuss the circumstances of Eckhart's life and career therefore, the influence of the women's spirituality of the age upon him, with whom he had such extensive contact, and that of his own German Dominican school. The analysis of his work, which comes in chapters 5, 6 and 7, will also seek to place his thought against the background of the scholastic and patristic theology which he inherited in order that its distinctness, as well as its indebtedness to tradition, can emerge. Chapters 8, 9 and 10 will evaluate Eckhart's use of language, his orthodoxy and character as a Christian mystic, and the matter of his influence. The epilogue will review general conclusions and attempt to evaluate the meaning of Eckhartian spirituality within the context of our modern world.

Before looking in more detail at the different ways in which Meister Eckhart has been understood over the centuries, we should turn our attention to a major question which arises at the very outset of this study, namely that concerning the *status* of Eckhart's work. Are we to regard him as a mystic or a theologian, or is he both? The answer given here is that he is both, but a mystic first and a theologian second.[3] This is an important point for it means that we shall read his theology as *an instrument for the articulation* of what is essentially a mystical, and therefore experiential, vision. Thus theology, and the language in which it is written, becomes a medium through which Meister Eckhart seeks to express and to convey the quality and character of his own sense of an existential encounter with God. It is by no means the case that all commentators accept an experiential basis to Eckhart's thinking, and it is evident that such a thing is not easy to 'prove'. But in the light of the fact that Eckhart seems to have been received in his own time as a preacher with a spiritual message, and certainly has been widely seen as such since his rediscovery in the modern period, the onus is upon those who would deny such an experiential basis to Eckhart's work to 'prove' their case. This too is not easily done. After all, what specific grounds do we have for denying to Eckhart what no one would think to deny for John of the Cross or Julian of Norwich? Moreover, as Kurt Ruh has written, to contest that Eckhart in some way experienced the realities of which he wrote is at the same time to contest his 'inner truth', and is to suggest that Eckhart's system, bereft of the inner life of experience, is a monstrous compilation of second-hand ideas.[4] Eckhart himself gives short shrift to those who write of things they do not themselves know when he says: 'a master of life (*lebemeister*) is worth more than a thousand masters of books (*lesemeister*)',[5] and the urgency of his communication ('If no one had been here, I should have had to preach it [this sermon] to this collecting box': W 56) demands to be understood as an appeal from experience to experience.[6]

To the extent therefore that Eckhart's teaching communicates lived experience, he stands within the classical Dominican tradition of *contemplata aliis tradere* ('handing on to others what has been learned through meditation'),

which is summed up in the words of another leading
Dominican, Humbert of the Romans: *In contemplatione
hauriunt quod postmodum in praedicatione effundunt* ('they
drink in through meditation those things which they later
pour forth in their preaching').[7]

But if Eckhart stands within the Dominican tradition of
sharing the fruits of *contemplatio*, then it is also true that
his conception of God as 'the Word which speaks itself'
lends a particular colour to his spirituality and his teaching.
Eckhart's thinking centres on the concept of God as a form
of knowing self-reflection, which flows out of itself and
floods back into itself as the divine Word.[8] The dynamic and
relational aspect of the divinity is thus conveyed through the
imagery of utterance, and it is the Word in its unbounded
fertility which becomes the medium for the creation of all
things. But our own essence, which is itself a form of
knowing, stands in a particularly close relation to the divine
self-knowing, and it is this, the area of our own inner
depths, which becomes the fertile place in which the Word
itself is born in us.

It is the communication of that sense or experience of the
birth of the Word in us which is the inspirational centre of
the Eckhartian system.[9] For the flooding energies of God
which are contained in the Word are the sign of his 'essential
relatedness' and 'substantial openness' to us.[10] The relatedness of God is speech and 'we know that in speaking we too
are drawn into the speech of God which supports us and
unites us and which as a free, personal relatedness to us
occurs ever anew'.[11] But the divine Word 'which speaks
itself' is in essence a trinitarian model, and so, following the
many Christian trinitarian mystics before him, Eckhart is
telling us that we too can be drawn up into the inner life of
the Trinity where we can enjoy God in his unity and his
diversity.

Eckhart is certainly unusual in the Christian mystical
tradition in that the paradigm with which he maps out our
union with God is an intellective one. It is a union founded
upon the mind and upon the act of knowing which is

intrinsic to the mind. Thus the experience which underlies
Eckhart's system and which he is constantly seeking to
convey *is itself a form of thought*,[12] albeit one which touches
on the fulness of our personhood. This fact leads to two
characteristic qualities of Eckhart's writing. The first is the
fact that Eckhart likes to disrupt our thought patterns in
order to lead us on to a higher, more essential form of
knowledge, which remains always elusive and a goal to be
reached. The use of contradiction, therefore, and the shifting
interplay of images that we find in Eckhart, are intentional
and serve this end. The second is the systematically abstract
nature of Eckhart's language together with his preference
for *verbal imagery*, which is to say themes and images
which derive from the processes of language itself. The
reasons for this are complex and shall receive due attention
at a later stage, but we can say here that they lead Eckhart
to believe that it is necessary to strip away all knowledge of
created things in order to release that part of the mind (what
he calls the 'spark') which is capable of knowing God as he
is in his essence. Eckhart systematically suppresses the
created dimension in his sermons therefore, both by making
his language rigorously abstract and by holding before his
audience the possibility of breakthrough, from images of the
created world, into transcendental knowledge of the
uncreated Creator.

Eckhart's use of language in an *intentional* way, turning
upon the use of contradiction, paradox and the suppression
of the created dimension, can further contribute to the
possibilities of misunderstanding. It is easy to see Eckhart
as being concerned with a mysticism of the mind alone, free
from any doctrinal input. But the combination of transcendental knowing and ordinary physical forms of knowing sets up
in his work a marked form of dialectical tension. The two
seem pure contraries: knowing the uncreated and knowing
the created, and yet they coexist, for Eckhart, within the
human mind. This interpenetration of the human and the
divine is thus a deeply felt tension in Eckhart's work, which
the rhetorical suppression of 'createdness' does little to

diminish. And it is a sign also of the fact that Eckhart stands closer to the paradox of God made flesh, and ultimately that of God crucified on the cross, than might at first glance appear.

NOTES TO INTRODUCTION

1. References to these trends in the interpretation of Meister Eckhart will be found in chapter 2 below, and in the Epilogue. We find extensive reference to Eckhart in Hanns Cibulka, *Wegscheide Tagebucherzählung* (Halle and Liepzig 1988), and Alois Haas has a discussion of the marxist view of Eckhart in his 'Maître Eckhart dans le miroir de l'idéologie marxiste' in *La Vie Spirituelle*, 53 (1971), pp. 62–79. See also 'Meister Eckhart im Spiegel der Marxistischen Ideologie' in Haas (1979), pp. 238–54.
2. Etienne Gilson sums up the problem of diversity in the field of Eckhart interpretation wonderfully well when he says in his Foreword to V. Lossky's important study (1960): 'The doctor from Thuringia does not lack historians, amongst whom there are some excellent ones. There is no difficulty in finding a good interpretation of Eckhart, the problem rather is to choose between so many interpretations which while coherent and founded upon irrefutable texts are sometimes so different as to be contradictory. In fact, nothing is easier than to reduce Eckhart to a system founded upon one's own evidence; the problem is that after having done so, one will see that one could just as easily have constructed quite a different system, even though based upon texts which are just as authentic as the other. This is certainly one of those occasions when an abundance of goods is a form of poverty' (p. 9).
3. This seems to be the opinion of Josef Quint, too, when he says: 'Eckhart is a scholastic mystic and not a mystical scholastic', Quint (1928), p. 674.
4. Ruh (1985), p. 189. See also Haas (1974), pp. 79–81. It seems astonishing that Bizet (DS, VII 1, 234) and Vandenbroucke (*History of Christian Spirituality* II, p. 391) can suggest that Suso alone of the Rhineland mystics actually experienced the realities of which he wrote. The grounds for this view must be the existence of a text in which Suso's visionary experiences are described! When Kurt Flasch

contests the status of Eckhart as a 'mystic', he does so on the basis of a suspect opposition between philosophy as rationality and mysticism as a form of irrationality (Flasch [1974], pp. 301ff.); see also the remarks of Alois Haas on this in Haas (1989b), p. 10, and (1984), pp. 200ff.

5. Pfeiffer, p. 599 (quoted in Haas [1974], p. 83).

6. In quoting from Eckhart's sermons, I am using the edition by Walshe (unless otherwise stated). The following figure refers to the number of the sermon from which the extract is taken *according to Walshe's own numeration.* Appendix III provides a table with which to collate the different editions and translations of the sermons.

7. Thomas Aquinas, *Summa Theologiae*, III, q. 40, a. I, ad 2. The second quotation is given in Haas (1984), pp. 69f. For Humbert of Romans, see Simon Tugwell, *Ways of Imperfection* (London 1984), pp. 138–51.

8. Kurt Flasch brilliantly captures this idea in his article 'Die Intention Meister Eckharts' (1974). See also Alois Haas' comments in 'Meister Eckhart und die Sprache' in Haas (1984).

9. There are difficulties with the word 'experience' of course in the context of mysticism. What I mean here is not the more dramatic epiphenomena of the interpenetration of human and divine life, but that which corresponds to the 'existential knowledge' of God of which Hans Urs von Balthasar speaks in his 'Zur Ortsbestimmung christlicher Mystik' in *Pneuma und Institution. Skizzen zur Theologie* IV, (Einsiedeln 1974), p. 302 and *Herrlichkeit* I (Einsiedeln 1961), p. 287.

10. Flasch (1974), p. 302; quoted in Haas (1984), p. 75.

11. Haas (1984), p. 77.

12. Haas (1974), p. 92.

PART ONE

MEISTER ECKHART'S BACKGROUND

1 • WAYS OF READING MEISTER ECKHART

The year 1857 might seem an appropriate place to begin a sketch of the different critical responses there have been to Eckhart's work. This was the year in which Franz Pfeiffer published his edition of the German sermons and treatises and, despite the many problems associated with this early edition, it marks the point at which a substantial part of Eckhart's works first became available to a large audience.[1] Modern interest in Eckhart predates this event however, and the rediscovery of his work must be seen in the light of the achievement of the Romantic movement, which made such a contribution to German life and letters. In England Romanticism is remembered today chiefly in terms of the poets it produced (such as Wordsworth and Coleridge), but in Germany, the movement as a whole penetrated and formed many aspects of national and cultural life during the late-eighteenth and early-nineteenth centuries. The intellectual leaders of Romanticism in Germany, figures such as Johann Gottfried Herder and the Schlegel brothers, were concerned to explore what was described as the 'national spirit'. There was a new interest in the folksongs of the countryside (e.g. *Des Knaben Wunderhorn* by Arnim and Brentano) and in folktales (e.g. the collection gathered by the Grimm brothers, which proved also to be so popular in the English-speaking world), and there was a determination to discover more of the medieval past. The centuries of the Enlightenment had left an appetite for what was mysterious, infinite and transcendent, and this new sensibility found an adequate expression not only in the work of German poets (typified by Novalis' *Hymns to the Night*) but also in the rediscovery of the texts of medieval piety. The point has been made that at first the interest was overwhelmingly a naive and spiritual one; only slowly was that other great achievement of Romanticism, the desire to order and catalogue the past, applied to the newly discovered texts.[2] Initially therefore we must see the rediscovery of Eckhart in the context of the German rediscovery of their national medieval past, together with a hunger for *mysticism*, which seemed to speak of new and exciting realities beyond the limits of the world and the self.

But in the case of Meister Eckhart a very specific kind of modern interest soon made itself felt. Unlike his better-known contemporaries, Johannes Tauler and Henry Suso (also known by his German name of Heinrich Seuse), Eckhart seemed to speak a philosophical language, and one which was uncannily like that of much contemporary philosophical discourse. One of the themes which greatly exercised thinkers of the day was the gulf which the Enlightenment had created between reason and faith. *Franz von Baader*, a philosopher from Munich, is the first to draw attention to Eckhart in the context of the modern struggle to draw faith and reason back towards a central unity. Baader saw in Eckhart a master of mystical speculation from the past who represented the reconciliation of philosophy and theology. Through speculative mysticism, Baader thought, life could be breathed again into contemporary religion, which would then draw upon both reason and experience. Franz von Baader can thus be seen as the founder of modern Eckhart studies. It was he, too, who encouraged *Friedrich Hegel*'s interest in Eckhart. Hegel is one of the great philosophers of the nineteenth century, and a life-long concern of his was to unite philosophy (or reason) with faith (or revelation). Once again, Hegel's interest in Eckhart stems from the fact that, though he was clearly a Catholic religious (and a medieval one moreover), Hegel judged Eckhart to have held views which were very similar to his own, and thus to support Hegel's theory that religion and philosophy were essentially one.

Hegel's efforts to unite his own Philosophy of Spirit with the received truths of the Christian religion constituted an attack, in the eyes of some Protestant scholars, upon the integrity of faith itself. The first major study of Meister Eckhart therefore, which was by a Protestant scholar from

Strasburg (Carl Schmidt, 1839), sought to distance Eckhart
from the Christian religion.[3] In Schmidt's study, Eckhart
emerges both as a brilliantly original thinker who freed
himself from the shackles of scholasticism, and at the same
time as an arch-pantheist, whose teachings, which sought to
relativize dogmatic truths, were ultimately no more recon-
cilable with the Christian religion than were those of Hegel
himself. And so we find even at the very beginning of
modern Eckhart studies that Eckhart is pulled to and fro by
the powerful currents of contemporary tendentiousness and
polemics although, as Degenhardt points out, the critical
study of Eckhart in fact owes more to his involvement in the
Idealist controversy than it does to the Romantic discovery
of his work as pious and edifying literature.[4]

Prior to the publication in 1857 of Pfeiffer's edition of
Eckhart's German works, virtually the only texts of Eckhart
which were available were those sermons which had been
included in the Basle edition of Tauler's sermons, itself a
rarity. The Pfeiffer edition therefore stimulated further and
generally more scholarly interest in Eckhart, who began to
attract the attention of historians and theologians alike.
Several themes emerge from this early stage of Eckhart
studies. Firstly, Eckhart was anti-scholastic (a positive
attribute in an age which was itself determinedly anti-
scholastic), and represented a living mysticism in the face of
a dry, bone-picking philosophizing. Associated with this
liberation from scholasticism, Eckhart is seen also as a
German thinker who freed (for the first time) the German
spirit from the fetters of an international and essentially
alien way of thought. He is thus the 'father of German
speculation'.[5] With this discovery of Eckhart as a specifically
German theologian/philosopher, who stressed neither the
clerus nor the value of works, he soon came to be seen as the
forerunner of that other German theology: the Lutheran
Reformation.[6] And indeed, some Protestant scholars came
to see Meister Eckhart, and German mysticism in general,
as being radically opposed to the forms of the Roman
Catholic Church. Two further perceptions of Eckhart emerge
in this period, which have exercised some considerable

influence down to the present day. The first is the view of Eckhart as a pantheist, who teaches that there is no distinction between God and his creatures, and the second is that approach to Eckhart which sees him as an advocate of a form of spirituality which is free of all dogmatic assertions and all forms of Church affiliation. As Degenhardt points out, this latter approach is one which undoubtedly has a dubious appeal to the secularity of our own time.[7]

The Catholic response to Eckhart up to this point had been muted. Joseph Bach and F. X. Linsenmann had shown an awareness of the fact that Eckhart belonged to the scholastic tradition, but it was the brilliant and formidable figure of Heinrich Seuse Denifle who discovered and published some of the Latin works of Eckhart and, for the first time, set the Meister fairly and squarely within the medieval philosophical context of Catholic scholastic thinking. Denifle, a Tyrolean Dominican whose mind was as sharp as his tongue, stripped away much that was shallow in contemporary thinking on Eckhart. He argued that Eckhart owed a great deal to the international Catholic tradition of which he was a part and that in no way did he represent a specifically German, Idealist or Protestant kind of thinking. What was valuable in Eckhart, Denifle argued, was the general scholastic achievement, while what was original in him was both bad and heterodox, and thus deserving of the Church's condemnation. In Denifle's hands, therefore, Eckhart emerges as 'a mediocre student of Thomas Aquinas'.[8] Although Denifle's judgement of Eckhart (from the perspective of a narrow neo-Thomism) has been entirely superseded, his recognition that the sharp distinction between 'mysticism' and 'scholasticism' was a spurious one and, above all, his passionate belief that Eckhart can only be properly understood within the context of scholastic thinking were of lasting value.

Denifle was particularly dismissive of Meister Eckhart's German works, and this, strangely, had positive results. Initially, the *Germanisten*, or scholars of German literature, had been lukewarm in their response to Eckhart's vernacular writings, which seemed so very different from the poetry of the High Middle Ages that was so much in fashion at the time, and they had left the field of Eckhart studies in general to those with theological and philosophical interests. Denifle's attacks on Eckhart as German thinker and writer awoke a new-found interest in Eckhart among the German literary scholars. Phillip Strauch, in particular, came to the defence of Eckhart as a wonderful and innovative German stylist and a founding father of the German prose tradition. Towards the end of the nineteenth century, there grew up around Strauch at Halle a thriving school of Eckhart studies, which did much to rehabilitate the mystic's name.

But it was not until the beginning of the twentieth century that the name of Eckhart began to be known in wider circles. This increased popularity, with all its attendant evils, was the result largely of a brilliantly modernised (though compromised) translation by Hermann Büttner, which became a best-seller and which succeeded in presenting Eckhart as a spiritual father of the modern neo-Romantic mood of anti-institutional and subjective religiosity. A number of writers and artists eagerly took up Eckhart's cause as a variety of 'Eckhart novels' and 'Eckhart poems' appeared during these years, plunging the Dominican into yet deeper mists of romance and notoriety. Büttner had argued that Eckhart stood for a new phase of the Christian religion, which was neither Catholic nor Protestant but which was founded upon our own innate spiritual powers. The whole apparatus of the Christian Church and of Christian doctrine becomes redundant when we are united with the ground of our own souls. This seriously distorted view of Eckhart himself was to become tragically grotesque when it came to the eager attention of the National Socialists. In the hands of Alfred Rosenberg (*Der Mythos des 20 Jahrhunderts*, 1933), the so-called 'philosopher' of the Nazi party, Meister Eckhart became the 'greatest apostle of the Teutons', whose work belonged in every German house.[9] The marked anti-Christian trend in Büttner's work becomes rabid polemic against the Churches in the Nazi appropriation of Eckhart, as the party seeks to found a new Germanic religion of vitalism, strength and racial purity on the basis of an ignorant and superficial reading of Hermann Büttner's interpretive rendering of selections from the works of the fourteenth-century Dominican.

During these dark years of a popular misrepresentation of Eckhart's thinking, some real progress was made however at the scientific level with the publication of a number of important documents relating to Eckhart's trial. And, for the first time, the disparaging judgement of Denifle was seriously questioned on the Catholic side. Otto Karrer (*Meister Eckehart: Das System seiner Religiösen Lehre und Lebensweisheit*, 1926) was the first to make the vital point that Eckhart is not a 'failed Thomist', but belongs rather to an alternative school of late medieval Neoplatonic and Augustinian scholasticism. Karrer also argued strongly for Eckhart's orthodoxy (as did Herma Piesch, a pupil of his, and Alois Dempf), while Herbert Grundmann, an ex-pupil of Denifle, stoutly defended his own teacher's position. Controversy reigned also in the Protestant camp. Here the clash was between those who wished to see in Eckhart a forerunner of the Reformation, and those Protestant theologians who believed that a form of mysticism which preached union of the soul with God in his essence was ultimately irreconcilable with the Christian gospel. This controversy to some extent turned on the relation between Eckhart and Luther.[10]

The fruit of this intensification of scientific interest in Eckhart led to the initiation of an ambitious project which aimed at editing his complete works. In 1934 R. Klibansky published the first of three fascicles of Latin texts and, in 1936, J. Koch (Latin) and J. Quint (German) launched an edition of the complete works under the auspices of the *Deutsche Forschungsgemeinschaft*, which is still under way at the present day (see Appendix I).

The last two decades have seen an expansion of critical comment on the work of Meister Eckhart. The contemporary interest in him within the context of Christian dialogue with other religions began as early as 1891. Rudolf Otto's comparative study of Eckhart and Sankara (*West-Östliche Mystik*) appeared in 1926 and this was followed by a number of studies which, with varying degrees of success, have sought to find common ground between Eckhart and either the Zen Buddhist or Hindu traditions.[11]

A second area of concern has been with the status of Eckhart as a mystic, with some dissenting voices e.g. H. Fischer (1974). A. Haas, in *Nim din selbes war*, Freiburg, Switzerland, 1971, showed that the process of self-knowledge in Eckhart is itself the discovery of the way of salvation, while D. Mieth (1969) has stressed the interdependence, even identity, of the ontological and ethical dimension in Eckhart, the 'social' mystic. In French, V. Lossky (1960) and F. Brunner (1969) have examined the mystical overtones of Eckhart's theory of analogy.

A third branch of concern has been to challenge the idea of Meister Eckhart as a *Randfigur* within the Christian mystical tradition and to argue, rather, for his centrality. Two books in particular have this as their aim: *Meister Eckhart als Normative Gestalt Geistlichen Lebens*, by Alois Haas (1979), and *Meister Eckhart: the Way of Paradox*, by Cyprian Smith (1987). Both these writers are leading Eckhart scholars, and these books well mediate the Meister's thought to a broader audience. It is also to this category of book that the several popular anthologies of Eckhart's work belong.[12]

A fourth line of research has been a close examination of Eckhart's metaphysics. This has concentrated on his ontology (theory of being) and system of analogy, the roots of which lie in a Neoplatonist metaphysics.[13] Eckhart has also come to be seen in relation to his own German Dominican school of radical Augustinianism. Researches into the work of Albert the Great and Dietrich von Freiberg in particular have cast much light on Eckhart's teaching on the human intellect.[14]

Finally we may mention one line of enquiry which has also proved valuable in recent years, and which is all too easily ignored. This is research into Eckhart the stylist, which has explored the distinctive character of Eckhart's language as a vehicle for the communication of mystical concepts and experience.[15]

Meister Eckhart in the English-speaking world

Interest in the Rhineland mystics began with Susanne Winkworth's translation of the *Theologia Deutsch* in 1854 (with a foreword by Charles Kingsley). This was quickly followed by translations of works by Tauler (1857) and Henry Suso (1865). Eckhart himself did not appear in English until C. de B. Evans translated Pfeiffer's edition in two volumes (1924–31). Meister Eckhart's German prose is not easy to translate, and the modern English reader is well-served with good recent translations of selections from the Latin works by Maurer (1974) and from the German and the Latin works by McGinn and Colledge (1981), and McGinn with Frank Tobin and Elvira Borgstädt (1986). The last two books in particular have valuable and substantial introductions. The complete German sermons and treatises are available in three volumes in an authoritative translation by M. O'C Walshe.[16]

Although it is true to say that the greater part of original Eckhart scholarship has originated from the German-speaking world, there are a number of figures from Britain and America who have made a valuable contribution to our understanding in their own right. Foremost among these are Bernard McGinn, Frank Tobin, Edmund Colledge and Reiner Schürmann, some of whom, including Richard Woods, have in particular presented a strong defence of Eckhart's orthodoxy.[17] A major study by C. F. Kelley (1977) attains an awesome degree of theoretical complexity, detached from any clear historical analysis, and has made as yet little impact on the scholarly world. At the other end of the spectrum, Matthew Fox's interest in Eckhart seems to be determined by his desire to represent him as a forerunner of his own 'creation-centred spirituality', which leads to a highly partial and selective reading of Eckhart's complete work.[18]

The achievement of Eckhart studies

This all too brief overview of the reception of Meister Eckhart during the last two centuries highlights two things. The first is that the least satisfactory readings of him occur where the interpreter is strongly committed to a particular ideological viewpoint. The following splendid quotation from the philosopher, Arthur Schopenhauer, is powerfully representative of just this kind of view:

> What Buddha, Eckhart and I teach is essentially the same, though Eckhart is burdened by the fetters of his Christian mythology. In Buddhism the same ideas exist, untarnished by any such mythology, and thus they are simple and clear, in so far as any religion can be clear. But in my work there exists total clarity.[19]

And from the earliest days to the present, Eckhart's teachings do seem to lend themselves to this kind of eccentric or imbalanced reception, whether in the cause of Idealism, an undoctrinal Universal Religion, 'creation-centred spirituality' or, less happily, forms of tendentiousness which derive from fascist or communist ideologies. The growth in understanding of Eckhart has been slow and has been achieved by the careful scholarly reconstruction of his life, his works and his world. Needless to say, these are the sole parameters within which Eckhart can be seen *on his terms*, as he was in actuality, and not as we would choose him to be.

NOTES TO CHAPTER 1

1. For this section I have drawn extensively on Ingeborg Degenhardt's invaluable study, *Studien zum Wandel des Eckhartbildes* (1967). Toni Schaller, in his 'Die Meister-Eckhart Forschung von der Jahrhundertwende bis zur Gegenwart' in the *Freiburger Zeitschrift für Philosophie und Theologie*, 15 (1968), pp. 262–316 and 403–26 and his 'Zur Eckhart-Deutung der letzten 30 Jahre' in *Freiburger Zeitschrift für Philosophie und Theologie*, 16 (1969), pp. 22–39 also provides a useful account of the Eckhart literature. See also L. Sturlese, 'Recenti studi su Eckhart' in *Giornale critico dalla filosofia italiana*, an. LXVI (LXVIII), fasc. II (Florence 1987), pp. 368–77. *The Thomist*, 42 (1978), pp. 313–26 contains an extensive bibliography. See also W. Fues (1981) for a

thematic bibliography (pp. 425–63) and a discussion of Eckhart criticism. For an examination of the response to Eckhart in the period up to the seventeenth century, see 'The Influence of Meister Eckhart', pp. 215–34 below.

2. G. Fischer, *Die Wiederentdeckung der Mystiker im 19 Jahrhundert* (Freiburg 1931), p. 29 (quoted in Degenhardt, p. 108).

3. 'Meister Eckhart: Ein Beitrag zur Geschichte der Theologie und Philosophie des Mittelalters' in *Theologische Studien und Kritiken*, 12 (1839), pp. 663–744.

4. Degenhardt (1967), p. 131.

5. e.g. J. Bach, *Meister Eckhart, der Vater der deutschen Spekulation* (Vienna 1864).

6. e.g. C. Ullmann, *Reformatoren vor der Reformation* (Gotha 1866).

7. Degenhardt (1967), p. 155.

8. Degenhardt (1967), p. 182.

9. Degenhardt (1967), pp. 261f.

10. For a discussion of some of the issues involved, see below, pp. 225–7.

11. Karl Eugen Neumann, *Die innere Verwandtschaft buddistischer und christlicher Lehre* (Leipzig 1891). It must be said that this kind of inter-theological exchange, while stimulating, is fraught with difficulty (see below, pp. 212–13). Rudolf Otto's book appeared in English in 1932 under the title *Mysticism East and West*. See also Reiner Schürmann, 'Trois penseurs du délaissement, Maître Eckhart, Heidegger, Suzuki' in *Journal of the History of Philosophy*, 12, 4 (October 1974), pp. 455–78, and 13, 1 (January 1975), pp. 333–418; Bernard Barzel, *Mystique de l'ineffable dans l'hinduisme et le christianisme: Sankara et Eckhart* (Paris: Editions du Cerf, 1982); Shizuteru Ueda, '"Nothingness" in Meister Eckhart and Zen Buddhism' in *The Buddha Eye: an Anthology of the Kyoto School* (New York, Crossroad, 1982) (repr. from *Tranzendenz und Immanenz: Philosophie und Theologie in der veränderten Welt*, D. Papenfuss and J. Söring, eds, [Berlin 1977]); D. T. Suzuki, 'Meister Eckhart and Buddhism' in *Mysticism Christian and Buddhist* (New York, Harper and Row, 1971), pp. 3–38.

12. For example, German: Josef Quint, *Meister Eckhart: Deutsche Predigten und Traktate* (1955); Dietmar Mieth, *Meister Eckhart: Einheit im Sein und Wirken* (1979); English: Ursula

Fleming, *Meister Eckhart: the Man from whom God Nothing Hid* (1988); my own *The Rhineland Mystics: an anthology* (1989); and on a more scholarly level Edmund Colledge and Bernard McGinn, *The Essential Eckhart* (1981), and Bernard McGinn, *Meister Eckhart: Teacher and Preacher* (1986).

13. Here we might mention in particular: Karl Albert, *Meister Eckharts These vom Sein: Untersuchungen zur Metaphysik des Opus Tripartitum* (1976); Alain de Libera, *Le problème de l'être chez Maître Eckhart: Logique et Métaphysique de l'analogie* (1980); Bernard McGinn, 'Meister Eckhart on God as Absolute Unity' in D. O'Meara, ed., *Neo-Platonism and Christian Thought* (1982), pp. 128–37; Burkhard Mojsisch, *Meister Eckhart: Analogie, Univozität und Einheit* (1983); Émilie zum Brunn and Alain de Libera, *Métaphysique du Verbe et théologie négative* (1984).

14. See Kurt Flasch, ed., *Von Meister Dietrich zu Meister Eckhart* (1984); Alain de Libera, *Introduction à la Mystique Rhénane d'Albert le Grand à Maître Eckhart* (1984); Burkhard Mojsisch, *Theorie des Intellekts bei Dietrich von Freiberg* (1984).

15. See Alois Haas, *Sermo Mysticus: Studien zu Theologie und Sprache der deutschen Mystik* (1979); and 'Meister Eckhart und die Sprache: Sprachgeschichtliche und sprachtheologische Aspekte seiner Werke' in *Geistliches Mittelalter* (1984); J. Margetts, *Der Satzstruktur bei Meister Eckhart* (1969); Joseph Quint, 'Mystik und Sprache' in Kurt Ruh, ed., *Altdeutsche und altniederländische Mystik* (1964), pp. 113–51; Frank Tobin, *Meister Eckhart: Thought and Language* (1986). There is an extensive bibliography of works on Eckhart's language in Toni Schaller's 'Zur Eckhart-Deutung der letzten 30 Jahre' in *Freiburger Zeitschrift für Philosophie und Theologie*, 16 (1969), pp. 31f.

16. It must be said, however, that despite the skills of his English translators, there is much in the vigour and expressivity of Eckhart's style which proves resistant to translation.

17. Woods (1986), pp. 151–219, and McGinn (1980), pp. 390–414. But see also E. Colledge, 'Eckhart's Orthodoxy reconsidered' in *New Blackfriars*, Vol. 71 (1990), pp. 176–84.

18. See my article in *The Tablet* (5 August 1989), pp. 890f.

19. Quoted in Degenhardt (1967), p. 158.

2 • MEISTER ECKHART: THE MAN

It requires some considerable imagination and not a little audacity to reconstruct somebody's personality from the bare bones of their biography. In the medieval period, this unenviable task is further undermined by the fact that more often than not what is presented as fact for the sake of convenience turns out on closer inspection to be mere supposition. This is certainly the case with Meister Eckhart who, despite the extent of his achievements, has left only fragmentary traces of his life's course.[1]

The uncertainty begins with his name, which is given variously in early manuscripts as Eckhart, Ekhart, Eggert etc. (or in Latin: Aycardus, Equardus, Eycardus etc.). The Latin form which is used in the only letter in Eckhart's own hand which has come down to us is Ekhardus. We possess no contemporary attestation for the first name Johannes (John). There has also been much uncertainty concerning his provenance. A sermon given on the occasion of the feast day of St Augustine refers to Eckhart as 'Echardus de Hochheim', and we can assume that Eckhart was born in Thuringia (in the eastern part of Germany), which is the province in which Erfurt is to be found, where Eckhart had his early education. But there are two villages called Hochheim in Thuringia, one near Gotha and one near Erfurt itself. Recent work strongly suggests that 'de Hochheim' was in fact a familial name by this time and that Eckhart came from the village of Tambach, which lies to the south of Gotha, and was of noble stock.[2]

The first sure date we possess for an outline of his life is 18th April 1294, the day on which Eckhart delivered the Easter sermon at the university of Paris.[3] The manuscript in which this sermon is preserved speaks of him as a *lector sententiarum* or 'reader of the sentences'. The 'sentences' referred to are Peter Lombard's *Sententiae*, the standard theological textbook of the Middle Ages. Young theology students who had completed their study of the Arts (grammar, logic and rhetoric) and were already Bachelors of Divinity would deliver a series of lectures explicating this lengthy work, which covered all aspects of theology. This commentary on the *Sentences* was often the first substantial work of the major medieval theologians. Unfortunately, it is still a matter of dispute as to whether Eckhart's own commentary survives.[4] What certainly is Eckhart's, however, is the *Collatio in libros Sententiarum*. This is the first part of the *principium*, which describes the themes of the sermon on the *Sentences* which was to follow. The *Collatio* can accordingly be dated to between the 14th September and the 9th October 1293.[5]

The above dates accord well with the usual supposed date of Eckhart's birth, around the year 1260. Although we have no evidence for this period, we would surmise that he joined the Dominican Order (the local priory at Erfurt) when he was fifteen years old. Josef Koch has argued that his early training in the Arts may have been at Paris, where in the year 1277 he would have witnessed at first hand Bishop Tempier's condemnation of 219 articles (including some drawn from the work of Thomas Aquinas).[6] In the Faculty of Arts, he would also have heard Siger of Brabant. The latter was a controversial figure and the leader of the Averroist movement, who lent greater weight to some of the principles of Aristotelian philosophy than was judged acceptable. The rules of the Dominican Order at this time allowed two students from each province to study at Paris, although it is not known with any certainty whether Eckhart was indeed one of these. We possess no firm evidence either that he later studied at the Dominican *studium generale* in Cologne, although it is generally assumed that he did so. This was a distinguished centre of studies which had been founded in 1248 by Albert the Great, one of the foremost theologians of the day, whose work exercised an undoubted influence upon Eckhart. Here Eckhart may actually have overlapped with Albert, who had himself taught the young Thomas Aquinas, and who died as a very old man in Cologne in 1280. Eckhart is likely to have been involved in elementary teaching within the Dominican Order, and possibly at his home priory of Erfurt, until his appearance as a reader of Lombard's *Sentences* at Paris in 1293.

Some light is thrown on Eckhart's subsequent career by his first surviving German work, the *Spiritual Counsels* or *Talks of Instruction (Rede der underscheidunge)*. A reference in the title of this collection of talks indicates that Eckhart was both the Prior of the Dominican convent in Erfurt and the Vicar of Thuringia. Both of these posts involved pastoral duties: the former within the convent itself, and the latter among a number of women's convents of the province for which the Dominican Order bore responsibility. After 1298 these two posts could no longer be held by the same person (one necessitated residence in the convent and the other travel away from it).[7] Since Eckhart cannot have remained Prior after 1300, when all the Priors in Teutonia were changed, and yet did not arrive in Paris for his second period of residence there until 1302, it is perhaps likely that he chose to renounce his position as prior in 1298 and stayed on as vicar. If this is the case, then it might point to an early preference on the part of Eckhart for pastoral work, which is a theme to which we shall later return. The *Talks of Instruction* can be dated to a period between the time of his departure from Paris in 1294 and 1298. In 1302, Eckhart returned to Paris as *magister actu regens* (professor with a teaching commitment).

On the basis of his previous studies, Eckhart took up for a year one of the two Parisian chairs of Theology.[8] Relatively few pieces of his work survive from this period: two formal disputes (*Quaestiones*), as well as a dispute with a Franciscan Master of Theology, Gonsalvus of Valvoa, and a sermon on the occasion of the feast of St Augustine.[9] Since it would also have been Eckhart's task at this point to lecture on Holy Scripture, it is possible that some of his extensive scriptural commentaries might go back in one way or another to this time.

The next stage in Eckhart's career had to do with organizational developments which were taking place in the Dominican Order. Since its foundation early in the thirteenth century, the Order had rapidly grown and, in 1303, at the General Chapter of Besançon, it was decided that a number of Dominican provinces which had grown too big would again be divided. Teutonia therefore was to become two provinces, the one retaining the old name and the other taking the name of Saxonia. This latter area essentially covered northern Germany, extending from the area around the modern German–Polish border to the Netherlands, and it included Eckhart's home area of Erfurt.[10] Later in 1303, Meister Eckhart was named the first Provincial of the new Saxonia, a post he held until 1311. The only letter we possess from the hand of Eckhart himself dates from this time, and has to do with the evident tension between the expanding Dominican Order and the towns in which the new and developing Dominican foundations were situated.[11] This gives us an, admittedly brief, insight into the kind of administrative and diplomatic duties which Eckhart must have been involved in at this time. A considerable degree of travelling was also the lot of a Dominican Provincial, and the extent to which Eckhart had to journey across Europe by foot can be judged from his presence at Chapter meetings in Strasburg, Toulouse and Piacenza. During this period, three new Dominican houses were founded in the province of Saxonia, with which Eckhart must also have been much concerned.[12] In view of his considerable duties as Dominican Provincial, it seems unlikely that this was a fertile period for Eckhart's own creative work.

There is every indication that Meister Eckhart carried out his administrative and regulative duties with success for, in 1310, the electors of Teutonia also sought to woo him as their Provincial. This move was stopped however by the General Chapter held in Naples in 1311, who chose rather to send Eckhart back to the same Dominican chair he had held in Paris, this time for a period of two years.[13] This must be seen as a great compliment to Meister Eckhart, who shares the honour of twice holding this Dominican chair of theology only with Thomas Aquinas. Eckhart's duties in Paris as a 'master' were again to comment on Scripture, and so it seems reasonable to suppose that his surviving commentaries on the Bible go back to this as well as the earlier period of scriptural exegesis in Paris.

The next stage in Eckhart's life again shows his involvement with pastoral concerns. It would have been normal for a Parisian master to return to his own native province which, in Eckhart's case, would have been Saxonia. But, in 1313, we find him in Strasburg, which lay in the Dominican province of Teutonia. Somewhat surprisingly, a number of documents survive which indicate that Eckhart did not in fact hold a teaching post at the Dominican convent there. The exceptional character of this appointment is explained by the fact that he seems to have been serving as Vicar-General of the province with oversight of the many women's convents in the South German area.[14] We shall return to this period when we come to consider the circumstances surrounding the condemnation in greater detail. It was in Strasburg that the *Liber benedictus* was written, which contains two works which were dedicated to Agnes, Queen of Hungary: 'The Book of Divine Consolation' and 'On the Noble Man'. Agnes' father King Albert was murdered in 1308, and her mother Elizabeth died in 1313, but K. Ruh has recently argued on textual evidence that the *Liber benedictus* was written on the occasion of Agnes' entry into the religious life.[15]

We possess scant information regarding Eckhart's time in Cologne. He cannot have arrived there earlier than the year 1323, and to judge from the sermons Eckhart gave in Dominican and other communities, he was involved in both pastoral and academic activity. Eckhart, the master of theology, must have been the head of the Dominican *studium generale* in Cologne and hence bore the responsibility, together with his *lector*, for the advanced theological education of some thirty to forty young Dominicans drawn from a number of provinces.[16] Eckhart's *lector* was Nicholas of Strasburg, who held the same special commission in Cologne that Eckhart had had in Strasburg, and who had been appointed Visitor to the province of Teutonia in 1325 by Pope John XXII. And around the year 1325 we find an extraordinary fact. Nicholas, who as Visitor was Eckhart's superior and yet as *lector* (whether in the *studium generale* or the Dominican convent in Cologne) was his academic inferior, conducted a critical examination into the orthodoxy of Eckhart's work. This examination appears to have concentrated primarily on the *Liber benedictus* together with some other material from the German sermons, and it was concluded early in 1326 with Meister Eckhart's complete exoneration. Again, we shall consider this event in greater detail when we come to examine the reasons for the condemnation.[17]

In the summer of 1326, Henry of Virneburg did indeed initiate inquisitorial proceedings against Eckhart.[18] Henry appointed a commission to examine Eckhart's work which consisted of Reinerius Frisco, a cathedral canon, and Petrus de Estate. The latter was replaced by Albert of Milan upon his death in 1326. Both Petrus and his successor were Franciscans. Joseph Koch points out that this was the first ever occasion that a teacher of Eckhart's standing and productivity had been accused under the Inquisition. With the sole exception of Meister Eckhart's case, established theologians suspected of heterodoxy during the Middle Ages only ever faced an examination of faith, and not the full force of an inquisitorial enquiry, the *inquisitio haereticae pravitatis*, with its heavy penalties. It is not surprising, therefore, that Reinerius Frisco and Petrus de Estate proceeded slowly.

The method they adopted was that which had been in use since the trial against Abelard (1140), which was to extract offending statements (*articuli*) and draw them up in lists (*rotuli*). The inquisitorial procedure then demanded that these be presented to the accused for their response. The first hearing came in September of 1326 when Eckhart was presented with a list of forty-nine articles extracted from the *Liber benedictus*, from the (lost) defence of this book which Eckhart prepared for Nicholas of Strasburg, as well as from a number of Latin and German texts. This was followed by a second list of fifty-nine articles taken only from the German sermons. A third list of unknown length included extracts from Eckhart's commentary on the Gospel according to St

John. There may have been one or even two further lists as
the final list of articles condemned in the bull of 1328
included six further articles which are not taken from the St
John commentary and which do not appear in the first two
of the Cologne lists. The latter have survived in a single
manuscript together with Eckhart's comments on the
accusations, a work, therefore, which is generally referred
to as his *Defence* (German: *Rechtfertigungsschrift*).[19]

Two further figures crop up at this point: Hermann de
Summo and William de Nidecke. Both were Dominicans in
Cologne and both seem to have put themselves forward as
witnesses for the prosecution. Neither of these two colourful
personalities seem to have enjoyed the respect of their
brethren. Hermann, attempting to flee the disciplinary
attentions of the Visitor to the province fled from Cologne to
Avignon where he was promptly arrested for leaving the
convent without permission. William seems to have suffered
a similar fate and, to cap it all, proclaimed that he wished to
fight in the army of Lewis of Bavaria, who was presently
engaged in a large-scale conflict with the Papacy. The
removal of these two dubious witnesses was an important
achievement by Eckhart's Dominican supporters.[20]

On 24 January 1327, after the trial had been under way
for some six months, Eckhart formally complained in a
letter to Pope John XXII at what he felt were the unnecessary
and vexing delays in the procedure, and pointed out that the
whole exercise was invalid in that the Pope's own Visitor
(Nicholas of Strasburg) had already 'long since' conducted
an enquiry into his work and had found it to be orthodox.
On 13 February 1327, Eckhart made a further move. After
preaching at the Dominican church in Cologne (known
today as the church of St Andreas), Conrad of Halberstadt,
a fellow-Dominican, read out a Latin document to which
Eckhart provided an oral commentary in the vernacular. In
this statement (as it was recorded by the notary), Eckhart
protested his rejection of heresy and stated that he was
prepared to retract anything in his teaching which might be
shown to be erroneous. He denied that he had ever taught
that his little finger had created all things, saying that he

had meant by this the little finger of the child Jesus. He denied that he had taught that there was an 'uncreated something' in the soul, but stressed that if the human soul were all intellect according to its essence, then it could be said of it that it is uncreated. Joseph Koch describes this as the 'most embarrassing document of the whole trial', and finds it purposeless.[21] It has recently been argued, however, that the clear and public statement by Eckhart that he was prepared to retract whatever might be erroneous was a strategic endeavour to counter the threat of his being judged a heretic, which could only be the case if he was shown to hold *wilfully* (*pertinaciter*) to erroneous theological positions. Indeed, Eckhart's *protestatio* in Cologne is probably one of the key reasons why in Avignon the trial for heresy became the lesser one of censure.[22]

Although the authorities in Cologne rejected Eckhart's request, they were in fact powerless to stop the transfer of the judgement, and of all the papers concerning the trial, to the Court of John XXII at Avignon. Eckhart did not travel alone, but went to Avignon in the company of Henricus de Cigno, the Dominican Provincial of Teutonia, and three lectors, a fact which well shows the degree of support which Eckhart enjoyed among those *confrères* closest to him. Koch points out that the two commissions set up at Avignon to examine Eckhart's work, one consisting of theologians and the other of cardinals, would not have had the power to scrutinize Eckhart's work as such again, but only to examine those articles which the Cologne commission had already judged to be heretical. These, originally 150 in number, were reduced to twenty-eight. Koch indicates that even this number was unusually large in cases of this kind and reflected a desire, apparent already in Cologne, to attack the whole body of Eckhart's work.[23] All twenty-eight articles were found to be 'heretical as they stand' (*hereticus, prout sonant*). In the final Bull however only fifteen articles are declared to be 'heretical as they stand', while eleven are said to be 'evil-sounding, rash and suspect of heresy' and it is acknowledged that Eckhart had denied teaching the final two. This shift in tone was presumably the result in part of

Eckhart's important protestation of his readiness to retract what might be shown to be erroneous, as well as the 'more favourable atmosphere' for him in Avignon.[24] It has been attributed to the influence of one of the commissioners, Cardinal Guillelmus Petri de Godino, who must have known Eckhart at Paris twenty-five years earlier, and who seems to have exercised a modifying influence on other such occasions.[25]

The Bull is not without its difficulties. One of the last two articles which Eckhart denies having taught actually forms part of his *Defence*, and in certain instances the distinction between 'heretical' and 'evil-sounding' seems quite arbitrary.[26] In any case, Meister Eckhart did not live to see the promulgation (only in the town, archdiocese and province of Cologne) of John XXII's Bull *In agro dominico* (27th March 1329); a letter sent by the pope to Henry of Virneburg on 30 April 1328, had assured the archbishop that the case against Eckhart would continue despite the latter's death. Eckhart died, in all probability, in the Dominican house at Avignon at some time during the winter of 1327 and 1328.

It is possible to gain a real sense of Eckhart as a person from the skeletal remains of his biography. He was evidently strong and with a robust constitution, or the extensive journeying which he undertook as Dominican Provincial would not have been possible. And the fact of his having received high appointments in the Dominican Order shows that he must have been an individual who inspired confidence in his brethren. The fact that he had some enemies could be a consequence of his own success, or perhaps of his challenging and uncompromising personal style (as is evident from many a turn of phrase in his sermons). Above all, we see in his life a perpetual tension between academic learning on the one hand and pastoral care on the other, particularly the care of religious women amongst whom he spent so much of his career. It is perhaps this same tension which finds resolution in his German sermons, which are intellectual in content but profoundly pastoral in form and for which, quite rightly, Eckhart is best remembered today.

The background to the Bull *In agro dominico*

In agro dominico has deservedly become the object of much scholarly interest over recent years. The reasons are not hard to find. Firstly, it was the first and only occasion when the full machinery of the Inquisition was used against a member of the Dominican Order, and it was similarly the first and only time in which a major theologian of the first rank was charged with the *inquisitio haereticae pravitatis*: the most serious accusation which the Inquisition had at its disposal and the one which carried the heaviest penalties. Despite its extraordinary character, however, Eckhart's trial remained fundamentally within the bounds of legality, as Winfried Trusen's recent study has shown, though Trusen also reveals the malevolence of his detractors and their determination to inflict maximum damage upon Eckhart within the strict letter of the law. Had they not conducted a trial for heresy against him (as distinct from an investigation of his teaching), for instance, his objections that he was not subject to their jurisdiction as a Dominican would have been good, as would his protestation that the case against him was invalid since the instigators had been shown to be wholly disreputable.[27] On the evidence of Trusen's conclusions, therefore, we immediately encounter the question of an antagonism towards Eckhart which animated his detractors from the outset of his trial in Cologne, and it seems reasonable in this case to enquire into the political and historical background of the trial in order to draw to light the possible motivation for those who wished to see Eckhart's public humiliation.

The very first sign of a movement against Eckhart comes around 1325, when he was in his sixty-sixth year. In 1323 or 1324 Eckhart arrived in Cologne to act as regent (*magister regens*) of the Dominican *studium generale* in that city. He was at the height of his career in that he had twice held a Parisian chair of theology, and he had successfully carried out his extraordinary brief in the troubled city of Strasburg (to which we shall return). Eckhart arrived in Cologne then, to one of the top teaching posts in his Order, as a powerful academic theologian and an accomplished administrator.

It is all the more surprising, therefore, that this should be the moment at which formal accusations are first levelled at him for teaching matters not consonant with the Catholic faith. And what is even more surprising is that it should have been Nicholas of Strasburg, a Dominican theologian, who initiated this procedure. Although Nicholas had admittedly been the Papal Visitor to the province of Teutonia since the year 1325 (and therefore was in a sense Eckhart's superior), he also held the post of *lector* either at the Dominican centre of studies or at the Dominican convent, and thus was Eckhart's academic subordinate. Unfortunately, we possess no documents from this first examination of Eckhart's teaching except certain statements from Eckhart's formal defence, which are taken up and used by other of his accusers at a later date.[28] But from remarks which Eckhart makes later, it is evident that the findings of Nicholas of Strasburg were that Eckhart was entirely innocent of having taught heterodox material.

It would be wrong to think of this examination of Eckhart's teaching as being an entirely isolated event however. The General Chapter of the Dominican Order held at Venice in the spring of 1325 made a statement castigating those 'brethren in Teutonia who say things in their sermons which can easily lead simple and uneducated people into error'. This statement is repeated at the General Chapter in Toulouse in 1328, at the very height of Eckhart's trial, and immediately prior to the publication of the condemnatory Bull. And, in this second instance, the dangerous material in the friars' sermons is defined as 'subtle matters' (*subtilia*), which seems a clear reference to Eckhart's inclination to present sophisticated theology to the common people.[29] What we find here then is a likely indication that clouds were gathering around the head of Eckhart in the early 1320s, and that the Dominican Order was seeking to distance itself, at least publicly, from his cause. Two further facts are possibly significant here: the first is that during the previous year, 1324, the Dominican Order had seen a change of leadership. Herveus Natalis, who must have held Eckhart in high esteem for he maintained his appointment (under

Berengar) as Visitor in Strasburg, had died in 1323 and he was followed by Barnabas Cagnoli, a man of less certain sympathies. The second consideration is that the initial statement expressing the Order's unease regarding events in Teutonia falls in the same year as Pope John XXII's decision to charge Nicholas of Strasburg, who was already the Dominican Visitor in Teutonia, with the added responsibilities of a Papal Visitor to that Dominican province. Here we find more than one indication, then, of the development of a situation of some considerable political sensitivity in the Dominican province of Teutonia, and centring on the figure of Eckhart himself.

The unparalleled brevity of Nicholas's inquiry in 1325/26 as papal visitor, together with the fact that he was himself so closely allied with Meister Eckhart, strongly suggests that it was in essence a stratagem, a defensive manoeuvre on the part of the Dominican Order against incipient attempts to discredit one of their chief theologians and administrators.[30] It seems very unlikely that Nicholas could have undertaken such an inquiry without the knowledge and complicity of the head of his own Order, and so the cautionary statement regarding certain preachers in Teutonia of spring 1325 is balanced by a determined attempt by the Order to head off the approaching attack. But, if this was indeed a ruse to protect Eckhart, then it was of course one which failed.

If the inquisitorial proceedings conducted by Henry II of Virneburg, the Archbishop of Cologne, were remarkable on account of the fact that Eckhart was both the sole Dominican to be charged with heresy during the Middle Ages and the sole theologian of the first rank to undergo this indignity, then it also seems exceptional that the papacy should persistently have upheld the rights of the Archbishop of Cologne to conduct such an examination into Eckhart's work, even though Eckhart himself represented no threat to Pope John XXII. Moreover, it cannot really have been in the pope's best interests to condemn a leading Dominican theologian. Perhaps one of the most striking things of all about this case is that the papacy pushed through the condemnation *even after Eckhart's death*. In contrast, the charges levelled against Nicholas of Strasburg by the archbishop are simply left in the files. More importantly, the case against William of Ockham, who placed himself in outright opposition to the papacy when he escaped from Avignon and sided with Lewis of Bavaria, was never formally concluded. In the eyes of John XXII, the subtleties of Meister Eckhart's teaching must have seemed far less threatening than the vehement and full-blooded attack on the papacy launched by William, and yet it is Eckhart who is condemned and not William; and, of course, the charge against William was only an examination of faith, and not a full inquisitorial proceeding.

There are three distinct questions therefore which emerge from this state of affairs. The first is who was the instigator of the attack upon Eckhart? The second is why was such an attack mounted? And the third is what factors led to Pope John XXII proving so amenable?

The first question is easily answered, and here all commentators are agreed. The letter sent by Pope John XXII to Henry II of Virneburg, assuring him that the case against Eckhart will continue, despite the latter's death, is clear evidence of the centrality of the Archbishop of Cologne in the whole affair. Here is the motivating mind, the fount of animosity.[31] We need then to explore in greater detail the experience and character of this archbishop in order to explain the possible reasons for his antagonism towards an elderly Dominican theologian who, prior to 1323, he had surely never met.

Henry II of Virneburg belonged to a noble family from the Eifel region of Germany (bordering on the present-day Belgian Ardennes).[32] It was a family which rose meteorically at the end of the thirteenth century only to vanish into obscurity, just as suddenly, two centuries later. Henry III, the Archbishop of Mainz between 1338 and 1346, belonged to the same Virneburg family. The young Henry II soon showed himself to be an ambitious man, although he had to wait until his mid-fifties before gaining election to the archbishopric of Trier in 1299. Unfortunately for him, Pope Boniface XIII had reserved the appointment for himself, and thus the election was proclaimed invalid. It took a direct personal intervention by the pope himself however to persuade Henry to give up the archbishopric. Henry was a candidate also for the seat of Cologne when the latter fell vacant in 1304 with the death of Wikbold von Holte. The vote however was split over three candidates. William of Jüllich was killed on the battlefield shortly afterwards, and Henry and Reinhard of Westerburg both turned to the Curia in order to gain a decision in their favour. Only after two years of intensive personal lobbying of the pope, first of Benedict XI and then of Clement V, was Henry able to secure his election to the archbishopric of Cologne.

Once in position, Henry applied his considerable abilities to remedying the financial ills of his archdiocese. Indeed, financial acumen is one of the hallmarks of his career, so that upon his death, in 1332, the Pope was able to praise him for the 'good order' of the archdiocese of Cologne.[33] There are occasions, however, when his aspirations in this direction appear quite grotesque. During the double election of 1314, for instance, Henry insists as part of his support for Frederick the Fair that the king should lend him martial aid, if necessary, at his own cost, while no such obligation was to fall to himself. The king should always permit him access, and should pay for the costs of the archbishop's lodging at the royal court. The king is required to maintain, at his own cost, two emissaries from the archbishop at the court who are permanently to ensure that the king does nothing that might be harmful to the archbishop's interests. Even Gregor Schwamborn, Henry's mild biographer who is prepared to tolerate his extensive and destructive nepotism as an old man's 'indulgence' describes these preconditions as 'schnöde Habsucht' or 'bare-faced avarice'.[34]

The second keynote of Henry's reign is his abhorrence of heresy. As soon as he took office in 1306, Henry addressed himself vigorously to the question of the so-called extra-regular groupings, the Beguines and the Beghards, who lived a life based on the evangelical precepts but who did not follow a formal religious rule. The women lived sometimes singly and sometimes together, and they took only temporary vows. The men were generally itinerant, mendicant people who, for one reason or another, did not become part of the regular mendicant orders. It was against these groups that Henry launched his attack. And it is of particular interest that he explicitly accused them of the antinomian heresy of the Free Spirit, which had been recorded by Albert the Great at Ries, near Augsburg, during the 1270s. Thus they are said to be guilty of teaching that the soul can become so totally one with God that we can no longer sin, and all is permitted. Fornication, in particular, is not to be thought of as a sin. The perfected soul is also free from the observance of Church practice. Henry threatened those who did not renounce their lawless ways with excommunication and the secular arm. Robert Lerner makes the point that Henry is the first to link the so-called heresy of the Free Spirit with the Beguines and Beghards; and Lerner also makes the point that we have no actual evidence from Cologne in this period for cases of Beguines or Beghards being put on trial for the errors of the Free Spirit.[35] The legislation issued in Mainz and Trier in 1310 follows Cologne by making specific reference to Beghards, but there is no mention in either case of antinomian principles. As with earlier complaints against the Beguines, those prior to Henry's decree of 1307, Mainz and Trier stress the complaint of unregulated mendicancy.[36]

In 1311–12, in two different Bulls (*Cum de quibusdam mulieribus* and *Ad nostrum*), the Council of Vienne also presented a link between the Beguines and the Free Spirit heresy. Here, it seems, there were two factors at work. The first is the case of Margaret Porete, who was burnt at the stake in 1310 for refusing to recant certain propositions she had put forward in her book *The Mirror of Simple Souls*. A reference in a contemporary chronicle suggests that she was a Beguine (probably of the more suspect, itinerant type). Whether her work contains heretical elements or not is a matter of some dispute, but it would certainly seem at least to permit antinomian readings.[37] But the second important

factor here is Henry himself. Neither the Archbishop of
Mainz, nor of Trier, were present at the Council of Vienne,
and thus Henry was the dominant German presence,
together with John of Zürich (also known as John of
Dürbheim), the Bishop of Strasburg (to whom we shall
return).[38] The first Bull, *Cum de quibusdam mulieribus*,
shows a keenness to differentiate between pious Beguines
and those who constituted a threat to Church orthodoxy.
Nor does it speak of the Beguines particularly in terms of an
antinomian sect. The second Bull, *Ad nostrum*, however, is
altogether harsher in tone in that it makes no attempt to
safeguard 'good' Beguines and it makes explicit reference to
their alleged antinomian practices. It is perhaps significant
that this second, more uncompromising Bull even makes
reference to 'the German lands' (*in regno Alemaniae*) as
being the geographical area concerned, which may well
point to the influence of Henry of Virneburg, the sole German
archbishop present at the Council, in the drawing up of this
document.[39]

In our examination of the reasons for the condemnation,
the next point to consider is why it was that Meister Eckhart
should have attracted the attention of Archbishop Henry
and, indeed, become the object of his indefatigable
animosity. The answer, or at least part of it, is to be found in
the fact that Eckhart, in the year 1313, moves from Paris,
where he has finished his second term as *magister regens*, to
Strasburg. Under normal circumstances, a Parisian master
would have returned to his own Province, which in Eckhart's
case was Saxonia, whereas Strasburg lies in the Province of
Teutonia. We may conclude, therefore, that Eckhart must
have been dispatched to Strasburg at the behest of Berengar
of Landora, the General of the Dominican Order. But a
number of documents survive which indicate that Eckhart
did not in fact hold a teaching post at the Dominican
convent in Strasburg. Rather, he seems to have been serving
as Vicar-General of the province with oversight of the many
women's convents in the South German area. This, at least,
is what we can deduce from the few instances in which his
name occurs on documents from this period (property

transactions and a disciplinary visitation to a convent).[40] Winfried Trusen is quite right to point out that the circumstances of Eckhart's move to Strasburg have not been adequately commented upon, and he is right, too, when he says that they have to do with the implicit threat to the Dominican Order brought about by the Vienne moves against the Beguines for whom, to a considerable extent, the Dominicans themselves bore pastoral responsibility.[41]

Since 1267, at the behest of Pope Clement IV, the Dominican Order had accepted responsibility for the many women's communities which had sprung up in Europe during the twelfth and thirteenth centuries and which, largely due to their numbers, had failed to find a home within the established monastic orders. These groupings were of diverse kinds, but many were communities of Beguines, some of whom became Dominican (or Franciscan) tertiaries, while others retained a high degree of independence. In the light of this special link between the Beguines and the Dominican Order, it is easy to see why Eckhart should have been sent to Strasburg, for it was in the Province of Teutonia, in which Strasburg was situated, that over half the 'Dominican' nunneries were to be found. A good many of these owed their existence to Beguine origins, and their number was constantly increasing as more and more Beguine communities sought affiliation with the Dominican Order, although the practical expression of Dominican pastoral care might take the form only of the appointment of a Dominican chaplain to the community. And in cities such as Strasburg and Cologne, where medieval records have been well preserved, it is noticeable that there was a marked tendency for the Beguine establishments to collect around the Dominican (and Franciscan) houses.[42] This was certainly the case in Strasburg where, during Eckhart's sojourn there (1313–23?), there were three Dominican nunneries in the immediate vicinity of the friars in the very centre of the city: Turm, Offenburg and Innenheim. All three of these convents had originally been Beguine houses which had been accepted by the Dominican Order sometime before the year 1276. In 1304 these three are joined by Mollesheim and in 1323 by

Spiegel. But the friars were also surrounded by a large number of religious women whose relations with the Dominican Order were less precise. Dayton Phillips, in his seminal study of Beguines in medieval Strasburg, suggests that in the period 1300–1310 there were some ninety Beguines living in the immediate vicinity of the friars. Many of these would have been women living alone, inhabiting the Schlauchgasse, which led directly off the friars' own house. It is recorded that by the end of the fourteenth century there were in Strasburg some eighty-five Beguine Houses attached to the Dominican Order.[43]

The decision of the leadership of the Dominican Order to send Eckhart to Strasburg was proved to be well-founded when, on 13 August 1317, and actually prior to the publication in Paris of the Vienne decretals on 25 October of that same year, the Bishop of Strasburg initiated a campaign against those extraregulars who identified themselves with the sect of the Free Spirit. It is by no means the case that the Bishop thereby intended those Beguines and religious sisters who were closely allied with the Dominicans and Franciscans; in fact, he specifically excluded the 'honest' Beguines (much in the spirit of *Cum de quibusdam mulieribus*) and those Beguines who were in the care of the Franciscans.[44] Nevertheless, his instruction of August 1317 seems to have been interpreted by the secular clergy of the area as an invitation to open season on the Beguines for, in August of the following year, the pope was forced to issue the Bull *Ratio recta* in which he determined that the distinctions of *Cum de quibusdam mulieribus* between 'good' and 'bad' Beguines must be respected. And, on 18 January 1319, 'accommodating himself to the wishes of the local clergy', the bishop actually called for the dissolution of the Beguines and their return to normal parish life.[45] This resulted in the papal Bull *Etsi apostolicae* (23 February 1319) in which John XXII explicitly stated that the Vienne decretals must not be extended to Third Order Franciscans.

There can be no doubt that the situation regarding the Beguines in Strasburg was both confused and acrimonious. Above all, it was the product of a long animosity between the secular clergy and the mendicant orders. Under the influence of the secular bishops, decretals issued at the Council of Vienne had decidedly reduced privileges accorded to the Franciscans and Dominicans alike, and the announcement on 5 August 1318 of the formation of an alliance between the cathedral chapter and the chapters of St Thomas and St Peter in Strasburg against the mendicants, who were regarded as being the supporters of those in error, is a clear instance of this conflict.[46] It is not to be wondered at, consequently, that within this context Meister Eckhart, who was one of the chief figures on the Dominican side during these turbulent years, must have appeared as a defender of the Beguine cause against the efforts and interests of the secular clergy, not least those of the Bishop of Strasburg, John of Zürich.

It is easy to see, therefore, why Meister Eckhart, upon his arrival in Cologne, should have been of interest to the Archbishop, who was a close ally of the Bishop of Strasburg and was well known for his zealous pursuit of groupings which he suspected of heresy. And in addition to Eckhart's role in Strasburg, it was during his Strasburg years that Eckhart began to present in German some of the radical ideas which had long been part of his Latin writings. The treatise 'On the Noble Man' from his *Liber benedictus* is a particular example of this, and it is perhaps not surprising that material from the *Liber benedictus* featured prominently in the first lists of Eckhart's suspect articles to be drawn up at Cologne. While being of a different nature altogether, such articles could easily be read by the uneducated or the unsympathetic as being perilously close to some of the precepts of the Free Spirit heresy which Archbishop Henry believed to be such a threat among the Beguines. It remains now for us to ask why it was that the archbishop should have found such a ready ear in Pope John XXII for his malignant intentions towards Meister Eckhart.

A brief glance at German history between the eighth and the fourteenth century shows that it is marked by the constantly shifting patterns of power involving the German emperor (not to forget his princes), the papacy, the French king and the provinces of Italy. In 774, Charles the Great became King of Lombardy and was crowned in Rome in the year 800. Otto the First invaded Italy in 951 and received the title 'imperator et Augustus' in Rome in 962. Frederick Barbarossa, from his base in Swabia, launched an extensive campaign in northern Italy which led him finally to exert considerable influence not only in Lombardy but also in the province of Tuscany and parts of central Italy. Frederick II's entrance on to the Italian stage in 1220 was certainly less felicitous and led to a serious weakening of the monarchy in Germany and the rise of the German princes. Lewis of Bavaria's active involvement in northern Italy from 1323, and his invasion of Italy in 1327 can be seen, therefore, to be merely the latest in a long-standing tradition of German kings seeking an extension of their empire and income in the lands of Italy.

But the papacy had already shown itself to be particularly sensitive in the matter of German incursions into Italy. Frederick Barbarossa's extensive gains there were never formally recognised by his friend, Pope Lucius III, fearful doubtless of an alliance with the Normans in Sicily. And the activities of Frederick II in Italy, likewise alienated the papacy. The evident reason for this unease was the implicit threat to the pope's Italian possessions, combined more often than not with the sound instincts of the papacy to maintain a proper balance between the French and German powers. But there were particular reasons why John XXII should have resented Lewis of Bavaria's incursion into Italy. From the very beginning of his reign, John XXII had shown himself to be greatly concerned with the Italian problem; and the constitution *Si fratrum* of March 1317, which was drawn up soon after John was elected pope, 'assumed that the empire was vacant and declared penalties against any who might meddle with it in defiance of the papal claim to administer during the vacancy'.[47] Although the initiation of the papal process against Lewis, which occurred on 8 October 1323, followed the battle of Mühldorf in 1322, in which Lewis defeated his rival Frederick of Austria, it also came immediately after Lewis's first direct intervention in the affairs of Lombardy through his lieutenant, Berthold of Neiffen, in March 1323.[48] It was Italy which was paramountly the bone of contention between pope and emperor, rather than the disagreement on the process of Lewis's election, and the reasons for this are not difficult to see. Lewis himself possessed virtually no funds; 'his lack of money was chronic and desperate to a degree which sets him apart from most of his contemporaries'.[49] His attempted assertion of imperial rights in Italy, therefore, was not just an act of aggrandizement but a policy for increasing his revenue, which was important not least for securing his position in Germany, which was never strong. The financial advantages of hegemony in Italy cannot have been far from John XXII's mind either, although it was in fact the cost of his wars in Italy which led to the stringent measures he took elsewhere in Europe in order greatly to increase the papal revenues.[50] Of far greater importance to the pope was the need to restore papal power in central Italy prior to a return to Rome. The papacy envisaged itself gaining a new independence based in Rome, with benign Habsburg rule in Lombardy: a plan which was wholly obstructed by the intervention of Lewis of Bavaria, who fought in open animosity to the pope, and who, after a successful campaign, had himself crowned king by a representative of the Roman people in the year 1328.

The relevance of Pope John's troubles in Italy, where he was confronted by an outrightly hostile and generally victorious German king, is crucial to an understanding of why it was that Meister Eckhart's propositions were condemned. One of the questions to be raised most insistently by the account of Eckhart's trial is why the papacy did not simply let matters drop? It could not have been in the interests of the Holy See to carry through the condemnation of Eckhart's teaching and yet, the Bull *In agro* was promulgated even after Eckhart's death. It seems imperative therefore to ask finally what were the circumstances which allowed Archbishop Henry of Virneburg to

exercise such a seemingly irresistible influence upon Pope
John XXII?

Henry was one of the three most powerful German
ecclesiastical electors of the German king. And already in
1308, with the contested election of that year, he had shown
himself to be in possession of a sharp political sense and to
be not at all afraid of isolating himself from the other
German archbishops. In that year Henry had sided with the
papacy by supporting Henry of Luxemburg against the
French candidate. The archbishops of Mainz and Trier,
both of whom were under French influence, had opposed
the pope and the Cologne archbishop, but in vain. In the
second contested election, of 1314, Henry had once again
shown himself to be a man of shrewd and opportunist
independent judgement. On this occasion, Mainz and Trier
initially supported John of Bohemia, Henry of Luxemburg's
heir, in their determination to keep out the Habsburg
candidate. In the face of John of Bohemia's youth, and the
unlikelihood of gaining papal acceptance for that reason,
they later switched their allegiance to another Luxemburg
candidate, Lewis of Bavaria. Henry of Virneburg, on the
other hand, resolutely supported the Habsburg, Frederick of
Austria. The result of the contest was a double election with
Lewis being crowned in Aachen by the Archbishop of Mainz,
and Frederick being crowned in Bonn by Henry of Virneburg
himself.[51] Henry of Virneburg, 'the chief supporter of the
Austrian party among the princes', was therefore the pope's
chief ally, and one whom he simply could not afford to
alienate.[52] A glance at the key dates in the pope's struggle
with Lewis, when the archbishop's influence over John XXII
would have been greatest, shows that these correspond
closely to the critical stages in Eckhart's trial. The process
against Lewis, which was initiated in 1323 (perhaps the
year of Eckhart's arrival in Cologne), reached a head in
1324, when the pope excommunicated him. And in January
1328, when Eckhart may already be dead but *In agro
dominico* has not yet been published, Lewis is crowned
emperor in Rome and as a further act of defiance, he

appoints an anti-pope, the short-lived Nicholas V. In fact, a clear insight into the nature of relations between the pope and the archbishop at this time is afforded by a letter which John wrote to Henry on 3 June 1324. In an earlier letter of 6 April, the pope had urged Henry to publish the first process against Lewis (which he had so far failed to do on account of opposition from the citizens of Cologne), and in this second letter, the pope promised the archbishop restitution of whatever toll-rights King Albrecht had removed from his diocese during the toll-war in the Rheinland area; all the archbishop was required to do was to notify the Pope of the present owners of such rights.[53] This document is the clearest evidence we possess so far of the far-reaching influence which the Archbishop of Cologne exercised over Pope John XXII in this period, and of the evident willingness of the pope to accede to the wishes of his German ally, and it is therefore of considerable consequence in our evaluation of the reasons for Eckhart's condemnation.

Different reasons have been put forward as to why Pope John XXII promulgated the Bull *In agro dominico*, thus condemning the work of a foremost Dominican theologian. Kurt Ruh has suggested that it was the result of the fact that much of Eckhart's teaching was in the vernacular, and thus might potentially exercise far greater influence among the masses.[54] Although this may well have been a factor, the fact that the condemnation was published only in the diocese of Cologne, and not in that of Strasburg, where Eckhart had preached and written in the vernacular for over ten years, suggests that it was not a primary one. The argument put forward by Otto Karrer, that Eckhart was 'sacrificed' in order to placate the Franciscans and to compensate them for the canonisation of Thomas Aquinas, also seems difficult to sustain.[55] In 1328 John XXII was in a relatively strong position with regard to the Franciscan rebellion. His Bull of 1323, *Cum inter nonnullos*, had pronounced the teaching of the absolute poverty of Christ to be heretical, a Bull which, however unpalatable to the Franciscans, was accepted by their General Chapter held at Lyon in 1325. In addition to this clear victory, at the beginning of 1328 we find Michael of Cesena, the General of the Franciscan Order, a virtual prisoner at the papal court of John XXII (together with William of Ockham). In the light of this balance of power, which was so favourable for the papacy, John XXII simply had no need to placate the Franciscan Order or to pander to their wishes.

As we have seen, the concerns of Pope John XXII during the critical period of Eckhart's trial lay chiefly with Italy, with his hopes for a return to Italy, and with his struggle against Lewis of Bavaria over the Italian lands. It is within this political context that Henry II of Virneburg, the Archbishop of Cologne, who was animated by a marked hostility towards Meister Eckhart, gained great personal influence over the Holy See. And the fruit of this animosity was that a distinguished Dominican theologian with a penchant for academic *subtilia* was dragged before the Inquisition in an affair which disgraced him and disgraces still, not a little, the Church of his day.

NOTES TO CHAPTER 2

1. Koch (1973), pp. 247–347 remains the standard study of Eckhart's life. For the relevant texts pertaining to his life, see L. Sturlese, ed., LW V, pp. 153–240.
2. Albrecht (1978).
3. This sermon was discovered in 1957 by Thomas Kaeppeli in a manuscript collection of Parisian academic sermons and *collationes* which survives at Kremsmünster. It has been published in LW V, pp. 136–48.
4. It will be published in Vol. 5 of the Stuttgart edition, but its attribution to Eckhart is not universally accepted. See Koch (1973), pp. 255–7.
5. LW V, pp. 3–26.
6. Koch (1973), pp. 252ff.
7. ibid., pp. 258ff. The title is universally translated into modern German as *Die Reden der Unterweisung*, which means 'The Talks of Instruction' and not 'Counsels of Discernment' (*pace* Colledge in EE). See J. Koch's remarks on the meaning of the MHG word *underscheidunge* in DW V, pp. 312f.

8. Tugwell (1988) has recently questioned the assumption that one Parisian chair of Theology was 'intern' and the other 'extern'. Tugwell shows that the principle of alternation applied to the sequence of *appointments* rather than chairs, and that this practice is more characteristic of the fourteenth rather than the thirteenth century (note 77, pp. 102ff.).

9. LW V, pp. 29–83 and 87–99.

10. Koch (1973), pp. 261ff.

11. ibid., pp. 268ff.

12. ibid., pp. 273ff.

13. Ruh (1985), p. 30.

14. These documents are listed in Koch (pp. 284ff.) and LW V, pp. 182–6. Two have to do with gifts of property formally received by the Dominican Order in Strasburg and a third with an administrative visitation by the Order to the convent of Unterlinden in Alsace. We also possess some slight references to Eckhart's activity in this period in contemporary nuns' lives (see LW V, pp. 187f.).

15. See Ruh (1985), pp. 115–35.

16. Koch (1973), p. 304.

17. There seems to be no reason to follow Trusen's judgement here (Trusen [1988], p. 66) that the investigation by Nicholas cannot have been such a manoeuvre because he did not himself possess the power to instigate proceedings of this type, but only to investigate accusations made by others. If Nicholas wanted such an investigation to take place, then it doubtlessly lay within his power to find individuals who were prepared to call Eckhart's orthodoxy into question.

18. See Laurent, Daniels and Théry for texts concerning Eckhart's trial. A detailed description and evaluation of Eckhart's trial can be found in Trusen (1988).

19. Trusen argues convincingly that the articles contained in MS Soest 33 are not likely to have been drawn up by the commissioners but rather by others, and thus cannot represent a 'Defence' in the strict sense of the term (p. 86).

20. Koch (1973), pp. 328f., and Trusen (1988), pp. 114f.

21. Koch (1973), pp. 332f.

22. Trusen (1988), pp. 104ff. and p. 118. It is also the case of course that Eckhart's readiness to retract whatever he had taught which could be shown to be erroneous is entirely consistent with the tone of his defence in general, which was that his teaching was catholic orthodoxy and was being

misunderstood. The 'retraction' delivered in Cologne (and this same 'retraction' or some other referred to in the Bull) do not constitute the recognition of error, but only the readiness to withdraw statements which can be shown to be erroneous. It is entirely likely that Eckhart meant by this statements which could be shown to be erroneous *by argument* and not by ecclesial condemnation.

23. Koch (1973), p. 335.
24. Trusen (1988), p. 118.
25. Koch (1973), pp. 342f.
26. See the fine article by McGinn in the *Thomist* (1980), which provides the best discussion of the theological misunderstandings surrounding the Bull, and Colledge and McGinn (pp. 14f.) for further discussion of the inconsistencies of the Bull.
27. With regard to Eckhart's objection that the trial was invalid in that Nicholas of Strasburg had already examined his work, Trusen points out that Nicholas, as Visitor, could not have conducted proceedings for heresy (p. 71), and with regard to his objection that the commissars had no authority over him as a Master of Theology, Trusen points to the precedent of the condemnations by Bishop Stephan Tempier and Archbishop Robert Kilwardby (p. 91). But Trusen believes that the commissioners may in fact have gone beyond the letter of the law in their determination to proceed against Eckhart on the grounds of heresy rather than the lesser charge of censure (p. 97).
28. See LW V, pp. 192f.
29. I am inclined to agree with Kurt Ruh (1985), pp. 171ff., therefore against Joseph Koch (1973), pp. 314ff., on this point. Koch argues that the 'error' concerned is of a political nature and to do with the role of the Dominican Order in the conflict between the papacy and the emperor. Ruh, on the other hand, argues that 'error' is generally the medieval shorthand for heresy. Ruh also makes the important point that 'simple and uneducated people' played no part in the political controversy between the papacy and the emperor. The repetition of the injunction in 1328, which uses precisely the same formula as the 1325 injunction ('ducunt populum in errorem': *Monumenta ordinis Fratrum Praedicatorum historica*, IV, p. 180) with the addition of the word 'subtilia', seems also to support Ruh's case.

Trusen argues forcefully for Koch's reading, providing new

and interesting material to illuminate the tensions in the Dominican Order surrounding the controversy. But his statement that it is now 'evident' that the 1325 declaration had 'nothing whatsoever to do with Eckhart' (p. 60) must be balanced by the fact that Trusen never actually addresses the two main points made by Ruh, nor the fact that the same formula is used in both injunctions. The matter appears, in any case, far from a resolution.

30. This observation seems first to have been made by X. Hornstein in his *Les grandes mystiques allemands du 14e siècle* (Lucerne 1922), p. 34. Trusen's view (p. 66) that this cannot have been the case on the grounds that Nicholas was not himself empowered to initiate such proceedings in the absence of other persons acting as accusers, seems strange. It cannot have been beyond the initiative of Nicholas to find just such persons if he did indeed wish to conduct an inquiry of this kind. Trusen makes the good point, however, that the legal status of Nicholas' enquiry was not sufficient to undermine the legality of the later trial, as Eckhart claimed (p. 71).

31. This seems the case even though the original source of the complaint against Eckhart is likely to have been those of his Dominican brethren who were envious of him and to whom he himself refers (*Rechtfertigungsschrift*, Daniels, 1; Théry, 185). But it is not at all clear that we need resort to the theory that Eckhart was the victim of internecine conflict within the Dominican Order between reformers and their opponents (*pace* Trusen, p. 70).

32. For the following, see Gregor Schwamborn's detailed study of Henry II of Virneburg (*Heinrich II: Erzbischof von Köln*, Neuss 1904, especially pages 8–12). I was wrong to state that Henry was a Franciscan in my own *God Within* (1988).

33. Schwamborn, p. 72.

34. ibid., p. 22.

35. See R. E. Lerner, *The Heresy of the Free Spirit in the Later Middle Ages* (London 1972), p. 78.

36. ibid., p. 67.

37. See Paul Verdeyen, 'Le procès d'Inquisition contre Marguerite Porete et Guiard de Cressonessart (1309–1310)' in *Revue d'histoire ecclésiastique* 81 (1986), pp. 47–94.

38. The list of those present at the Council of Vienne is given in Carl Müller, *Der Kampf Ludwigs des Baiern mit der römischen Curie* (Tübingen 1879), vol. I, pp. 73ff.

39. This is the view also of Schwamborn (p. 66, n. 2). Lerner (p. 81) records that the Vienne decrees were drawn up by commissions and not at plenary sessions, which again supports the theory that *Ad nostrum* may have been the expression of a small, radical German faction, motivated by animosity towards the Beguines. It is also noteworthy in this respect that the Pope was obliged to promulgate the Bull *Ratio recta* in 1319 in order to counteract excessive persecution of the Beguines in Germany and to reinforce the distinction between 'good' and 'bad' Beguines which was made in *Cum de quibusdam mulieribus*, the earlier of the two Vienne decretals.

40. See LW V, pp. 182–86.

41. Trusen (1988), pp. 19–61. What Trusen does not notice however is the network of relations which connect Archbishop Henry with the Vienne decretals against the Beguines, and Archbishop Henry with John of Zürich, Bishop of Strasburg. Henry and John were also united in their support of the Habsburg candidate against Lewis of Bavaria (see Hauck, *Kirchengeschichte Deutschlands*, vol. 1, p. 495). It is also possible that there is a parallel to Eckhart's move in the appearance of the leading Franciscan theologian Duns Scotus in Cologne in 1307 (the same year in which the archbishop made his first attack upon the extraregulars of that city). This possibility has been disputed (see E. McDonnell (1954), p. 519, where there is also a good bibliography on this question), but there is certainly a tradition going back to the early seventeenth century which suggests that Duns Scotus might have been sent to Cologne to combat heresy among Beguines and thus, by inference, to defend the Franciscan Order. See Wadding, *Annales Minorum* (1636), vol. III, p. 71 and Ferchius, *Oratio in Ionnem Dunsium Scotum* (1634), p. 10.

42. See Langer (1987), pp. 36–8. R. W. Southern, in *Western Society and the Church in the Middle Ages* (Harmondsworth, Penguin, 1970), pp. 327f., writes: 'Of the hundred and sixty-seven individual beguines whose exact address in Cologne is known between 1263 and 1389 a hundred and thirty-six lived in the neighbourhood of the Dominicans and Franciscans'. See also McDonnell (1954), pp. 203f.

43. D. Phillips, *Beguines in Medieval Strasburg* (Palo Alto 1941), pp. 90ff.

44. McDonnell (1954), pp. 528ff. There is also a good discussion

of the situation in Strasburg in Ruh, pp. 112ff. and Trusen, pp. 24ff.

45. McDonnell (1954), p. 533.
46. Trusen (1988), p. 26. See A. Patschovsky, 'Straßburger Beginenverfolgungen im 14 Jahrhundert' in *Deutsches Archiv* 30 (1974), pp. 94–161, for relevant documents from this period.
47. H. S. Offler, 'Empire and Papacy: the Last Struggle' in *Transactions of the Royal Historical Society* series 5, vol. VI (1956), p. 25.
48. *Monumenta Germaniae Historica* Const., v, nr. 729, p. 568 (quoted in Offler, p. 24).
49. Offler, pp. 31f.
50. Between the years 1320-1 and 1325-6 the papal income advanced from 112,490 to 528,857 florins, of which some 336,000 florins were used for the war in Lombardy. See Offler, p. 27.
51. See Schwamborn (pp. 13ff.) for an account of Henry's role in the imperial elections.
52. Carl Müller (1879), p. 151.
53. ibid. Müller's reference for this letter is *Oberbairisches Archiv* I, 64, no. 25f.
54. Ruh (1985), p. 173.
55. See Koch (1973), p. 321, n. 195.

3 • MEISTER ECKHART AND THE RELIGIOUS WOMEN OF THE AGE

There are particular reasons for wishing to examine Eckhart in the context of the spiritual writings of religious women and the abundant spiritual life of the women's communities of his age. The first is that it was largely women who, perhaps on account of their lack of a formal education in the Latin language, were the first to write spiritual works in the vernacular as, of course, Eckhart himself did. Mechthild of Magdeburg (German) and Margaret Porete (French) in particular stand at the very beginning of spiritual writing in the vernacular languages of Europe, and both have been linked with the name of Eckhart.[1] Secondly, we need to consider Eckhart's work in the light of the particular forms of spiritual life which predominated in the German convents during the late thirteenth and early fourteenth centuries, since Eckhart himself had such long-term and immediate contact with these communities.

Hildegard of Bingen

We begin this section, however, with a study of a twelfth-century woman who wrote not in the vernacular but exclusively in Latin. Hildegard was born in the year 1098 in the German province of Rheinhessen, although she lived for most of her life at Disibodenberg and Rupertsberg, and founded a community of Benedictine nuns at Eibingen. Rupertsberg today is in the Rhineland town of Bingen, and Eibingen overlooks Rüdesheim, on the opposite bank of the Rhine. Disibodenberg is a short distance away on the river Nahe.

Hildegard herself received visions from an early age (from her third year according to her *Vita*), which formed the basis for her three visionary works: *Scivias, Liber vitae meritorum* (*The Book of Life's Merits*) and *Liber divinorum operum* (*The Book of Divine Works*). In addition, Hildegard wrote medical and scientific treatises (*Physica, Causae et Curae*), a corpus of songs (the *Symphonia*, which she herself set to music), a variety of shorter theological and biographical treatises and a good number of letters, some three hundred of which survive. She also became an important and well-known figure of her own age, and corresponded with four popes, the Emperor Frederick Barbarossa, Henry II of England and Bernard of Clairvaux as well as numerous archbishops, clergy and nobility. Hildegard also conducted four preaching tours, opposing the Cathar heresy in Cologne for instance at the invitation of the local hierarchy. Hildegard died in the year 1179.[2]

Hildegard was a very remarkable visionary theologian whose work, while incorporating much of the concerns of twelfth century Christian cosmology with its considerable debt to Platonism, includes elements which are brilliantly original. There are three key areas of her thought which serve in particular to distinguish Hildegard's work from that of her contemporaries. Firstly, we find that she makes extensive use of feminine personifications when discussing both the creation and the Church so that, as Barbara Newman has observed, she explores 'the eternal feminine [who] in her several guises, links God's coming into the world with the world's own coming to be'.[3] A second area of originality in Hildegard is her belief that the abundant life of the physical world forms a continuum with the inner life of the spirit. The basis of this continuum is the Holy Spirit itself, which is the life-principle at work within the living things of the world, and is at the same time the principle of our own spiritual and moral health. This view is epitomized in the image of *viriditas* or 'greenness', of which Hildegard makes extensive use. It is, at this level of reflection, peculiar to her and, in the words of Peter Dronke, 'is the earthly expression of the celestial sunlight; greenness is the condition in which earthly beings experience a fulfilment which is the blithe overcoming of the dualism between earthly and heavenly'.[4] For Hildegard, we are united with the world by the principle of life, which manifests as fertility at the level of nature and which is Christian virtue and love of God at the level of grace-filled humanity.[5] Thirdly, we find in Hildegard a highly developed view of humanity as the *imago Dei*, or 'image of God'. If God is the Creator, then men and women are capable either of assisting him in the 'creation' (where this word carries the fullest possible Christian resonances), or not. This view is summed up in a passage from Hildegard's *Vita* (II, 35) where we find: 'Humanity is the work of God along with all other creatures. But humanity is also called to be the workman of God'.[6] It is the belief that humanity can choose whether or not to co-operate with God in his creation which lends Hildegard's work its profoundly didactic character.[7]

Before proceeding to an analysis of texts, it needs to be stated that there are good reasons for thinking that the young Eckhart would have been familiar with at least some of Hildegard's writings. At first glance there would seem to be little in common between Hildegard, the visionary, and Eckhart, the scholastic. And yet, in historical and geographical terms, they do overlap. After her death there existed a thriving cult around the figure of Hildegard in the diocese of Mainz, and in the surrounding areas of the Rhineland, to such an extent, in fact, that her community were obliged to ask the Archbishop of Mainz to command the saint not to perform any further miracles (!).[8] Very importantly, in 1324 (the likely year of Eckhart's arrival in Cologne), Pope John XXII gave express permission for her 'solemn and public cult'.[9] Around the middle of the fourteenth century, Johannes Tauler, who was based in Strasburg (where Eckhart himself had lived from 1313 to 1324) and who had been a close follower of Eckhart, mentions Hildegard by name, calling her a 'noble creature', and states that he has seen an illumination of the 'fear of God' in 'her book'.[10] There is evidence, however, that Hildegard was known closer to Erfurt (which was Eckhart's provenance and where from 1294 he was prior). There are passages in Mechthild's own book, the *Flowing Light of the*

Godhead, which suggest that, even as a Beguine in Magdeburg, she herself knew Hildegard's *Book of Life's Merits*, amongst other of her works.[11]

From a historical perspective, therefore, there is every reason to think that the young Eckhart had access to one or other of Hildegard's works, and that she was a figure of sufficient stature to warrant his interest. And we find in a number of his sermons elements which may arguably derive from his reading of Hildegard's work. The sermons in question are all contained in the collection known as *Paradisus animae intelligentis*. This is a corpus of sermons which comes down to us in two manuscripts from the middle of the fourteenth century.[12] The Thuringian dialect in which it is written strongly suggests that the source of these sermons is the same Erfurt Dominican house in which Eckhart spent his early years. The collection contains sixty-four sermons, thirty-two of which are attributed to Eckhart, and they are believed to date from between the years 1303 and 1311.[13] To some extent this selection portrays a rather different Eckhart from the one we glean from the new critical edition in that these sermons contain virtually no reference to the condemned propositions (which formed the criteria for authenticity in Quint's critical edition). One reason for this may be, of course, that the compiler of the selection avoided material of that kind, but it may well be also that these sermons represent an earlier stage in Eckhart's thinking and that, above all, his rhetorical style, which was the cause of so many of his problems, had not yet fully developed. A considerable number of the sermons in *Paradisus animae intelligentis* show a greater interest in the created order than is the case in Eckhart's later work.

Individual sermons also include thematic material which closely parallels key concepts in Hildegard's works, as is the case in sermon number eighty-two of Quint's critical edition (Pfeiffer, No. 62; Walshe, No. 62). Here we encounter two elements which are central to Hildegard's thought: the belief that humanity is both the 'work' and the 'tool' or 'instrument' of God, and the idea that the Holy Spirit underlies both the vitality of living things and the fruitfulness of spiritual grace:

> The third point to note is the wondrous work that God performs in the soul, as it says: 'What wonders shall come of this child?' It is needful that every tool is adequate to the work the craftsman performs, if that work is to be perfect: for man is God's instrument, and the tool works according to the nobility of the craftsman. Therefore it is not sufficient for the soul that the Holy Ghost works in her, because he is not of her nature. And as I have often said, he has given her a divine light which is like him and as it were of his nature, and he has given it to the soul so much for her own that it is a part of the soul, so that he may work joyfully within her: just as we can see in the case of light, that it works according to the quality of the material it falls upon. In wood it performs its own work, creating heat and fire; in trees and moist things it produces growth, not heat or its own work, but it makes them green and bear fruit. In living creatures it produces life from dead matter, as when a sheep eats grass and that is turned into an eye or an ear. But in man it promotes blessedness. This comes from God's grace which raises the soul up to God and unites her with him and makes her God-coloured. If the soul is to be divine, she must be raised up. If a man were to reach to the top of a tower, he would have to be raised as high as the tower: in the same way grace has to raise the soul up to God. The work of grace is to draw and to draw completely, and whoever does not follow will come to grief. But still the soul is not satisfied with the work of grace, because even grace is a creature: she must come to a place where God works in his own nature, where the craftsman works according to the nobility of the instrument, and that means in his own nature, where the work is as noble as the craftsman, and he who is poured out and that which receives the outflowing are all one.

In this sermon Eckhart is commenting on the reading for the Nativity of St John the Baptist (24th June): *'Quis, putas, puer iste erit? Etenim manus domini cum ipso est'* (Luke 1.66: 'What will this child turn out to be? And indeed the hand of the Lord was with him'). Following tradition, Eckhart interprets the 'hand of the Lord' as the Holy Spirit and he stresses the role of God as a 'craftsman' (*werkmeister*)

who perfects his 'work' (*werk*) through the 'hand' of the
Holy Spirit. There are echoes here therefore of God the
Creator, and of Hildegard's description of humanity as the
plenum opus dei ('the complete work of God') and as the
operarius dei ('God's workman'). But Eckhart's interest,
typically, lies chiefly in the idea that men and women can
become united with God, through that within them which is
most like him: they can become the perfect 'tool' (*gezouwe*)
of God in so far as their nobility matches that of the
'craftsman' himself. The emphasis then is upon personal
union with the Godhead, which contrasts with Hildegard's
characteristic emphasis upon humankind as the agent of
ethical action within the world, and yet there is a
convergence here in the kind of imagery which both writers
employ.

We find also in the above passage that the action of the
Holy Spirit is compared to that of light, which both sustains
the life of the natural world, its greenness, growth and
fruitfulness, and also works 'blessedness' in the soul.
Although the precise relation between the Holy Spirit and
light is not made clear, we cannot fail to note the
juxtaposition (in terms virtually of a continuum) of the inner
world of spiritual virtue with the outer world of natural
fertility, which is a theme much beloved of Hildegard, as
when she speaks of the Holy Spirit as that which 'poured
out this green freshness of life into the hearts of men and
women so that they might bear good fruit' (DO: 10, 2).
What underlies this transference is, of course, the idea that
it is the same divine life which establishes the vital growing
energy of the natural world and the spiritual vigour of the
life of grace. Although the juxtaposition of the two orders of
being is more hesitant in Eckhart and less clear than it is in
Hildegard, we find once again in this sermon a convergence
in their ideas and imagery.[14]

In sermon seventy-two (W 95), when he is speaking of the
ontological status of creatures, Eckhart makes specific
reference to the image of 'greenness':

The prophet says: 'God will lead his sheep into a green pasture'
. . . All creatures are green in God. All creatures proceed first
from God, and then through the angels . . . In the heights all
things are green: on the 'mountain top' all things are green and
new: when they descend into time they grow pale and fade. In
the new 'greenness' of all creatures our Lord will 'feed his
sheep'. All creatures that are in that green and on that height, as
they exist in the angels, are more pleasing to the soul than
anything in this world. As the sun is different from night, so
different is the least of the creatures, as it is there, from the
whole world.

Therefore, whoever would receive God's teaching must ascend
this mountain: there God will make the teaching perfect in the
day of eternity where all is light. What I know of God, that is
light: what touches creatures is night.

The term 'greenness', as we have seen, is one which enjoys
a special place in Hildegard's writings, and it is an image
which is specifically hers.[15] It is her original coinage in
spiritual usage (*viriditas*), and she applies it repeatedly in
order to convey both the burgeoning life of the physical
world which reveals God, and the order of grace, which is
the operation of the Church and the rich fecundity of a
virtuous life founded on the Spirit. In the light of this,
therefore, we cannot but read the occurrence of this word in
the above passage as a conscious reference to Hildegard.

It is interesting to note in this regard the way in which
Eckhart comes to the noun 'greenness' in the above passage.
The text on which he is preaching is *Videns Jesus turbas,
ascendit in montem* ('When he saw the crowds, Jesus went
up to the mountain', Matt. 5.1), and it is the reference to a
mountain which prompts Eckhart suddenly to interpolate
the line: 'The prophet says: "God will lead his sheep into a
green pasture"' (Ezek. 34.11). From this he progresses to a
discussion of 'greenness' as a concept. From an original text
therefore which presents an image of ascent, Eckhart
proceeds to an evaluation of the theme of 'greenness', which
he interprets within the context of 'height' and his own
exemplarist metaphysics of essential being. It seems
reasonable to suppose therefore that the 'greenness' of
creatures was a concept already familiar to Eckhart, and

that he was taking the opportunity to appropriate it as an image for the purposes of conveying his own metaphysical system.

If this is indeed the case, then we discover here a marked difference in Eckhart's understanding of the creature from that which we find in Hildegard's work. Hildegard teaches repeatedly and uncompromisingly that God's creation reveals the Creator: 'all creatures are the garment which God wears' (DO: IX, 14). The earth clothes God, she writes, as the body clothes the soul (DO: IX, 14), and we have already noted references to the 'radiance' and abundant life of the physical world. This view contrasts strongly then with the position we find in the mature Eckhart that creatures represent a form of specific and determinate being which is an obstruction to us as we ascend through our own divine image into the indeterminate, essential being of God. Rather than interpreting the created order in mystagogical terms, Eckhart opposes the order of creation to that of the divine, with the result that he can say: 'all creatures are a pure nothingness' (W 68) and in them there is 'no truth' (W 17).

There are a number of points at which the theology of Eckhart and Hildegard overlap. They are both keenly interested, for instance, in the original point of creation from the Godhead, and in the genesis of creatures through the Word. Both comment extensively on the opening of the Fourth Gospel. Both are also concerned to construct an ontology, which centres upon the Incarnation. And even at the level of imagery there are a number of parallels. Thus we find in Hildegard the image of the soul as a 'living spark' (DO: IV, 105), which recalls Eckhart's 'spark of the soul'. We find in her also the language of 'bubbling' when she speaks of creation from the primal 'spring' or source of the Godhead (DO: VIII, 2: *fons saliens*; cf. Eckhart's play on *bulliens—ebulliens*: LW II, pp. 21ff.). Such parallels ultimately reveal their common concern with the *fertility* of God. Here the similarities cease, however, for as we have seen in Eckhart's use of the term 'greenness', his understanding of the status of the creature is very different from that of Hildegard. For Eckhart, the creature, localised in time and place, is that which we must transcend as we advance into universal and indeterminate being, close to the Godhead which is the source of all being. For Hildegard, however, creatures reveal the Creator through their very createdness; they are the garment which he wears. Their *localised* being is itself a form of radiance. When the early Eckhart states that 'all things speak God', then he follows up this phrase with the words 'but it is precious little that they are able to reveal' (W 22); while the former sentiment remains for Hildegard the very kernel of her theology. Eckhart's use of the term 'greenness' seems more of a critique of Hildegard's position therefore than a mere adaptation of her language for the purposes of his own metaphysics. In the final analysis, God's fertility is shown, for Hildegard, not only in the life of grace within the soul, and within the Church and her sacraments, but also at the level of nature and the creation, while for Eckhart the created order obstructs and obscures our connaturality with the uncreated God, and so God's birth in us is simultaneously our birth 'out of the world' (W 7).

Mechthild of Magdeburg

The primary source for Mechthild's life is what she herself tells us in her classic work *The Flowing Light of the Godhead* (*Das vliessende lieht der gotheit*). She was born around the year 1212 in the diocese of Magdeburg.[16] Her familiarity with the *Minnesang*, the German chivalric tradition of 'courtly love', which is evident in the imagery and style of her work, suggests that she may have been from a noble background; a view which is supported by the tradition that her younger brother was well-educated and became sub-prior at the Dominican priory of Halle. Mechthild herself left home for Magdeburg in 1230, where she joined a community of Beguines. Around the year 1270, when she was already an old woman, Mechthild entered the convent of Helfta, which was a great centre of learning and of spiritual writing. It was in Helfta that Mechthild wrote the final book of her work. She is likely to have died, in Helfta, around the year 1294.

The Flowing Light of the Godhead is the first full-length spiritual work in the German language. Although the text has come down to us in an Alemannic translation made by the Dominican Henry of Nördlingen between the years 1343 and 1345, it was written in Mechthild's own Low German dialect under the supervision of her Dominican confessor, Henry of Halle. It was also translated into Latin at an earlier date, around the year 1285.[17]

There are a number of reasons why it seems possible that Eckhart had read Mechthild's work. The first is that Magdeburg and Helfta are both relatively close to Erfurt. The second is that Mechthild's own dialect, and the language of the original composition, would have been easily comprehensible to Eckhart, himself a Saxon. A third reason is that the important Latin translation of *The Flowing Light of the Godhead* was made during Eckhart's own lifetime, and a fourth is the evident involvement of the Dominican Order with the genesis and the later fortunes of the book. Positive evidence of a link between Mechthild and Eckhart's own community at Erfurt exists in the person of Dietrich of Apolda, who wrote a life of Saint Dominic which enjoyed great popularity during the thirteenth century.[18] Dietrich's work includes passages taken from the Latin version of the *Flowing Light of the Godhead* (one of which eventually found its way into Dante's *Divine Comedy*).[19] Dietrich, who was born around the year 1228 and died circa 1298, was a member of Eckhart's own Dominican community at Erfurt.[20] Moreover, his *vita* of Dominic is dated to the last decade of his life (1287–98), which substantially overlaps with the period during which Eckhart was Prior of the convent at Erfurt (1294–1302). It seems inconceivable that Meister Eckhart should not have known of the work of Mechthild of Magdeburg if her work was of sufficient status to be used in a life of St Dominic, which was itself being produced in the selfsame convent of which he was prior.

Like Eckhart, Mechthild is concerned to trace the union of God with the soul. Again, like Eckhart, she uses the resources of her own imagination as well as elements of the secular tradition of which she was a part in order to articulate spiritual experience, even if the Courtly Love elements within her seem to convey a very different sensibility from that of Eckhart's scholasticism. And indeed, there are a number of occasions when the style or content of Mechthild's work seems strikingly close to that of Eckhart himself. In the section which follows we will look first at areas of similarity between the work of Mechthild and Eckhart, which may, however, be seen to be themes and topics common to a number of other mystical writers from the period. Secondly, we will look at elements in their work which appear to be more specific areas of congruence.

The first parallel we might mention is Mechthild's use of the language of bareness and union:

Soul: What do you require, Lord.
God: You should be naked!
Soul: But Lord, what will happen to me then?
God: Lady soul, you share my nature so far
 That nothing can come between you and me.
 No angel has ever been so honoured
 As to know for a single hour
 What is yours from eternity
 Thus you should lay down
 Both fear and shame
 And all the outer virtues.
 Only those which live in you by nature
 Should move you in eternity . . . . (I, 44)[21]

Although the imagery of this passage is decidedly that of *Brautmystik* ('nuptial mysticism'), the underlying concept, which is that of our essential being within God from eternity, is close to a theme we find many times in Eckhart, who stresses repeatedly that we must return to an essential bareness of being. Mechthild's soul strips itself of all that comes between itself and God, even the 'external virtues', in order to attain simplicity of being, in which state of essence it enjoys union with God. This serves to parallel Eckhart's repeated appeal to a life of metaphysical detachment which, while grounding the virtues, necessarily remains transcendent.

Elsewhere, too, Mechthild uses the language of self-stripping, and in particular of the soul's divestment of 'creatures' in order to attain the inner, unitive state: 'She [the soul] is stripped of all things' (III, 10). In one passage Mechthild speaks of the three places in which God speaks to us: the first is in the senses, the second is in the soul, and the third (not quoted here) is in heaven. She writes:

> In the first place the Devil too often speaks to the soul, which in the other two places he cannot do. The first place is a person's senses. These are open to the penetration and speaking of God, the Devil and all creatures alike, according to their will. The second place, where God can speak to us, is the soul. No one can enter this place but God alone. But when God speaks in the soul, then this happens without the consciousness or awareness of the senses in a great, violent and sudden union of the soul with God. Thus the senses cannot hear the blissful speech [of God]. They become so humble that they cannot endure the presence of any creature. (VI, 23)

Here creatures fall away as the soul enters the unitive state and transcends the creaturely dimension. In this passage the idea of the soul as the place which nothing and no one but God can enter also seems to echo closely the comments Eckhart makes on the 'spark of the soul' as that into which no 'power' can gain entrance but God alone (W 8).

We find also that Mechthild develops the theme of divinisation in ways that remind us of Meister Eckhart. In the following passage, Mechthild stresses the *metaphysical* aspects of our union with God and, like Eckhart, she is prepared to use the radical language of our deification (although 'detached' here translates *mit also ellendiger sele* and not the Eckhartian *abegescheidenheit*):

> When we pray in Christian prayer, with a heart so humbled that it cannot tolerate the presence of any creature, and with a soul which is so detached that all things must fall away from it in prayer but God alone, then we become a divine God with the heavenly Father. (VI, 1)

In another passage, Mechthild stresses the *volitional* aspect of our union with God, which is to say the extent to which our will becomes one with his, another important theme to the Dominican (e.g. W 65):

> But the dust of sin which falls on us almost unawares is destroyed by the fire of love as quickly as the gazing upwards of the eye of our soul touches God in painful but sweet desire, full of sighs, which no creature can withstand. As the soul begins to rise, then the dust of sin falls away from it and it becomes one God with God so that it wills what he wills, and they could not be united in any other way. (ibid.)

And in a third passage, Mechthild speaks of union again in uncompromising terms. Here there are further echoes of Eckhart's theory of the divine spark by virtue of which we know God (e.g. W 66):

> However good a person's eyes may be, they cannot see for more than a mile into the distance. However sharp our powers of understanding, we can comprehend things beyond the senses only through the power of faith, or we would be like a blindman groping in the darkness. The loving soul, which loves all the things that God loves, and hates all that God hates, possesses an eye which God has illumined. With this eye it can see into the eternal Godhead and can see what the Godhead with its nature has performed in the soul. He has formed it in his own image, he has rooted it in himself, he has united himself to it more closely than any creature, he has enclosed it within himself and has poured into it so much of his divine nature that when in union with him it can say only that he is more to it than a father. (VI, 31)

In other passages Mechthild highlights themes which are much rarer within the spiritual tradition and which she nevertheless has in common with Meister Eckhart. Thus Mechthild states on at least two occasions that God *must* descend into the soul when it has prepared itself to receive him (e.g. W 60). And God must do so because this is his nature: 'Only to those who are simple and pure and who intend God alone in all that they do, God must incline himself according to his nature'. (II, 23) And again:

> Then he [God] spoke: 'Truly if you go before me in humble complaint and holy fear, then I must follow you as the high

flood enters the deep basin. But if you come towards me in the
blooming longing of flowing love, then I must come to meet you
and touch you with my divine nature as my sole Queen.' (III, 15)

Elsewhere Mechthild makes use of that same imagery of
height and depth which we find in Eckhart (e.g. W 46). In
the following passage God is the 'all-highest', and the 'lowest
valley of all' is the soul in its humility:

Soul: Who are those who oppose God?
Love: People who burden themselves and others with their
wickedness.
Now I shall tell you who he [God] is:
He is the all-highest height,
And the same highest height has descended
To the lowest valley of all,
And the lowest valley of all
Has been raised to the all-highest height. (II, 23)

And again:

Whenever I [God] gave exceptional graces
I always sought the lowliest places,
The very least, most hidden places.
The highest mountains cannot receive
The revelations of my graces.
For the flood of my Holy Spirit
Flows by its nature into the valleys. (II, 26)[22]

Mechthild also has a preference for extreme forms of
comparison as a rhetorical device, much beloved of Eckhart.
In the following passage she writes:

The least truth
Which I saw, heard and knew there [in heaven]
Is higher than the greatest truth
Which was ever uttered on earth. (III, 1)

And elsewhere we find both a proportional construction and
a content of meaning which bears close comparison with a
number of similar passages from Eckhart's *Talks of
Instruction*:

No one enters this state [of union with God] who does not
undertake a total exchange with God so that you give God all

that you have, both internal and external. Then truly God will give you all that is his, both internal and external. (IV, 15)

It is, of course, exceedingly difficult to prove that one writer has been influenced by another, unless there is strong testimony from a third source. What we have sought to show is that there are strong historical reasons for thinking that Eckhart is very likely to have had access to works by Hildegard and Mechthild and that he would have had good reason, in view of their current reputation, to engage with them. This theory is supported by internal evidence from Eckhart's own early work which, in the case of Hildegard's *viriditas*, appears to constitute a critique and, in the case of Mechthild, to represent points which display congruence or even influence.

Margaret Porete

The *Mirror of Simple Souls* is a mystical treatise which exercised a considerable influence during the Middle Ages. Written in French around the beginning of the fourteenth century, it was translated early on into Latin (two versions), English and Italian (two versions). Not until 1946 however was it discovered that the *Mirror* was in fact the work which had been publicly burned in Valencienne on the orders of Guy II, the Bishop of Cambrai, and for which its author Margaret Porete, a Beguine from Hainaut (in modern-day Belgium), had been burned at the stake in Paris in the year 1310.[23] There are two reasons why this work is relevant to our present concerns. Firstly, the *Mirror* highlights certain mystical themes which occur also in Eckhart's own work and, secondly, there exists an indirect but nevertheless real historical connection between Eckhart and its author.

It was Herbert Grundmann who first pointed out that when Eckhart arrived in Paris in 1311 (the year following Margaret's death), he lived in the same Dominican Convent of St Jacques as William Humbert of Paris, who had been Margaret's Inquisitor.[24] In addition to this historical connection, Kurt Ruh has also raised the possibility that Eckhart may have heard of the *Mirror* at an earlier date through Godefroid de Fontaine. This canon lawyer was *magister actu regens* in the Faculty of Theology at Paris from 1285–86, and he was one of the three theologians who delivered a positive verdict on Margaret's text. Godefroid went to Rome in 1300, but returned to Paris prior to Eckhart's second teaching period there in 1302.[25] It is, therefore, highly probable that if Eckhart did not have a first-hand knowledge of the text itself, then he must at the very least have known the propositions for which the book and its author were condemned.

It was Edmund Colledge and J. C. Marler who first published an account of the elements in Eckhart's sermon *Beati pauperes spiritu* which closely resemble certain themes in Margaret Porete's *Mirror*.[26] For some of these they suggested there might be a common source and they did not 'postulate an immediate influence'.[27] But one theme suggested a greater affinity. This is the matter of metaphysical poverty, and it is central to Margaret's spirituality. Time and again, she describes how the 'annihilated', 'liberated' or perfected soul is one which is united with God through being entirely stripped of its own will and knowledge. Hence such a soul 'knows of only one thing: that she knows nothing, and wills only one thing: that she does not will anything' (ch. 42). This can be seen to parallel closely the theme which Eckhart develops in his sermon *Beati pauperes spiritu* and which is expressed in the line: 'A poor man is one who wills nothing, knows nothing and has nothing' (W 87). Margaret's view that even our willing the good is wrong (ch. 48)[28] is also matched by Eckhart's words: 'For I declare by the eternal truth, as long as you have the will to do the will of God, and longing for eternity and God, you are not poor: for a poor man is one who wills nothing and desires nothing' (ibid.).

There is strong textual evidence, therefore, that Eckhart had read the *Mirror* and that he made use of its central theme of 'non-willing' in the composition of his sermon *Beati pauperes spiritu*. Kurt Ruh speculates that Eckhart took up these elements and gave them a 'more precise, theologically defensible formulation'.[29] It is certainly the case that the isolated spiritual dicta of the *Mirror* are given a rich metaphysical context in *Beati pauperes spiritu* as the shedding of will and knowledge are seen as being a necessary part of our return to an 'uncreated' source. But Ruh is also right when he points out that the ideas of this sermon do not represent a radical departure from ideas already present in Eckhart's earliest work.[30]

In the light of the fact that the *Mirror* had been condemned before 1306 (Guy II was Bishop of Cambrai between 1296 and 1306), that Margaret was burned in 1310, and that condemned propositions of hers appeared in the Bull *Ad nostrum* in 1311/12 (published in 1317), some questions must be asked as to what Eckhart might have intended by making use of elements from her book in his own work. If Colledge and Marler are right when they assert that *Beati pauperes spiritu* was still forming in Eckhart's mind in 1326, then it is indeed likely that the uncompromising nature of the sermon makes it 'a gesture of defiance'.[31] But the extent to which we should view it as being also a statement of solidarity with the condemned Margaret Porete, as does Kurt Ruh, seems altogether more questionable; unless, that is, we are to assume that Eckhart knew her work only from the condemned propositions.[32] If he had access to the whole of her work, Eckhart would undoubtedly have found positions which contrasted with his own. Whereas Eckhart himself stresses the inner content of 'works' rather than any 'external' value, he does not advocate that we should leave such works behind (cf. *Mirror*, ch. 85). Nor do we find in him a direct opposition between the life of 'virtue' (i.e. external observance) and the life of 'spirit' (cf. *Mirror*, ch. 55); rather, in *Beati pauperes spiritu*, he wishes those people well, who practise virtue while remaining innocent of its higher meaning. Nor do we find Eckhart anywhere making a distinction between a 'true' Church of perfected souls and another of external observance, whereas for Margaret the former is 'Church the greater' and the latter 'Church the lesser'. And, finally, at the biographical level Margaret made an outright challenge to the Catholic Church which led her, tragically, to a cruel death; while Eckhart appeals to the final judgement of the Holy See and declares himself with feeling to be innocent of heresy, which is a matter of the will. While recognizing the affinity between the writings of Eckhart and Margaret Porete, therefore, which may well have taken the form of a direct influence in the case of the sermon *Beati pauperes spiritu*, we should be careful not to assimilate the work of the one to that of the other.

Eckhart and the pastoral care of women

There is no scope here for a full discussion of the historical circumstances of the *Frauenfrage*, that nexus of problems which surround the sudden flowering of numerous communities of women during the twelfth and thirteenth centuries. Nevertheless, we must at least cast a glance at the history of religious women during this period, as it forms an essential background to Eckhart's own career.

The sharp increase in women seeking a religious vocation during the twelfth century is not easily explained; perhaps it was connected with urban development, or with the losses among the male nobility on account of the Crusades, or perhaps it was largely the result of a movement of the spirit which led many men and women to embrace evangelical poverty, as we find exemplified in the life of St Francis of Assisi.[33] Whatever the causes, the result was that from the late twelfth century onwards an increasing number of women sought entrance to the religious life. Such women were at first received by the Premonstratensian order, which had been founded in 1120 by Norbert of Xanten. This order quickly felt itself to be overburdened by the influx of women, however, whose pastoral needs necessarily made considerable demands on their own manpower. From 1228, the Cistercians, to whom the women had subsequently turned, also forbade the foundation of further women's communities.

One result of this reluctance on the part of the established orders to accommodate the growing numbers of women seeking the religious life was that independent, loose-knit communities began to develop which stood outside the existing and accepted forms of religious community life.

One of the chief forms that this new expansion took was that of the Beguine movement, a phenomenon which was particularly strong in Germany and the Low Countries. In fact, women calling themselves 'Beguines' were first recorded in the diocese of Liège (in modern-day Belgium) as early as the latter part of the twelfth century. One theory concerning their name is that they were the successors of a group of devout women who had been inspired by the Church reformer, Lambert le Bègue, who had been falsely accused of belonging to a heretical sect known as 'the Apostles'. The nickname 'le Bègue' comes from the French *li beges*, or 'one dressed in grey', after the colour of the Apostles' undyed penitential dress, and it was synonymous with 'heretic'. A second possibility, less likely and no more flattering to the Beguines, is that the term derives from 'Albigensian', another heretical group, associated with the Cathar heresy of Southern France. There is nothing to link the Beguines with this heresy, however, and a distinguished figure in the early Beguine movement, Marie of Oignies, was active in her support of the Albigensian Crusade.[34]

Although 'Beguine' was and remained an imprecise term, it was generally applied to those women who chose to lead a common life of prayer and service:

> Although some beguines remained with their parents or in their own homes, they often set up house together, referred to as a 'convent', sometimes in the vicinity of a hospital or a leprosarium, or clustered around an established religious community. As the beguine movement gathered strength, there was a tendency for these settlements, which became known as 'beguinages' (Flemish: *begijnhoven*) to increase in size and complexity. The women, who might be single, married or widowed, commonly made an informal vow to remain celibate whilst living as a beguine, but retained the use of private property. They were free to change their status and were not under the obligations of a monastic rule.[35]

Despite initial Church support, these communities of women, who were rather on the margins of Church control, soon attracted the attention of tidy-minded individuals for whom their innovative life-style seemed an affront. The first rumblings of disapproval came in 1273, when the German Bishop of Olmutz complained of the Beguines whose sins, he suggested, included failing in their duty to get married.[36] The following year, the Council of Lyons reaffirmed the Church's opposition to the foundation of new religious Orders, and the Council urged those which had been founded since the original ban of 1215 to integrate as soon as possible into an established Order.[37] A more aggressive line was taken at the Council of Vienne in 1311, as we have seen, with the drawing up first of *Cum de quibusdam mulieribus* and then *Ad nostrum*.

The failure of the older orders to cope with the women's religious fervour created a vacuum which might naturally have been filled by the new mendicant orders, the Franciscans and Dominicans. Since its formation however the Dominican Order had shown a high degree of ambivalence towards undertaking pastoral responsibilities for the women. In the constitutional decree of 1228, it was clearly stated that pastoral care of women's communities might prejudice the true aims of the Order, which were the furthering of education and the correction of error.[38] But after a long struggle between the advocates of this view and their opponents, a formula was found 'whereby the friars were to exercise spiritual control over the sisters without being absorbed by this new ministry' and, in 1267, at the behest of Pope Clement IV, the Dominicans finally accepted responsibility for the womens' houses.[39]

The nunneries were particularly numerous in the Province of Teutonia, in Germany, where Hermann of Minden had no less than seventy such houses in his charge. Their charters show that a good many of these establishments owed their existence to Beguine origins, and their number was constantly increasing as more and more Beguine communities sought affiliation with the Dominican Order. In cities such as Strasburg and Cologne, where records are good, it is noticeable that there was a marked trend for the Beguine establishments to seek ties with the Dominicans and to collect around the Dominican (and Franciscan) convents.[40] In the city of Strasburg, for instance, three of the Dominican convents had originally been Beguine houses, and there were a further eighty-five Beguine establishments for which the Dominicans held some degree of responsibility.[41] As well as ecclesiastical respectability, the Dominicans, for their part, offered the women administrative supervision, the services of a chaplain and those of a learned preacher, who would deliver a sermon on the occasion of important vigils.[42] And it was a formula which, though conceived for political reasons, bore substantial spiritual fruit.

There is some evidence that in as early as 1298 Meister Eckhart may have expressed a preference for work as what we would today term a spiritual director.[43] At the very least, the early *Talks of Instruction* shows a considerable facility in the expounding of spiritual ideas and a keen *engagement* with the spiritual life of those who were in his charge. Certainly, the exceptional circumstances surrounding Eckhart's mission in Strasburg strongly suggest that Berengar of Landora, the General of the Dominican Order, believed that Eckhart was well-qualified to deal with what was both a political and a pastoral problem.

The duties which Eckhart exercised in Strasburg were extensive. Some idea of them can be gained from a passage from the acts of the General Chapter held in Carcassone in 1312, which concern the sending of two Vicars General to the Province of Hungary. They are given complete authority 'to investigate, to punish, to absolve, to confirm, to reform, from convent to convent and from province to province, both as concerns the heads and the members'.[44] Otto Langer comments that Eckhart functioned not only as:

confessor and pastor, but also as visitor. He takes disciplinary measures, which are confirmed by the General of the Order. He determines the tasks and conditions of the convent chaplains; he forbids unauthorized movement between the communities; he fixes the number of confessors and lays down codes of behaviour for them; he approves time-honoured customs of the convent and gives instructions which concern the status of an absolved sub-prioress or procurator.[45]

It is true to say, therefore, that Eckhart's involvement with the life of the convents was both extensive and substantial. Finally, the point also needs to be made that after his departure from Strasburg for Cologne, where he certainly held a major teaching post, Eckhart still appears to be giving sermons to sisters. Several sermons contain references which indicate that they were delivered to religious women in Cologne itself: numbers 12 and 15 (in the Stuttgart edition) were delivered to the Benedictine nuns of St Machabaeorum, number 22 to the Cistercian nuns of St Mariengarten, and numbers 13 and 14 were possibly preached before the Dominican nuns of St Gertrud.[46]

In view of the extensive contact which Meister Eckhart had during his life with the ferment of spirituality which the newly-founded women's communities represented, it is now time to consider the character of that spirituality and the nature of its possible influence upon him.

The spirituality of the 'holy women'

The character of the spirituality which prevailed in the women's convents of Northern Europe (principally Germany and the Low Countries) is most accessible to us today in the works of individual writers from that period who have deservedly won an honoured place in the anthologies of Christian writing. Chief among these are Mechthild of Magdeburg, whom we have already considered in part above, Beatrice of Nazareth and Hadewijch of Antwerp (or Brabant). Much of their writing is visionary, but they also represent a subtle and fascinating coalescence of the spiritual and the secular in their adaptation of motifs from the world of Courtly Love to the sensibilities of an intense inner experience of spiritual union with God.[47] Their piety is accordingly one that is based paramountly on the experience of love, and it is strongly Christocentric. These writers make free use of erotic imagery in order to convey their sense of intimacy with the divine, and their writings are flowing, organic works in which the individual mystic explores the full range of human sensibility in her faithful devotion to the mystical reality of *minne* or 'Lady Love' (Mechthild).

A more representative picture of life in the convents is offered, however, by the strikingly vivid *Nonnenvitae* or 'Lives of Nuns', which have survived in a substantial number.[48] Sometimes they were written by men close to powerful and charismatic women with the intent of establishing the spiritual credentials of these holy women (e.g. Jacque of Vitry and Marie of Oignies). Alternatively, they were composed with the purpose of reforming the communities of women by presenting them with an ideal model of the spiritual life. This emphasis upon spiritual achievement led to many descriptions of miraculous happenings and supernatural graces, as when Thomas of Cantipré recounts the wounds which were discovered on the hands of Christina Mirabilis after her death (thus, of course, raising the possibility that Christina may have received the stigmata before St Francis of Assisi). These *Vitae* characteristically depict a radical point of conversion in the life of the saint who, though generally high-born, now chooses a life of poverty. Part of her new existence is the practice of severe ascetical exercises, involving fasting, the keeping of vigils and even self-flagellation. She embraces a life of absolute chastity and, where the structures are strict, subordinates herself rigorously in obedience to her superiors. Her prayer-life is extensive and is dominated by the practice of petitionary prayer. But this intense striving for perfection of life leads to special graces for the saint, who receives ecstasies and what we might term liturgical visions (of the Saviour during the Eucharist, of Christ as a child during the feast of Christmas, of the Passion during Easter, and so forth). She may feel even that she has been taken up into a mystical marriage with Christ, with whom she is united both through her intense suffering and her abundant joy. In sum, the kind of spirituality which this literature represents, and whose provenance is largely the Dominican convents of Southern Germany, is one based upon uncompromising forms of self-abnegation, sometimes involving acts which we would describe today as self-mutilation. Extreme poverty and exercises in asceticism lead to extraordinary graces and the sense of a state of union with God which may take visionary form.

Recent research by Peter Ochsenbein has provided us with a particularly graphic illustration of the spiritual *mores* which prevailed precisely within the Dominican convents for which Meister Eckhart carried pastoral responsibility. The texts in question are the writings of Elisabeth of Oye, who entered the Dominican convent of Ötenbach around the year 1286.[49] What makes her testimony particularly valuable for our purposes is the fact that Ötenbach, near Zürich, was one of the convents which Eckhart visited. Indeed, the subprioress of the same convent, Elisabeth of Beggenhofen, actually records a conversation which she had with Meister Eckhart during a pastoral visit to the convent, which must have happened during Elisabeth of Oye's own lifetime (to which we shall return).[50] The texts which Peter Ochsenbein has identified as being the work of Elisabeth of Oye therefore represent an insight into the heart of the Dominican world in which Meister Eckhart was active over a period of many years.

The spirituality which Elisabeth of Oye's writings represent has aptly been called *Leidensmystik*, or a 'mysticism of suffering'. Her ideal is that of 'greatest likeness' (*glîchste glîcheit*) to God, which she attempts to realize through a *compassio cristi*, or sharing in the physical sufferings of Christ. Accordingly, Elisabeth describes the many forms of asceticism which she practises in order to achieve this end. She employs, for instance, a *krûze*, which is a cross of nails that she carries on her back as a radical interpretation of Luke 9.23 ('If any man will come after me, let him deny himself and take up his cross daily and follow me'). The blood which flows from the wounds caused by this instrument mixes with the blood that Christ shed on the cross, and flows back into the 'ground of the Father'. Despite the considerable pain she has inflicted upon herself, and despite her great desire at times to relieve herself of this cross, Elisabeth has visions of God, Christ, the Holy Spirit, John the Evangelist or Mary, which urge her to remain steadfast in her suffering. Only in this way can she become united with God; and indeed the mystic is granted a sense of being pervaded with the presence of God.[51]

Of course, the experience of Elisabeth of Oye may well represent an extreme form of the asceticism of the age, though she was certainly not unique, and a composition of her works (which Ochsenbein calls 'K-Redaktion') won considerable popularity. The *Life of Suso*, which is an account of the life of one of Eckhart's closest followers, describes how Suso initially led a life of great ascetical hardship before casting all his instruments of self-torture into the river Rhine as the result of a divine vision, and seeking to embrace the more abstract and metaphysical path of a true Eckhartian detachment of soul.[52] This story well illustrates the extent to which the two ways of extreme ascetical practice and of an internal metaphysical detachment coexisted in Dominican circles during this time. In fact, we find that Elisabeth uses a number of Eckhartian terms in her writings (e.g. birth of Christ in the ground of her soul); and it is highly likely that Eckhart preached at Ötenbach. The overall impression we gain, however, is that such terminology sits lightly and is simply adapted to the purposes of a *Leidensmystik* which has mystical union as its aim. Certainly we do not find the sophisticated metaphysical context to such terms which are germane to Eckhart's use of them. Further evidence of this juxtaposition of two very distinct types of spirituality is found in the fact that Elisabeth's writings, in fragmentary form, were often included in manuscripts which contained largely the works of Meister Eckhart and his follower Johannes Tauler.[53]

Meister Eckhart and the spirituality of the 'holy women'

The German-speaking women's convents of the thirteenth and fourteenth centuries not only saw an explosive period of growth, but also represent a flowering of medieval piety. Although the distribution of the surviving manuscripts (the so-called *Schwesternbücher*) which contain descriptions of the nuns' lives may owe a certain amount to chance, this powerful movement of religious piety seems to have been particularly strong in the Dominican convents of South West Germany: Unterlinden, Adelhausen, Ötenbach, Katharinenthal, Engeltal, Kirchberg, Töβ, Schönensteinbach, Weiler.[54] And, of course, it was precisely these convents for which Eckhart, in the period from 1313 to 1323/24, held ultimate pastoral responsibility. In fact we possess two accounts from this period which record Eckhart's visits to the convents of Katharinenthal and Ötenbach respectively. The former survives in the *Schwesternbuch* of Dieβenhofen and records simply Eckhart's hearing of Anna of Ramswag's confession (the contents of which Anna was wisely determined not to divulge!). In the second, however, we are given more detail of how Elisabeth of Beggenhofen sought advice from Meister Eckhart on the matter of her purification through ascetical practices (in which she had been inspired by Elisabeth of Oye). His advice to her was that 'No earthly wisdom belongs to it. It is a pure work of God. All we can do is trust God in a free detachment of the spirit'.[55] Seemingly as a result of this, Elisabeth found an inner detachment and submission to God's will which afforded her release from her suffering.

Elisabeth of Beggenhofen seemed to be confused as to whether she is right to pursue her ascetical practices or not. Eckhart responded, we may note, not by urging her to abandon her ascetical practices altogether, but by pointing to the absence of an inner dimension. And his mildly reproving reply well illustrates the gulf which separates his own metaphysical and internal spirituality from the asceticism of his charges. The 'formlessness', the 'waylessness' and the interiority of which Eckhart speaks contrast greatly with the visions and 'exercises' of the holy women; and over the years there have been different attempts to make sense of this relation. The link between the Dominican mystical theologians of the thirteenth and fourteenth centuries and the Dominican *cura monialium* (pastoral responsibility for religious women) was first spotted by the acute Heinrich Seuse Denifle in 1886.[56] Denifle argued that the German sermon as a genre was born within the context of the pastoral responsibilities which the Dominican theologians bore towards the women in their charge. The need to address such mystically orientated women necessarily meant, he argued, that these theologians had themselves to develop a mystical persona while, in essence, they remained scholastic thinkers. By this argument the mystical sermons of Eckhart and his Dominican brethren are merely simplified and vernacular renderings of scholastic theology. And, as we have already seen, it is Denifle's view that the extent to which these sermons differ from the work of Thomas Aquinas is the extent to which they are confused and debased.

This partial and indeed prejudiced view was superseded some fifty years later by the work of the distinguished Church historian, Herbert Grundmann. Grundmann believed that the German sermons were the product of a fusion of Dominican theological training with the raw mystical experience of the women. According to this approach, therefore, the work of a figure such as Eckhart becomes 'theology for religious women'.[57] The mysticism of Eckhart and of the convents are differing forms of expression of the same movement, which is the embrace of poverty that so powerfully influenced European spiritual life during this period. If, for Denifle, the German preachers simply introduce the women to the treasures of scholastic philosophy, then for Grundmann Meister Eckhart and his fellows appropriate and extend the organic spirituality of the women into the conceptual sphere. Eckhart's theological system is the exposition of 'poverty' not in terms of the abandoning of possessions but as the highest form of an inner self-abandonment: an exalted poverty of spirit.

Other scholars, notably F. W. Wentzlaff-Eggebert and more recently Kurt Ruh, have seen an opposition between the system of Eckhart and the spirituality of the convents. Meister Eckhart, it has been suggested, is adopting a critical stance towards the spirituality of the women in his charge, and is challenging them to pursue a more interior form of life.[58]

In his own discussion of this question Otto Langer

attempts to steer a middle course. He agrees with
Grundmann that Eckhartian 'poverty of spirit' and the
radical physical poverty of the Beguines are to be seen
together as being part of a broader evangelical movement
centring on poverty. But at the same time, Langer argues
that Eckhart's work is an extensive critique of the exteriority
of the spirituality in the convents. Indeed, Langer reads
virtually all the characteristic positions of Eckhart as being
an intentional critique (implicit or explicit) of the character
of the nuns' mysticism. These points include his cautioning
against the 'ways' of asceticism, his questioning of visions
and mystical 'experience', his comments on prayer and his
belief in a given, existential state of union with God as
distinct from momentary fusion through the uniting of our
will with God's will (what Langer calls the *unum* rather
than the *unitum*). For Langer, therefore, it is essentially
Eckhart's pastoral situation and the need to adopt a critical
position with respect to the exuberantly active and visual
spirituality of the women which determines the character of
his theology.[59]

The failure to grasp the significance for his work of Meister
Eckhart's role as preacher in the convents of south-western
Germany is certainly one of the elements which has led to a
misreading of Eckhart's thought. He has been understood to
be advocating a form of spirituality which is divorced from
the normal sacramental and doctrinal life of the Church
(whether as a distillation or a transcendence of Christianity).
This view of him is based largely upon the relative absence
in his work of explicit reference to the 'externals' of Christian
living in combination, of course, with his great emphasis
upon interiority. Whatever the precise balance of relations
between his own spirituality and that of the women in his
charge may be (and this, *pace* Langer, can only be guessed
at in the light of the other undoubted channels of influence
affecting Eckhart's thought), there is ample evidence that
his virtual silence on sacramental life is the result of his own
critical distance to what he perceived to be imbalanced
forms of sacramental piety. The impression we gain when

reading Eckhart in the light of the nuns' experience is that he was a man with a very different spiritual temperament, whose own spare, existential and conceptual mysticism was thrown into sharp relief by the devotional and ascetical enthusiasm of his charges. If we remove his German work, therefore, from the pastoral context which produced it, and if we understand Meister Eckhart to be advocating a form of 'universal' religion which is free of the forms of Christian devotional and sacramental practice, then we shall be doing the Dominican Meister a disservice.

It is not only the exuberant sacramental spirituality of his pastoral charges, however, which is a determining influence upon his work. More fundamentally, the women's convents provided a context which proved a fertile ground for the evolution of Eckhart's distinctive preaching style. His sermons are not so much cool evaluations of certain points of Christian thinking; rather they are calculated attempts to move his audience along certain lines, to open for them new spiritual horizons, and as such they could only have been given to a body of people who were as alive, as responsive and as aware as were the fourteenth-century communities of Dominican nuns and Beguines.

NOTES TO CHAPTER 3

1. It seems unlikely that Eckhart could have known the work of Hadewijch (or indeed the corpus attributed to Hadewijch II), to whom Ruusbroec owes so much. Hadewijch flourished in the area of Antwerp during the middle decades of the thirteenth century. She wrote in a Middle Flemish dialect which would not have been easily accessible to the Thuringian Eckhart, and we find in him no real echo of the *Wesensmystik* of love which is most characteristic of Hadewijch's work.
2. See F. Bowie and O. Davies, eds, *Hildegard of Bingen: an anthology*, London: SPCK; New York: Crossroad, 1990, for a summary of Hildegard's life and thought. For her life, see also Sabina Flanagan, *Hildegard of Bingen: A Visionary Life*, London and New York, Routledge, 1989.

3. Barbara Newman, *Sister of Wisdom* (California, Scolar Press, 1987), p. 64.
4. Peter Dronke, 'Tradition and Innovation in Medieval Western Colour-Imagery' in Dronke, *The Medieval Poet and his World* (Rome 1984), p. 84.
5. Hildegard's originality lies in her extensive development of this theme, although it is echoed in Abelard's identification of the platonic *anima mundi* with the Holy Spirit (*Theologia christiana*, I, 72).
6. 'Unde et homo opus Dei cum omni creatura est. Sed et homo operarius divinitatis esse dicitur' (PL 197, col. 116).
7. See Margot Schmidt, 'Hildegard von Bingen als Lehrerin des Glaubens' in Anton Brück, ed., *Hildegard von Bingen, 1179-1979. Festschrift zum 800 Todestag der Heiligen* (Mainz 1979), pp. 95-157.
8. Reported in J. P. Schmelzeis, *Das Leben und Wirken der heiligen Hildegardis* (Freiburg im Bresgau and Leipzig 1879), p. 602.
9. The relevant document is discussed by H. Hinkel in 'St Hildegards Verehrung im Bistum Mainz', in Brück, ed., pp. 385-411.
10. See G. Hoffman, ed. and tr., *Johannes Tauler: Predigten* II (Einsiedeln, Johannes Verlag, 1979), p. 526 (Sermon 68). The illustration to which Tauler refers is the first of the illustrations contained in the original Rupertsberg manuscript of *Scivias*.
11. The vision of the virgins in the future life (together with the preachers and martyrs) with their 'singular clothes, their songs of love and their wonderful chaplets' and who are 'suspended in the breath of God like air in the sun', remind us of Hildegard's vision of the virgins in the next life which she describes in chapter 6 of her *Book of Life's Merits*. The vision of the Church as a young woman, beautifully adorned, in *The Flowing Light of the Godhead* (IV, 6) is paralleled also by the similar passage in Hildegard's letter to Werner of Kirchheim. In VI, 29, we find the metaphor of angels as 'sparks' leaping from the fire of God, which closely follows Hildegard's description of angels in her *Book of Divine Works* (4, 11).
12. The critical edition of this text by P. Strauch was published in Berlin in 1919. For a discussion of the corpus, see Ruh (1985), pp. 60-71, and VL 7, pp. 298-303.
13. See Ruh (1985), pp. 61ff. Ruh dates these sermons in part on the basis of their privileging the intellect above the will, which

is characteristic of Eckhart's *quaestiones* which date from his period as *magister actu regens* in Paris in 1302/1303. They also contain a reference to an address by a Parisian master, who is presumably Gonsalvus of Valvoa, against whom Eckhart conducted a formal dispute specifically on this theme. Ruh makes the point that some individual sermons may be of a still later date.

14. A further sermon (W 81) draws the same parallel between the light which sustains natural life and that which is the source of inner virtue: 'Therefore these [faith, hope and love] are called divine virtues, because they perform God's work in the soul, just as we can see by the power of the sun which performs living works on earth, because it makes all things live and sustains their being.' This sermon also belongs to the *Paradisus animae* collection.

15. See Bowie and Davies, *Hildegard*, pp. 31ff. Peter Dronke, pp. 84f., points to some minor parallels (in, for instance, Hugh of St Victor) but stresses the essential originality of the image in Hildegard. The ultimate origin of 'greenness' must lie, of course, in scriptural usage, such as we find in Jeremiah 11.16.

16. Jeanne Ancelet-Hustache, *Mechthild de Magdebourg* (Paris 1926) remains a valuable study of the circumstances of Mechthild's life. See also Hans Neumann, 'Beiträge zur Textgeschichte des "Fließende Licht der Gottheit" und zur Lebensgeschichte Mechthilds von Magdeburg' in *Nachrichten der Akademie der Wissenschaften in Göttingen* (Göttingen 1954), pp. 27–80 (republished in Kurt Ruh, ed., *Altdeutsche und altniederländische Mystik* [Darmstadt 1964], pp. 175–239).

17. See Neumann for an exhaustive history of the text.

18. The text can be found in *Monumenta ordinis Fratrum Praedicatorum historica*, III, 1931.

19. Dante, *La divina commedia*, Paradiso, XII, pp. 37–45. For a history of the scholarship surrounding this observation, see E. Zum Brunn and G. Epiney-Burgard, *Femmes Troubadours de Dieu* (Belgium, Editions Brepols, 1988), p. 77 and n. 19.

20. LTK, III, pp. 383–4 and VL 2, pp. 103–10. In his article in the VL Helmut Lomnitzer dates the conclusion of the work to between 1296 and 1298 on the basis of its dedication to Nicholas Boccasini, the General of the Dominican Order.

21. My own translations are taken from the new critical edition of Mechthild's work by H. Neumann, ed., *Mechthild von*

Magdeburg, 'Das Fließende Licht der Gottheit', vol. 1, Munich 1991.

22. These lines strongly recall the passage from Tauler's sermons in which the Dominican preacher compares the Holy Spirit to the river Rhine: 'As if it were to break its banks with its mass of flooding waters, roaring and threatening to submerge all things, filling all the valleys and inclines . . . and thus he fills the valleys and depths which are opened up to him' (Hoffman, Sermon 25).

23. R. Guarnieri, ed., 'Il movimento del Libero Spirito' in *Archivio italiano per la storia della pietà* 4 (Rome 1965), pp. 353–708. See also the critical edition of the Latin version (with facing French text) by Paul Verdeyen, *Corpus Christianorum continuatio mediaevalis LXIX* (Turnhout 1986). It is to this edition that the chapter references for Margaret Porete refer.

24. 'Ketzerverhöre des Spätmittelalters als quellenkritisches Problem' in *Deutsches Archiv für Erforschung des Mittelalters*, 21 (1965), pp. 519–75. Quoted in Colledge and Marler (1984), p. 15.

25. Ruh (1985), p. 104.

26. The argument is to be found in Colledge and Marler (1984), pp. 25–47.

27. ibid., pp. 25–7.

28. The French actually reads at this point: '*quelque chose qu'il vieulle*', while the Latin has: '*quantumcumque sit bonum illud quod vult*'.

29. Ruh (1985), p. 104.

30. ibid., p. 108. Cf. TI, 23 (DW V, pp. 300–1).

31. Colledge and Marler (1984), pp. 44–7.

32. Ruh (1985), p. 107.

33. See H. Grundmann, 'Zur Geschichte der Beginen im 13 Jahrhundert' in H. Grundmann, *Ausgewählte Aufsätze* I (Stuttgart 1976), pp. 201–21 (first published in *Archiv für Kulturgeschichte*, 21, 1931, pp. 296–320) for the origins of the Beguines.

34. See F. Bowie, ed., and O. Davies, tr., *Beguine Spirituality: an anthology* (London: SPCK; New York; Crossroad), pp. 12f.

35. ibid., p. 30.

36. R. W. Southern, *Western Society and the Church in the Middle Ages* (Harmondsworth, Penguin, 1970), p. 329.

37. See c.23 *Conciliorum Oecumenicorum Decreta*, ed. J. Alberigo, p. 302 (quoted in Southern, p. 329).

38. McDonnell (1969), p. 187.

39. ibid., p. 194.
40. See Langer (1987), pp. 36ff. Southern, pp. 327f., writes: 'Of the hundred-and-sixty-seven individual beguines whose exact address in Cologne is known between 1263 and 1389 a hundred-and-thirty-six lived in the neighbourhood of the Dominicans and Franciscans'. See also McDonnell (1969), pp. 203f.
41. See McDonnell (1969), pp. 203f., and H. Grundmann ('Deutsche Mystik, Beginentum und Ketzerei des "Freien Geistes"' in *Religiöse Bewegungen im Mittelalter* (Hildesheim 1961), p. 533. See also D. Phillips, *Beguines in Medieval Strasburg*, Palo Alto 1941.
42. Sermons on the feast days themselves might have proved too popular an attraction for the local townspeople. See McDonnell (1969), p. 199.
43. The title attached to the *Rede der underscheidunge* indicates that Eckhart was both prior of the Dominican convent in Erfurt and Vicar of Thuringia. Both of these posts involved pastoral duties: the former within the convent itself and the latter among a number of women's convents of the province for which the Dominicans bore pastoral responsibility. After 1298 these posts could no longer be held simultaneously by the same person; one necessitated residence in the convent and the other travel away from it (see Koch [1973], pp. 258ff.). Since Eckhart cannot have remained prior after 1300, when all the priors in Teutonia were changed, and yet did not arrive in Paris for his second period of residence there until 1302, it is perhaps likely that he chose to renounce his position as prior in 1298 and remained vicar of Thuringia. If this is the case, then it might point to an early preference on the part of Eckhart for pastoral work among the women's communities.
44. *Monumenta Ordinis Praedicatorum Historica* IV (Rome), p. 28 (quoted in Langer [1987], p. 44).
45. Langer (1987), p. 44.
46. Langer usefully sums up the results of research on this point (pp. 45f.), but see Koch (1973), p. 302, where it is suggested that sermons 13 and 14 were given in the Dominican Church at Cologne.
47. See Bowie, *Beguine Spirituality*, with translations by myself for discussion of and examples from these writings.
48. For this synopsis of the medieval German *Nonnenvitae* I have drawn upon Otto Langer's fascinating study.
49. See Peter Ochsenbein, 'Leidensmystik in dominikanischen

Frauenklöstern des 14. Jahrhunderts am Beispiel der Elisabeth von Oye' in P. Dinzelbacher and D. R. Bauer, eds, *Religiöse Frauenbewegung und mystische Frömmigkeit im Mittelalter* (Cologne, Bohlau Verlag, 1988), pp. 353-72. Ochsenbein estimates her dates at around 1280-1350.

50. ibid., pp. 366ff. For the relevant text, see LW V, p. 188.

51. I am summarizing from Ochsenbein, pp. 360-4.

52. J. M. Clark, tr., *The Life of the Servant* (London 1952), pp. 55ff.

53. Ochsenbein, p. 358; for relevant manuscripts see also P. Ochsenbein, 'Die Offenbarungen Elisabeth von Oye' in K. Ruh, ed., *Abendländische Mystik im Mittelalter* (Stuttgart, Metzler, 1986), p. 425.

54. P. Dinzelbacher, 'Rollenverweigerung von Frauen im Mittelalter' in Dinzelbacher and Bauer, eds (1988), p. 30.

55. See LW V, pp. 187f. for texts.

56. 'Über die Anfänge der Predigtweise der deutschen Mystiker' in *Archiv für Litteratur und Kirchengeschichte des Mittelalters*, 2, 1886, pp. 616-40. I am indebted again to Otto Langer for his summary of this theme (pp. 9-20).

57. Grundmann, 'Zur Geschichte der Beginen im 13. Jahrhundert' in *Ausgewählte Aufsätze* (1976), p. 221.

58. F. W. Wentzlaff-Eggebert, *Deutsche Mystik* (Tübingen 1947), p. 99, and Ruh (1985), p. 111.

59. Langer (1987), pp. 18-20. A difficulty with Langer's view is that it seems to exclude the other undoubted channels of influence upon Eckhart, especially his Neoplatonist inheritance. Further, the oppositions between Eckhart and the women are clear but, although heightened through a critical alignment, they may well simply reflect a different spiritual temperament. After all, there are striking parallels between Eckhart's German and Latin works (which were composed for an audience very different from that of the Dominican convents).

4 • MEISTER ECKHART AND THE GERMAN DOMINICAN SCHOOL

We have seen something of the social and pastoral context of Eckhart's work, which determined its emphases; we need now to turn to the immediate intellectual tradition which he inherited and which formed him. Much of the following material is philosophical and at times unavoidably technical. And yet it is necessary that we come to terms with these ideas if we are to understand the theoretical building blocks from which Eckhart constructed his own mystical 'system'. This should not cause us to lose the sense of Eckhart's originality, but it will show the extent to which he belonged to a particular school within the Dominican tradition, and thus allow us to understand better his own distinctive contribution.

The theology of the thirteenth and fourteenth centuries was to a great extent determined by the Christian assimilation of classical Greek philosophical thinking. This resulted not only from the translation of works by Aristotle and the Neoplatonists, but also from the continuing reception of the 'Dionysian corpus', which is to say those works which were (wrongly) attributed to St Paul's Athenian convert (Denys, or Dionysius) and which had exercised a powerful influence upon the Western theological imagination since their translation in the ninth century. In particular, it was those individuals who were interested in how we can speak of God and how the soul can know God that were drawn to Denys' works and to the writings of his several commentators. But the debates which centred upon this theme of the *knowability* of God raised profound and intractable problems.

It is the judgement of Simon Tugwell that the penetration of Greek theology led in the West to an exaggerated form of negative theology which came to question the very possibility of knowing God in this life and in the next.[1] Thus we find both in Abelard and Gilbert of Poitiers the idea that the radical transcendence of God undermines any meaningful use of language with regard to him, while Thierry of Chartres and Hugh of Rouen also wish to remove the theological use of language from that of normal discourse. Similarly, Alan of Lille describes the language we use of God as 'miraculous' and beyond the parameters of normal usage.[2] This radical form of negative theology gave birth to the doubt as to whether the soul could ever know God in any real sense since he was beyond the grasp of concepts and language. Alexander of Hales initially put forward the view that we shall know God only through the intermediary of his intellectual creatures, while the Dominican Master Guerric of St Quentin and Hugh of St Cher both argued that we shall not see the essence of God even in the beatific vision.[3]

It was in opposition to such positions that in 1241 William of Auvergne, the Bishop of Paris, condemned the proposition that 'the divine essence will not be seen in itself either by any human being or by any angel'.[4] From now on the theologians were to proceed from the principle that it would be possible to know God's essence in the beatific vision, although the theoretical precepts underlying such an idea were far from clear. It was within this context therefore that Albert the Great, a leading Dominican theologian of his age, who stands at the beginning of a distinctively German Dominican school, took up the question of our knowledge of things human and divine.

St Albert the Great

Albert was born in Lauingen at the end of the twelfth century. He probably became a Dominican in around 1229 while engaged in philosophical studies at Padua. After a period in Cologne he became *lector* at Hildesheim (from around 1233) and eventually taught at the University of Paris, where he became Master of Theology in 1245. In 1248 he returned to Cologne where he was involved in the foundation of the Dominican *studium generale* there. After holding a number of senior academic and administrative

posts in the Order, he was elected Bishop of Regensburg in
1260, but resigned after two years. In 1269 or 1270 he
returned to Cologne to teach, where he died on 5 November,
1280, at over eighty years of age.[5]

Albert is important within the history of philosophy for a
number of reasons. He is for instance a great encyclopaedist,
whose extensive works on natural history guarantee him a
special place. But he also represents an important early
stage in the western reception of the works of Aristotle; he
was in fact the first major western thinker to be confronted
with the problem of how to reconcile the sophisticated (but
'pagan') philosophy of Aristotle with the precepts of the
Christian religion.

One of the key areas of medieval enquiry was that of
epistemology, which is the branch of philosophy that asks
the question how it is we are able to know things. And it is
in this area, with its questioning of the nature of human
intellect (by which the medievals meant something much
closer to what we mean today by 'consciousness') that we
find important features of Albert's assimilation of Aristotelian
principles. Aristotle had argued that the essential property
of our human nature is intellect, and among the Arabian
Aristotelians we also find the view that the actualization of
intellect is determined by the object of its knowledge. This
latter is an important point and, in combination with the
former, it provides an outline for Albert's theory of how the
soul knows God.

In his treatise *On the Intellect and the Intelligible* Albert
argues that our intellect is what is most essential to us:
'human beings, precisely as human, are essentially intellect',[6]
and he maintains that the intellect is realized ('becomes
actual') in a higher degree according to the intelligibility of
that which it knows. Through knowing objects in the world,
the intellect comes to a knowledge of itself; then through
knowing the principles by which it orders its perception of
objects, it rises to a more complete possession of itself and
so, finally, when it has become fully 'actual' the human
intellect rises to the point at which it fuses with that which

is the source of all intelligibility, and which is the 'divine intellect' itself.[7] The ultimate beatitude for Albert, therefore, is our all-consuming 'knowledge' of God at the end of time:

> Since all human beings naturally desire knowledge, and desire is not unlimited, it must be possible to bring this desire to an end in some form of knowing. And this can be nothing other than the knowledge of that which is the cause and light of all beings and all objects of knowledge, and this is no other than the divine intellect. . . .[8]

The achievement of Albert, therefore, is to have established a theory of intellect which on the one hand could explain those ordinary levels of knowledge which characterize our everyday experience and, on the other, our knowledge of 'divine things' together with the more remote (though theologically central) possibility of our union with God in the final beatific vision. This latter, of course, was not something which impinged much upon our existence here below, but remained only the ultimate condition of our final end.[9]

The Albertian school

Albert's ideas on the nature of the human intellect were taken up enthusiastically by the young German Dominicans whom he taught, and were developed in different directions. Hugh Ripelin of Strasburg, who died before 1268, was one of the first to attempt a synthesis of Albert's ideas in his *Compendium theologicae veritatis*. This work, written between 1260 and 1268, extends over seven books, which range from the nature of God to the sacraments and the end of the world. A characteristic emphasis within Hugh Ripelin's work falls on God as Being and on the Unity of God. The former idea leads to a pointed opposition between the Divine Being and the being of creatures, which can in fact be said not to exist at all.[10] This is an idea which is also strongly present in Eckhart. It was another of Albert's pupils however, Ulrich of Strasburg, who composed the main presentation of his system. Ulrich was born some time between 1220 and 1225 and died around the year 1277. In his work, the *Summa de summo bono*, we find a coherent and succinct statement of the progressive 'divinization' of the human intellect as it ascends through the different stages or conditions of knowledge until finally it is illumined by the Divine Mind itself.[11] Unlike the angels, Ulrich tells us, we are not intellect by essence, and so our progress towards God and our eventual 'divinization' takes place as our nature becomes ever more purely intellective.[12]

The chief figure among the followers of Albert, however, was Meister Dietrich of Freiberg, in Saxony. Dietrich was born around 1250 and died between 1318 and 1320.[13] He was one of the most illustrious leaders of the Dominican Order during this period, holding high administrative positions and becoming a Parisian Master of Theology in 1296-7. Like Albert before him, Dietrich's interests extended to the natural sciences as well as theology, and his works include treatises on colours, light and the rainbow.[14] Dietrich, who was much influenced by the writings of the Neoplatonist Proclus and whose work is a radicalization of Albert in many ways, emerged as the main Dominican opponent of Thomism. Like Eckhart, Dietrich also preached in German, though presumably not with the same popular impact, since his sermons have not survived.

The distinctive characteristics of Meister Dietrich's thought are, firstly, his explicit identification of the Augustinian *abditum mentis* (the secret interior of the mind) with the Aristotelian agent intellect. For Ulrich, the intellect had been only a property or *habitus* within the soul, while for Dietrich it becomes the essential soul itself. Intellect therefore is substance and is the very causal principle of the soul.[15] In his *On the Beatific Vision* Dietrich writes:

> That is what we find in the philosophers, albeit in different terms but without difference in doctrine, when they distinguish within our intellectual being the agent intellect from the possible intellect: the agent intellect of the philosophers is the same as Augustine's secret depths of the soul. . . .

Secondly, the intellect is the true image of God, who is likewise intellectual substance. The human (agent) intellect is not only the image of God, but it also approaches him without intermediary. In its creation, the agent intellect *proceeds* from God, unlike all other creatures, and can be thought of as an emanation from him: 'The intellect emanates intellectually from God in such a way that its substance is nothing other than a concept by which it conceives of and knows its Source, a concept without the knowledge of which it could not know its own essence'.[16] Thus it always looks towards the Divine Mind and is maintained in its being by him. We might even say that the human intellect, in its active mode, actually participates in the Divine Mind.

Thirdly, for Dietrich the intellect is entirely simple and self-contained, and yet at the same time it is wholly dynamic. The essence of intellect is its own perpetual self-knowing. It is a unity of that which knows (the subject) with that which is known (the object), where the object is itself the self-knowing of the subject. Thus, in one sense, the intellect cannot know anything outside itself. It knows by its own essence, by intuition, and not discursively. No created thing can impinge upon it therefore. Rather, since it is the image of God, it contains all that is within itself. When we perceive something, then its similitude which exists already within our own mind is activated, and that is what we perceive. Here Dietrich is breaking with the Aristotelian tradition espoused by Albert, according to which the mind emphatically knows things which are beyond itself (and is thus brought to knowledge of itself), and he prefers the Augustinian model, which locates the source of knowledge within the mind itself.[17]

Fourthly and finally, Dietrich believes that the process of thought, which is the very essence of intellect, is at the same time productive. Here Dietrich is following Proclus, for whom beings proceed from Intelligences.[18] In the Proclean world, however, the ultimate principle of creation is the One, from whom the Intelligences themselves proceed while, for Dietrich, the process whereby the One (or God) creates is intellective, for 'this One, whom Proclus put in first place and above all things, has the fecundity of an intellect'.[19] Thus we find in Dietrich a strong sense of God as (creative) *intellect*.

Meister Eckhart and the German Dominican school

The highly speculative theology of the German Dominican School, which centred on Albert the Great and his pupils during the second half of the thirteenth and first years of the fourteenth centuries, turned on the Augustinian insight that the mind (as 'memory') possesses depths which are unknown even to itself. A second, fundamental Augustinian precept was that of illumination from the Divine Intellect which, particularly in the teaching of Meister Dietrich, came to dominate in the analysis of how the human mind works. For these thinkers, the mind itself is caught up in a dynamic relationship with God, who is himself the source of all knowing.

Secondly, we find in the Albertian school the belief that we are ourselves intellect by our very essence. It was the important Arabian philosopher Avicenna, whose work was well known in the Latin Middle Ages, who identified the soul as intellectual substance and who aimed through his psychology 'to identify the human soul with the human intellect'.[20] It is from Avicenna also that the Dominicans learned of the idea that the intellect is actualized by the actuality of the object of its perception. This is a complex notion which Libera explains in these terms: 'The subject and object are therefore, according to Avicenna, in a relation such that the subject is actualized by becoming its object.'[21]

Thirdly, we find among the Albertians the belief that the end of human existence is our divinization. We are transformed in a final vision of God which entirely transcends all prior forms of knowledge. This is an idea which was powerfully represented in the *Mystical Theology* of Pseudo-Dionysius, which was much read during the Middle Ages and upon which Albert himself wrote a commentary.[22]

The young Eckhart, educated in Cologne, cannot but have come strongly under the influence of Albert's ideas. He is unlikely to have known Hugh Ripelin or Ulrich of Strasburg personally (although Ulrich was the Provincial of the German Dominican Province when Eckhart entered the Order), but he may well have known Albert himself, who died in the same year that Eckhart arrived at the *studium generale* in Cologne.[23] And certainly the young Eckhart had direct contact with Dietrich of Freiberg, who was the Provincial of Teutonia when Eckhart was prior in Erfurt. It is not far fetched to speculate even that they may have been friends.

It is evident from the description of the Albertian school given above that Meister Eckhart inherited a number of important philosophical ideas from his fellow Dominicans. The first is that the nature of God himself is intellect. The second is that we in our own essence are intellect and the third is the principle of ascent, from the lower levels of cognition (i.e. of created things) to the highest level of cognition, which is the knowledge of God himself. In so far as we have freed ourselves from the knowledge of creatures, and have come to know the uncreated God, thus far we have become pure intellect and thus far we ourselves participate in the nature of the divinity. All these ideas are strongly present in Eckhart's own teachings. And there are many echoes in particular of Dietrich of Freiberg in Eckhart's thought: the primacy of knowing over being, the wholly dynamic and transcendent character of our intellectual substance and, not least, the belief that we are at our core linked in an immediacy to God through the principle of participation in his divine knowledge. One of the chief differences between the work of Dietrich and Albert is that for the former we are already fully 'intellectual' in our essence and thus already by our inner nature in close communion with God. For Albert, on the other hand, there is much more of a gradual ascent from the everyday areas of our experience to the highest states of the next life, as we move from the knowledge of things earthly to things divine. It is clearly the former, more radical position of Dietrich which is closer to that of Eckhart, and it seems entirely appropriate here to suggest that the older man may have exercised a considerable influence upon his younger confrère on this as on other issues of current interest and debate.

Meister Eckhart needs fundamentally to be seen within the context of the German Dominican school which fashioned him. And when we do so, we will see that elements which had seemed to be entirely his own are actually the common property of a number of theologians who were all working at approximately the same time and in the same geographical area. At least part of the reason for the very diverse ways in which Eckhart has been understood in this century is the fact that the intellectual context to which he belonged and which educated him seemed absent. It had, in fact, been long eclipsed by the triumph of St Thomas Aquinas and the Thomist school, which obscured the memory of a once vigorous movement which forcefully presented a number of metaphysical positions that were very different from those of Thomas himself. Indeed, it has only been in recent years that the principal texts of these early German Dominicans have begun to be published in modern critical editions.

And yet, while we have established Eckhart's debt to many of his contemporaries, which would seem to underline what he has in common with them, we are left wondering finally why it was that his own writings touched the hearts of so many, as they still do today. Only those of a decidedly philosophical frame of mind are likely to feast upon the demanding academic speculations of an Ulrich of Strasburg or a Dietrich of Freiberg, while Eckhart's works are widely translated and avidly consumed. It is only part of the answer, it seems, to point to the fact that Eckhart preached in the vernacular, for Dietrich did so too. Far more important is the fact that what for his brethren was theory, for Eckhart was very much a matter of experience. The whole of his work is permeated with the immediacy of God's presence to us, and the many ideas and paradigms which he has in common with the Albertian school simply serve as the theoretical underpinning and assist in the articulation of what is felt to be a fresh and exciting encounter with the living God.

NOTES TO CHAPTER 4

1. See Tugwell (1988), pp. 44 and 50.
2. ibid., pp. 44–50.

3. ibid., p. 51.
4. H. Denifle and E. Chatelain, eds, *Chartularium Universitatis Parisiensis* (Paris 1889–97), I, pp. 170–2 (quoted in Tugwell [1988] p. 51).
5. Tugwell (1988), pp. 3–39.
6. *De Intellectu et Intelligibili* II, pp. 6–9, quoted in Tugwell (1988), p. 59, whose translation I have used.
7. See Tugwell (1988), pp. 57–61.
8. *Metaph* 1.1.5, quoted in Tugwell (1988), p. 60, whose translation I have used.
9. Like Augustine, Gregory the Great and later Thomas Aquinas, Albert does not believe the experience of God in this life, without the intermediary of creatures, to be a possibility except in cases such as that of St Paul (see Tugwell [1988], p. 74 and n. 195).
10. The text of the *Compendium* is to be found in vol. 34 of the *Opera omnia* of Albert the Great (A. Borgnet, ed., Paris 1895, pp. 3–261). For details of Hugh's life and thought, see de Libera (1984), pp. 73–98, and T. Kaeppeli, *Scriptores Ordinis Praedicatorum Medii Aevi*, II (Rome 1970ff.), pp. 260–9.
11. It is intended to publish a new critical edition of the text in the CPTMA series. For details of the current editions, see de Libera (1984), pp. 146f. There is a biography of Ulrich of Strasburg in M. Grabmann, *Mittelalterliches Geistesleben* (Munich 1926), I, pp. 147–67. De Libera (1984) includes a study of his life and work (pp. 99–162).
12. De Libera (1984), p. 114.
13. For a biography of Dietrich by L. Sturlese, see *Deutsche Literatur des Mittelalters: Verfasserlexikon*, II (Berlin 1979), pp. 127–37. The same author has also written *Dokumente und Forschungen zu Leben und Werk Dietrichs von Freiberg*, Beiheft 3, CPTMA (Hamburg 1984), pp. 1–63.
14. See W. A. Wallace, *The Scientific Methodology of Theoderic of Freiberg: A Case Study of the Relationship between Science and Philosophy*, Studia Friburgensia N.F. 26 (Freiburg, Switzerland, 1959).
15. This view of Ulrich is to be found in the *De sum. Bon.* I, 1, 8, quoted in de Libera (1984), p. 114. For Dietrich on the agent intellect and *abditum mentis*, see *De vis. beat. Prooemium* 5, (CPTMA II, 1) p. 14, quoted in de Libera (1984), p. 178.
16. *De vis. beat.* 1.2.1.1.7., 2; p. 43 (quoted in de Libera, pp. 192–3).

17. There is a good summary of this in B. Mojsisch, *Die Theorie des Intellekts bei Dietrich von Freiberg*, Beiheft 1, CPTMA, Hamburg 1977.
18. Proclus, *The Elements of Theology*, E. R. Dodds, ed., 1963, p. 23, prop. 20.
19. E. Gilson, *History of Christian Philosophy in the Middle Ages* (London, Sheed & Ward, 1955), p. 435.
20. ibid., p. 204.
21. de Libera (1984), p. 51.
22. There is a translation of this commentary in Tugwell, pp. 133–98. De Libera (1984) discusses all three of these thinkers and their respective influence upon the Albertian school (pp. 37–72).
23. Eckhart refers to a speech mannerism of Albert's in his Easter Sermon of 1294, published in P. Kaeppeli, 'Praedicator Monoculos: Sermons Parisiens de la Fin du XIII siècle', in *Archivum Fratrum Praedicatorum* 27 (1957), p. 162.

PART TWO

MEISTER ECKHART'S THOUGHT

5 • THE THEOLOGY OF UNION

In the preceding chapters we have traced some of the key influences upon Eckhart, which formed the context of his work and which were the source for many of his ideas. In this section we shall look at Eckhart's own system in depth. It is at this point that the critical balance in Eckhart's work between analysis and experience, touched upon in the introduction, will come into view.

We are inclined to think of the work of the philosopher or academic theologian as an attempt to elucidate and ultimately to *understand*. Such writing is discursive and analytical as such thinkers proceed from one point to another. Their work is architectonic, established on the foundation of sound principles and persuasive arguments so that the final result can be like an elaborate and towering edifice, rather in the style of the Gothic cathedral. At the other end of the scale there is the mystic, touched by God, led forth by him into new areas of awareness, ravished, transformed, transfigured. Such a spirit will utter poetry, or will perhaps give expression to this inner state through dance, or tears, or song.

Despite his great training and erudition, Eckhart belongs in essence among the latter and not the former. His is a mystical spirit which possesses a deep sense of union with God and which speaks out of the experience in a way which will move others to receive it. He is therefore in essence a mystic who sings, and theology is his song.

But if we are to understand the nature of that song, in its depths, then we must turn to those areas of his work where Eckhart is borrowing, and adapting, the theological themes of his age. And we cannot do better than to begin with the technical though all-important field of analogy.

Eckhart's theory of analogy

According to the categories of logic, a term which has only one meaning (though it can be applied to more than one object) is said to be *univocal*, while a term which has different meanings is said to be *equivocal*. There is a third category, however, that of a term whose meanings, while distinct, nevertheless have something in common with each other, and this type of relation we call analogy. Thus we might argue that when we use the adjective 'good' of God and of people, the word 'good' has essentially the same meaning (univocal). Conversely, we might argue that since God and humankind are such different realities, the term 'good' cannot mean the same in respect to both (equivocal). Thirdly, we might say that 'good', while different with respect to God and people, nevertheless straddles both and has some degree of common meaning in its application to both. This is the relation of analogy.

The technical discussion of the nature of analogy is a vitally important area within medieval theology. This might surprise us a little today, for analogy seems quite alien to our modern concerns. And yet the importance of analogy during the medieval period stems from the fact that it describes the nature of the relations between the Creator and his creation. To what extent can we actually know God, and how viable is it to apply to him, the Creator, the language of his creatures ('good', and so forth)? More importantly still, what is the relation between the being of God and the being of his creatures? If we say that being only properly belongs to God, then the creature disappears, and yet if we say that being belongs as much to the creature as it does to God, then God is undermined in his transcendent distinctness from creatures. In order to understand what Meister Eckhart himself has to say about this, it would perhaps be wise firstly to outline the views of his thirteenth-century confrère, Thomas Aquinas, since it was these which were to become normative within the Dominican Order and to a great extent within the Catholic Church at large.

Analogy according to Thomas Aquinas

The system of analogy which is commonly associated with
the name of Thomas Aquinas owes as much in fact to the
mind of Cajetan. Cardinal Cajetan (Thomas de Vio) was a
Dominican theologian who lived during the turbulent
fifteenth and sixteenth centuries and who decided to attempt
to expound systematically the complex area of Aquinas'
various statements on the nature of analogy. In his *The
Analogy of Names* (1498) Cajetan stated that there were
three types of analogy (in Thomas). He called the first the
'analogy of inequality'. This is 'a generic perfection unequally
shared by the species within the genus'.[1] Thus while a man
and a dog are both animals, a man is a more perfect animal
than a dog. This form of analogy is of less importance for
the following discussion. More important is the second kind
of analogy which Cajetan identified in St Thomas: the
'analogy of attribution'. The example he gave for this is that
of the adjective 'healthy' which is applied to a man, his
medicine and his urine. The quality of 'health' only truly
resides in the man, Cajetan argued, and so we apply the
adjective 'healthy' to all the other things only by virtue of an
association we make in our own minds. We attribute 'health'
extrinsically to his medicine (which is the *cause* of his
health) and his urine (which is the *sign* of his health),
although health cannot properly be said to reside in either of
these. The third type of analogy Cajetan calls the 'analogy of
proportionality'. In this instance 'it is not diverse realities
which fall under consideration but diverse modes of
existence of the self-same reality'.[2] An example of this is
when we use the term 'to see' of both the eye and the
intellect. The principle is the same but the context is
different. In the teaching of Thomas Aquinas, Cajetan
argued, it was this third type of analogy which was alone
the way in which we could use language of God and explore
his relation to the creature.

Although in general Cajetan's systematic reading of
Thomas held sway for several centuries, there was soon
heard at least one dissenting voice. The Spanish Jesuit
theologian Suarez argued that Cajetan was wrong on two

counts. Firstly, what Cajetan called 'analogy of proportion' was in truth metaphor (i.e. the 'seeing' of the eyes is not properly but only metaphorically used of the intellect), and therefore this could not have been what Aquinas meant when he sought to outline the relation of the creature to God. That would mean that God exists truly while creatures exist only metaphorically, while Aquinas had always sought to protect the status of the creature though at the same time safeguarding God's transcendence. Suarez therefore suggested that, when he talks of God, Aquinas is using a form of analogy which he calls 'the analogy of intrinsic attribution'. This means that although being (and other qualities) can more perfectly be attributed to God than to his creatures, creatures possess being too. In other words, although the source of the being of creatures is God's own being, nevertheless, they do in a real sense possess being themselves.

Modern interpreters of Aquinas' teaching on analogy agree with Suarez that the actual ideas of Thomas are rather different from Cajetan's immensely influential systemization of him.[3] The key type of analogy to emerge is that of a 'one to one' relation of 'intrinsic attribution'. The 'one to one' simply means that God and his creature are not related by the appeal to some third term, and the 'intrinsic attribution' is likeness between God and his creature based upon the principle of cause and effect. Our Creator made us in his own likeness. And yet it is still a relation of 'attribution', which means, for example, that the being which we truly possess derives from God and is dependent upon him. The 'analogy of intrinsic attribution is able to signify both that *there is a likeness* between primary (God) and secondary analogate (creature), and that *the secondary analogate is an imperfect imitation* of the primary'.[4] The advantage of the Thomist system of analogy in its application to the relation of the Creator and the created is therefore that it guarantees the reality of the latter, while safeguarding the transcendence of the former.

Meister Eckhart and the theory of analogy

In his *Commentary on the Book of Wisdom* we find the
following passage:

> These three are to be distinguished: 'the univocal, the equivocal
> and the analogous. Equivocals are divided according to different
> things that are signified, univocals according to various
> differences of the [same] thing'. Analogous things are not
> distinguished according to things, nor through the difference of
> things, but 'according to the modes [of being]' of one and the
> same simple thing. For example, the one and the same health
> that is in an animal is that (and no other) which is in the diet
> and the urine [of the animal] in such a way that there is no more
> of health in the diet and urine than there is in a stone.[5]

The phrases enclosed in single quotation marks are from
Thomas Aquinas (*In Sent* I d. 22 q. 1 a. 3 ad 2); but we
should note the difference in Eckhart's meaning. Eckhart
agrees with Thomas that in analogy there exist different
'modes of being', but his final sentence suggests that he
understands something very different from Thomas here.
Whereas in Thomas's analogy of proportion or analogy of
intrinsic attribution the second part of the analogy actually
does possess the quality concerned, albeit imperfectly, *in
itself*, in Eckhart's formulation it does not: 'there is no more
of health in the diet and urine than there is in a stone'. This
is further drawn out by his next remark, which is that 'urine
is said to be "healthy" only because it signifies the health,
the same in number, which is in the animal, just as a
circular wreath which has nothing of wine in it [signifies]
wine.'[6] Although the character as sign of healthy urine is
based causally on the health of the person, in the case of the
wreath (which traditionally hung outside German taverns)
there is no such connection. The character as sign of the
wreath is entirely an arbitrary one. Here Eckhart seems to
be explicitly stating that the property of the first part of an
analogical proposition (the first analogate) does not properly
belong to the second part, but inheres in it by imputation.[7]
Confirmation of this view comes in two further passages
from the same text in which Eckhart states that the

transcendental quality at issue (e.g. goodness, justice, wisdom, being) exists properly only in the first part of an analogical predication (i.e. God):

> [Secondary] analogates have nothing of the form according to which they are analogically ordered rooted in positive fashion in themselves, but every created being is analogically ordered to God in existence, truth and goodness. Therefore, every created being radically and positively possesses existence, life and wisdom from and in God and not in itself.[8]

> Being or existence and every perfection, especially general ones such as existence, oneness, truth, goodness, light, justice and so forth are used to describe God and creatures in an analogical way. It follows from this that goodness and justice and the like [in creatures] have their goodness totally from something outside to which they are analogically ordered, namely, God.[9]

This same idea is spelled out in the Latin sermons, where we find:

> Once again it must be noted that all things are ready to serve God, because in the analogical relation of cause and effect, there is only one thing which differs only according to its modes [of being]. This is what is meant by the word analogy itself, that is a single thing which exists both here and there, but in a prior and a posterior way. Therefore, just as the wreath serves the wine by proclaiming its presence, and the urine proclaims the health of the animal, although it has nothing of the animal's health within itself, similarly the creature serves God. This is why in Augustine the creatures are the signs of God and show that we should love him who made them.[10]

What Eckhart is stressing here, time and again, is that we should not think of creatures as possessing any of the so-called transcendental properties (goodness, justice, wisdom, unity, being)[11] *in themselves*. Rather, God *lends* such qualities to them:

> God does not give creatures any goodness, but he lends it to them. The sun gives the air heat, but it only lends it light, and so when the sun sinks, the light vanishes from the air while the heat remains in it, for heat is given as its own possession.[12]

Joseph Koch, therefore, is quite right when he says that if, for Thomas Aquinas, the being of the creature is a gift given by God which God might at any point take back, then, for Eckhart, being is *on loan* to the creature, and never properly comes into its possession.[13]

In statements of the type given in the pages above, Eckhart is attempting to show that creatures do not represent a reality *in themselves* (viewed outside their relation to God, that is). His meaning is not that God exists while creatures do not exist, but that the existence of creatures is given them immediately by God, that it still remains in God, and that creatures have no existence other than this.[14] He explores this same idea moreover in the *Commentary on John* and in the *Liber benedictus* by deliberately substituting for analogy the paradigm of the Nicene *generatio*, which is to say that model of an immediate generation which, according to the Nicene Creed, governs the relation between the Father and the Son. This affords him an even more striking paradigm for emphasizing the immediacy of relation of the principle as it exists in God and the transcendental quality as it exists in the individual creature.

Let us begin first of all with Eckhart's discussion of the generation by the Father of the Son in his *Commentary on John* in which Eckhart explicitly rejects the model of analogy on the grounds that this would fail to express the identity of being, or nature, between the first and second Person of the Trinity:

> The Son or Word is the same as what the Father or Principle is . . . Here it must be noted that in analogical relations what is produced derives from the source, but is nevertheless beneath the principle and not with it. It is of another nature and thus is not the principle itself.[15]

> What follows expresses this — 'The Word was with God.' It does not say 'under God', or 'descends from God', but says 'The Word was with God'. The phrase 'with God' bespeaks a kind of equality. In things that are analogical what is produced is always inferior, of lower grade, less perfect and unequal to its

source. In things that are univocal what is produced is always equal to the source. It does not just participate in the same nature, but it receives the total nature from its source in a simple, whole and equal manner. Thus . . . what proceeds is the son of its source. A son is one who is other in person but not other in nature.[16]

Eckhart rejects therefore the model of analogy (here based on cause and effect) in order to explicate the relation of the Son and the Father. The concept of *generatio* within the Trinity must convey the identity of essence which prevails between them. And it is this principle of the 'generation' of the Word which Eckhart then applies to the relations between the perfections as they exist in visible form in the creature and their source in God. In the following passage, 'justice' and the 'just man' stand for all the transcendental perfections:

> The just man proceeds from and is begotten by justice and by that very fact is distinguished from it. Nothing can beget itself. Nonetheless, the just man is not different in nature from justice, both because 'just' signifies only justice, even as 'white' signifies only the quality of whiteness, and because justice would make no one just if its nature changed from one place to another, just as whiteness does not make a man black or grammar make him musical. From this it is clear . . . that the just man is the offspring and son of justice. One is and is called a son in that one becomes other in person, not other in nature. 'The Father and I are one' (Jn. 10.30) — we are distinct in person, because nothing gives birth to itself; we are one in nature, because otherwise justice would not beget the just man, nor would the Father beget the Son who became other in person, nor would generation be univocal . . . If the Father and the Son, justice and the just man, are one and the same in nature, it follows . . . that the just man is equal to justice, not less than it, nor is the Son less than the Father.[17]

Here Eckhart speaks of one formal distinction between God and his creation, or justice and the just man, which is that the justice of the just man is 'begotten' and not 'begetting'. But essentially justice as a principle and the justice of the just man are the same. The real distinction between God and his creation for Eckhart, then, resides in the fact that the just man and justice are identical only *in so far as* (*inquantum*) the just man is just. In other words, God is entirely good, just, wise, and so on, while we are only partially so.[18] Among the Latin works, the *Prologue to the Book of Propositions* furnishes many examples of the way in which Eckhart assumes the perfections of the creature into the substance of the Creator Himself, but it is in the German *Book of Divine Consolation* and *On the Noble Man* that these ideas are most consistently expressed:

> Goodness is not created, not made, not born; rather it is what gives birth and bears the good man; and the good man, in so far as he is good, is unmade and uncreated, and yet he is born, the child and the son of goodness. In the good man goodness gives birth to itself and to everything that it is.[19]

Arising from the *inquantum* principle outlined above is the further important principle of unity and division. Essentially, the transcendentals, or 'perfections', exist in God in a condition of unity. There is no division in him, but truth, goodness and being form an indivisible unity. In created things, however, which only possess the transcendental qualities in finite proportions, there is necessarily division. For Eckhart, therefore, God represents the principle of absolute unity in distinction to the diversity of his creation:

> It is the nature of the first and superior, being 'rich in itself', to influence and affect the inferior with its properties, among which are unity and indivision. What is divided in the inferior is always one and undivided in the superior. It clearly follows that the superior is in no way divided in the inferior; but, while remaining undivided, it gathers together and unites what is divided in the inferior.[20]

GOD AND BEING

Being as God

Meister Eckhart, like so many medieval theologians, is fascinated with the question of *being*, its nature and its origins. Yet being in his work is not viewed as a phenomenon within itself, as is generally the case in existentialist philosophy today, but it is seen exclusively in relation to God. Some of Eckhart's statements on this relation can appear paradoxical, and he has even been accused of pantheism, which is that type of theological error (in Christian eyes) which effaces the distinction between God and his creation.[21] The complexity of Eckhart's teaching on God and being is much reduced, however, if we keep two factors clearly in mind.

The first point is that Eckhart's teaching on this must be seen initially within the context of his teaching on analogy, which we have discussed above. If we understand how Eckhart believes that the difference between the prior and transcendental properties (one of which is being), as these exist in God and in objects, is that they exist in God infinitely and only finitely or partially in created things (according to the *inquantum* principle) then many of his statements on being will fall naturally into place. Secondly, we need to grasp the significance of Eckhart's refrain 'being is God' (*Esse est Deus*), which sounds throughout the prologues to his *Three-Part Work*. This has sometimes been interpreted as meaning that 'God is being', but Karl Albert is quite right when he points out that this statement reveals the fact that Eckhart paramountly wants to say something about being, and not about God.[22]

Eckhart tells us that there are, as it were, two kinds of being. The first he calls 'being' (*esse*), 'absolute being' (*esse absolutum*), 'simple being' (*esse simpliciter*) or 'being itself' (*esse ipsum*), while the second he calls 'being this or that' (*esse hoc et hoc; esse hoc aut aliud; esse huius et huius*), 'being such and such' (*esse tale*) or 'determinate being' (*esse determinatum*). The former is the being of God, which is infinite and uncontaminated by any form of admixture, while the latter is the specific and local being of entities within the world:[23]

> God alone is in the proper sense being, one, true and good. Every other thing is *this* being, for example, a stone, a lion, a man, and so on, and *this* one, *this* true, *this* good, for example, a good mind, a good angel, and so on.

We must judge differently concerning being as such and the being of this or that, and also about other terms such as one, true and good. Thus there is only one being, and this is God; but there are many beings that are this or that.

1) God alone is properly being, one, true and good. 2) From him all things are and are one, true and good. 3) All things immediately owe to him the fact that they are and that they are one, true and good. 4) When I say this being, or this one, or that one, this or that true, this or that good, 'this' or 'that' adds absolutely nothing, or makes no addition, of entity, unity, truth or goodness, to being, one, true, good.[24]

The clear statement that 'being is God' indicates that Eckhart's application of the word 'being' to both God and creatures is univocal (has the same meaning), and that the distinction between God and his creation is maintained by the fact that the being of God is infinite while that of his creatures is finite and particular. This is thoroughly consistent with the *inquantum* principle of Eckhart's theory of analogy.[25]

In Eckhart's view of metaphysics as outlined in the prologues to the uncompleted *Three-Part Work*, this distinction between the local, determinate, diversified being of things and the free, undifferentiated, 'uncontaminated' being of God is central, for all the transcendental properties which exist in creatures in the diversity of their created state, exist also in God but in a condition of absolute oneness, which is the particular character of the divine nature. Eckhart finds subtle ways of designating the nature of God, which he variously calls the 'purity' or 'fulness' of being (*puritas* or *plenitudo essendi*), the 'negation of negation' (*negatio negationis*), the 'One', 'intellect' or 'nothing of anything' (*nihtes niht*).[26] The 'purity' of being (which is a phrase Eckhart has from Thomas) expresses the fact that God's nature is entirely united, and free of any form of addition, while the phrase 'negation of negation' expresses the infinity of God. To define the nature of something created is at the same time to say what it is not, while in defining the nature of God, the uncreated, we negate the principle of negation itself. The negation of negation thus becomes 'the purest form of affirmation as applied to God'.[27]

Despite the abundance and fluidity of Eckhart's terminology, however, certain themes do remain the same. The whole of his thinking on God seems to move between two poles, one of which represents the utter transcendence of God with respect to his creatures while the other is the immanence of God, who is the very foundation of the being of creatures and, therefore, of our own being.

God as Intellect

There are numerous occasions when Eckhart seems to put forward a very different view of the relation between God and being from that which we find in the *Three-Part Work*, where Eckhart sets up a distinction between God as 'absolute being', 'simple being' or the 'purity of being' and his creation as 'determinate being' or 'being this and that'. In his *Parisian Questions* Eckhart makes a simple opposition between God as 'knowledge' and his creation as 'being'. Thus it is not God any more who is 'being' but his creation. If Eckhart's system of analogy and the *generatio* tends to stress the continuity between God and creature in a theology of immanence, then the prologues to the *Three-Part Work* and the *Parisian Questions* stress more the extent to which God transcends his creation. And so we are not dealing with a process of evolution in Eckhart's thinking here so much as an attempt to hold a dialectic of immanence and transcendence in balance.[28]

Let us firstly consider what Eckhart has to say in the first of his *Parisian Questions* about the relationship between 'being' and 'knowledge' in God (by which, of course, Eckhart does not mean 'things learned' but rather that form of 'knowing' which is 'understanding' or indeed consciousness itself). He begins by stating that they are the same in reality: 'God is an intellect and understanding, and his understanding itself is the ground of his existence'.[29] As his argument develops, however, it becomes clear that Eckhart sees a basic disjunction between knowledge/understanding and being: 'my first claim is that understanding is superior to existence and belongs to a different order'.[30] In support of this argument, Eckhart points to the intelligent ordering of the universe and to the beginning of St John's Gospel: '"In the beginning was the Word", which is entirely related to an intellect'.[31] More importantly, he quotes the idea (from Proclus) that 'the first of created things is existence'.[32] This means that God as the cause of being must be prior to being. At this point Eckhart turns away from the model of causality which he used so extensively in the *Three-Part Work*, the *Liber benedictus* and the *Commentary on John*, according to which the cause effects its own likeness (i.e. the Good causes goodness), and he adopts instead a model according to which the cause is different from, or higher than, its effect. Eckhart uses the image of a line drawn from a point in order to illustrate what he means by this latter theory of causality: 'a principle is never the same as that which follows from a principle, as a point is never a line'.[33] But Eckhart still wishes to reconcile understanding and being within God by emphasizing that understanding is God's manner of being. He says, therefore, that 'existence is not in God but purity of existence' and at one point Eckhart tells us frankly, 'Of course, if you wish to call understanding existence I do not mind.'[34]

The second of the *Parisian Questions* shows a sharper distinction between understanding and being than we have seen in the first. Although Eckhart is discussing the theme with respect to angels, there are clear indications for the development of his thought both with regard to God and to the human intellect. He begins by quoting from Aristotle to the effect that the intellect is 'unmixed with anything' and 'has nothing in common' with anything so that it can 'know everything'. He concludes: 'If the intellect, therefore, in so far as it is an intellect, is nothing, it follows that neither is understanding some existence.'[35] Just as previously Eckhart had found the indeterminacy of 'absolute being' important in the ascription of this term to God, now it is the indeterminacy of the intellect which appeals to him, its 'non-existence': 'The intellect, as such, is neither here, nor now, nor a definite thing. But every being or existence is in a definite genus and species. So the intellect, as such, is not a being, nor does it have an existence.'[36] This leads on to statements such as we find in a German sermon:

> Foolish teachers say that God is pure being, but he is as far above being as the highest angel is above a gnat. If I spoke of God as being, I would be saying something which is as untrue as if I had said that the sun is pale or black . . . When we receive God in being, then we receive him in the forecourt in which he dwells. But where is he then in his temple, where he appears in holiness? Intellect is the temple of God. Nowhere does God dwell more truly than in his temple. In the words of another master: God is intellect which lives in knowledge of itself alone, which remains within itself, where nothing has ever touched it, for there it is alone in its stillness. In his knowledge of himself, God perceives himself in himself.[37]

And there are echoes of this in another (Latin) sermon:

> Intellect properly belongs to God, and 'God is one'. Therefore, anything has as much of God and of the One and of 'One-existence' with God as it has of intellect and what is intellectual. For God is one intellect and intellect is one God. Nowhere and never do we find God as God save in intellect.[38]

God as the One and the 'negation of negation'

The two last quotations given above reveal to what extent the idea that God is intellect guarantees the unicity or oneness of God for Eckhart. This is an important aspect of Eckhart's thinking to which he refers in a number of passages. In one of these, he argues that all the transcendental perfections exist in God as one:

> Thus in God every perfection is one because in him there is no number of perfections. This is the reason why anyone who would see God himself through himself, that is through his essence and not from other things nor through some other medium, would see a single perfection and would see all perfections in it and through it rather than it through them . . . If the onlooker were to give a name to that which he sees and through which and in which he sees, it would necessarily be the One . . .[39]

Eckhart then tells us that 'the One and being are inter-changeable' and that 'what falls from the One falls from existence', recalling the identification of knowledge and being that we find in the first of the *Parisian Questions*. He goes on in the same passage to state that 'division, in so far as it is a fall from the One, is a privation of existence, of oneness and goodness',[40] and elsewhere that 'existence always stands in the one; multiplicity as such does not exist'.[41] But Eckhart can also assert that the One is itself beyond being,[42] revealing the same fluidity of terms that we have seen in his approach to God as 'intellect' and 'being'.

It would seem that Eckhart's remarks on God as the One express a more radical rupture between God and the creation than was the case even with the paradigm of God as intellect and the creature as being. And yet the transcendence of God is once again balanced by his immanence in that Eckhart's exploration of the absolute unicity of God sets up another form of dialectic: that of the Neoplatonic scheme of emanation whereby all things derive, or 'descend', from the One in which they nevertheless continue to participate. Thus the principal, all-inclusive being of God, whereby he is omnipresent in the world through his metaphysical priority, serves precisely to distinguish him from all things and all beings in the world. God is distinct therefore from all creatures precisely by not being distinct from any.[43] Although a complex notion, this formula is a restatement in the terms of a Neoplatonic metaphysics of unicity of the same dialectical configuration of God within us and God beyond us which determined Eckhart's manipulation of analogy, 'intellect' and 'being' in his theology of God.

But if at times Eckhart is content to call God the One, then there are also occasions when he seeks to expound the theme of the oneness of God in terms of a further concept: the 'negation of negation'. Here Eckhart is denying that 'oneness' affirms anything *positively* of God, as this would tend to 'add' something to him and thus to conceal his true nature, as he is in himself:

St Paul says: 'One God'. *One* is something purer than goodness or truth. Goodness and truth do not add anything, but they add

in *thought*, and when it is thought, something is added. The
One adds nothing, where he is in himself before flowing forth
into the Son and the Holy Ghost. Therefore he says: 'Friend,
draw up higher.' A master says: 'One is the negation of the
negation.' If I say God is good, that adds something. One is the
negation of the negation and a denial of the denial. What does
one mean? One means that to which nothing is added. The soul
receives the Godhead as it is purified in itself, with nothing
added, with nothing thought. *One* is a negation of the negation.
All creatures have a negation in themselves: one negates by not
being the another. An angel negates by not being another. But
God negates the negation: he is one and negates all else; for
outside of God nothing is. (W 97)

Oneness, as 'negation of negation' therefore emerges as a
negative way of speaking of God which is nevertheless
wholly affirmative in that it does not *deny* anything of other
beings. Eckhart's point is that to define a creature is
simultaneously to say what it is not; while to define God as
the 'negation of negation' is to define him in terms which
neither add anything to him (thus concealing his true nature)
nor deny anything of anything else. But in another passage
Eckhart puts forward the contrary view that to speak of
God as the 'One' is in fact to 'add' something to him:

But being, goodness and truth are co-extensive, for as far as
being extends it is good and it is true. Now people take goodness
and attach it to being: that covers up being and gives it a skin,
for it is something added. Or they take God as he is truth. Is
being truth? Yes, for truth depends on being, for God said to
Moses: 'He that is has sent me' (Ex. 3.14). St Augustine says,
'Truth is the Son in the Father, for truth depends on being.' Is
being truth? If you were to ask many a master, he would say
'Yes', but if you were to ask me, I would have said, 'Yes', but
now I say, 'No!', for truth too is something added. Now they
take God as he is one, for one is more truly one than that which
has been unified. Whatever is one, from that all that is other has
been removed: but precisely that which is removed, is something
added, because it denotes otherness.
    But if God is neither goodness nor being nor truth nor one,
what then is he? He is pure nothing (*nihtes niht*): he is neither
this nor that. If you think of anything he might be, he is not that.
(W 54)

Passages such as these show Eckhart's clear preference for speaking of God in radically negative terms, so that nothing is 'added' to him. The inadequacy of using names and affirmative language of God, which conceal rather than reveal him, is to some extent resolved by using negative formulations which appear to subvert the linguistic process itself, and thus God becomes 'nothing of anything' (*nihtes niht*), 'solitude' and 'wilderness' (*einoede, wüestunge*: W 66) and is the 'hidden darkness of the eternal Godhead, which is unknown and never has been known and never shall be known' (W 53).

Conclusion

Eckhart identifies God as being, purity of being, intellect, the One and absolute nothingness. For each passage in which he affirms the identity of God as one of the first four of these, there are alternative passages in which he specifically denies that that particular term is applicable to God. Even the last term, which seeks to convey the total transcendence of the unknowable God, must be balanced by Eckhart's view – expressed in his teaching on the 'birth of God' – that this unattainable God pours forth his essence into the human soul. The reader might be forgiven for thinking then that Eckhart is guilty of a certain confusion of terms here, and it is no wonder that Etienne Gilson commented to the effect that while the interpreter of Eckhart is easily able to construct a system from his work, he is just as able to construct another – entirely different – system from the same works.[44] But such confusion, while wholly understandable, results largely from the fact that we approach Eckhart often with the wrong assumptions. Scholastic philosophy (indeed most philosophy) is a mapping out of an area of thought or experience whereby understanding leads to fixed points of reference. We demand not only clarity and precision from our thinkers, but we expect from them also that they will hold firm positions which provide shape and purpose in an overall design. But if we think of such philosophy as being the attempt to produce an account of the world which is like a still-frame snapshot, then Eckhart's thinking provides us with a moving frame. This means that his view of truth is that it is itself dynamic, generative, insightful. Truth is, in his own terms, 'break-through' into a new kind of *awareness* or cognitive being. This is why as soon as Eckhart has taken up a position (i.e. 'being is God'), he subverts it by collapsing it towards a centre. Thus the mind is drawn from the being of creatures to the purity or fulness of being in God, to the principle of Mind or unicity which is prior to being in God and from there to God as absolute nothingness and negation, beyond the reach of either concept or word. The effect of this strategy is to create a kind of metaphysical black-hole into which the ordered structures of the created universe, thinking and language, encountering the very limits of their own createdness, will collapse and vanish. Eckhart's ontology is a metaphysical journey, which begins with the ordinary created being of the creature and ends – through strategies of linguistic and conceptual subversion – in the 'hidden depths of the Godhead'.

Such a process is inevitably one which involves much paradox, fluctuation of terms and seeming inconsistency. The notion of being, for instance, undergoes a dramatic change: in the creature it is the signature of divine life (and thus reveals God), while in the divinity it masks the divine nature (and thus conceals him). Being is God *ad extra*, that is as viewed from the standpoint of the creature, but if our minds ascend through being into the Godhead itself, then being will be shown not to have been the divine nature at all but rather that which flows from a superessential ground which is more akin to intellect, desert or darkness. Being is therefore 'in' God, but is visible to the creature outside God and invisible to us as we become united with him.[45] Put in other terms, being is the garment which God wears and which simultaneously reveals and conceals him; it is the 'forecourt' to the 'sanctuary' in which God dwells.

The second crucial element which informs and fashions Eckhart's thinking is that of dialectic: a structure of unity and opposition which turns on the principle that God is both infinitely beyond us and infinitely present to and within us. Indeed, these two themes of transcendence and immanence provide the two poles between which Eckhart's thinking is suspended. Thus, if our being is God, then we are God only *in so far as* we truly possess being. If God is intellect and thus infinitely beyond being, then we too possess the power of intellect and can be one with him *in so far as* we are intellect. If God is beyond all words and concepts, hidden in impenetrable darkness, then it is this same God who gives birth to himself in us, in the ground of the soul. Indeed, Eckhart sums up this pervasive sense of dialectic in his work when he says in his Commentary on Exodus: 'You should know that nothing is as dissimilar as the Creator and any creature. In the second place, nothing is as similar as the Creator and any creature.' Eckhart justifies the first part on the grounds that God, as 'Existence Itself', is distinct from any particular existing thing. He justifies the second part on the grounds that the creature receives its existence from God and asks: 'What is as similar to something else as that which possesses and receives its total existence from the order and relation it has to something else?'[46]

To say, as Eckhart does, that God is both infinitely beyond us and yet intimately present within us, is a complex, contradictory truth which points beyond itself to a deep mystery. But perhaps we should not be so surprised at its presence in Eckhart, for dialectical thought (where dialectic denotes a kind of creative thinking which attempts to hold together two apparently contradictory truths in the service of a truth which is deeper and more elusive) is a kind of thinking which is germane to Christian doctrine and experience. It is after all evident in such paradoxical formulations as the Trinity in Unity, the belief in God made flesh or that those who lose their lives shall gain them. And it gains strength too from the notion that we are both 'like' God and 'unlike' him. To paraphrase a statement from the Fourth Lateran Council, the closer to God we become, the more distant we are from him.[47] We shall fail entirely to grasp Eckhart's 'point' then if we fail to understand the

dialectical nature of his thinking that is itself based upon
the primary Christian mystery which is the interpenetration
of the human and divine. This mystery radiates out from the
centre of Eckhart's own experience and serves to 'bend' the
formal theology which Eckhart received from his intellectual
world in accordance with its inner momentum.[48] Thus, in
his hands, scholastic theology becomes what de Certeau
calls a *manière de parler*, which is to say a medium for the
expression of a personal and mystical vision of a unitive
encounter with God.[50]

God as Creator

We cannot leave the field of Eckhart's fundamental theology
without considering another of those areas which exercised
a fascination over many minds in the Middle Ages. And yet
the question of the creation was a delicate issue. The reason
for this was that Aristotle, whose rediscovered works
enjoyed the greatest esteem and influence, had taught that
the world was not created but had existed from all eternity.
This evidently clashed with the Judaeo-Christian tradition
of *creatio ex nihilo*, or the creation of the universe out of
nothing. Some of the Arab thinkers who, as we have seen,
initially mediated Aristotelian thought to the West also
followed Aristotle in his teaching on the eternal existence of
the world. In 1272 Stephen Tempier, the Bishop of Paris,
condemned a number of radical Aristotelian propositions,
including that of the eternal existence of the world.

   In the light of this, anything which appeared to undermine
the principle of the creation was sensitive, and Eckhart's
teaching on the doctrine of the creation was one of the chief
areas for which he was condemned. The first three articles
of *In agro dominico* all suggest that Eckhart taught the
eternal existence of the world. This is emphatically not the
case, although certain of his statements, when removed
from their proper context, might seem to suggest this. In his
remarks on the creation Eckhart happily states that God
creates the world 'from eternity',[51] but what he evidently
means is that since God is himself outside time, then nothing

he does can be thought of as being within time. All that God does is, in this sense, from eternity. This becomes quite clear in his remarks on the charge of having taught the eternity of the world in his *Defence:*

> Creation indeed and every activity of God is the very essence of God, and yet it does not follow from this that if God created the world from eternity, the world is therefore from eternity, as the uneducated think. For creation is not an eternal state, just as the thing created itself is not eternal.[52]

Eckhart also makes the point that creation is not something we should think of as having happened in the past with consequences reaching into the present but that it is, in fact, continuous. To this end Eckhart is fond of quoting from St Augustine's *Confessions:* 'There is no other vein by which being and life flow into us except this, that you, O Lord, have made us'.[53] Summing up Eckhart's understanding of creation, Maurer writes: 'God so created all things that he nevertheless always creates in the present. The act of creation does not fade into the past but is always in the beginning and in process and new.'[54]

The classic instance in which Eckhart pursues this idea, however, is in his *Commentary on the Book of Wisdom* when he is interpreting the line: 'They that eat me, shall yet hunger' (Si. 24.29), and places creation, as the mediation of being, firmly within the context of his thinking on analogy:

> It is evident, therefore, that every being and everything that belongs to the number of beings does not possess the existence it thirsts for from itself, but from some superior. Therefore, existence is not fixed and does not inhere or have its source in it, nor does it remain when the superior is absent, even if only conceptually. This is why it always thirsts for its superior's presence, and it is better and more proper [to say] that it continually receives existence than that it has existence itself in a fixed or even initial way.[55]

The nothingness of creatures

Having clearly evolved a theology of creation whereby the creature is maintained in existence by a continuous inflow

of being from God, there are numerous instances in which
Eckhart speaks of the radical *nothingness* of the creature:

> All creatures are a pure nothingness. I do not say that they are
> only worth little, or that they are anything at all. They are
> absolutely nothing. Whatever has no being is nothing.
>   All created things have the shadow of nothingness.
>   Thus every created thing, in itself, is from nothingness and is
> nothingness.[56]

The final quotation above, however, hints at what Eckhart
means by such statements, and it tells us why Eckhart's
judges in Avignon were wrong to include the proposition
regarding the nothingness of creatures as number twenty-
six of the condemned articles. In a passage from his
Commentary on Exodus Eckhart gives a quotation from
Jerome in support of his view in which the nothingness of
the creature *in comparison with* the being of God is clearly
stated: 'Our existence is not compared with God's'.[57] And,
in the same passage, Eckhart makes quite clear that this is
what he himself means:

> Perhaps a more subtle reason can be given why there is no
> comparison between God and a creature, and it is this. Every
> comparison implies that there are at least two things and that
> they are distinct, for nothing is compared to itself or is like itself.
> Every created being taken or conceived apart *as distinct in itself
> from God* is not a being, but is nothing. What is separate and
> distinct from God is separate and distinct from existence,
> because whatever exists is from God himself, through him and
> in him.[58]

NOTES TO CHAPTER 5

1. G. Phelan, *St Thomas and Analogy* (Milwaukee 1943), p. 27.
2. M. S. L. Penido, *Le rôle de l'analogie en théologie dogmatique*
   (Paris 1931), p. 77 (quoted in Phelan, p. 41).
3. Phelan's *St Thomas and Analogy* still reflects Cajetan's view.
   It was Etienne Gilson's important paper 'Cajetan et l'Existence'
   (in *Tijdschrift voor Philosophie* (1953), pp. 267–86) which
   marked the turn. See Battista Mondin's excellent study *The*

Principle of Analogy in Protestant and Catholic Theology
(The Hague 1963), pp. 40-2.
4. Mondin, p. 101.
5. LW II, p. 280 (TP, p. 178). This passage is quoted and
analysed also by Koch (1973), pp. 371ff.
6. ibid.
7. Koch (1973), p. 379, quite correctly seeks to put Eckhart's
teaching on analogy in the context of his teaching on creation
and justification, while Brunner (1969), pp. 342ff., argues
that the Eckhartian system of analogy is essentially the
Thomist analogy of proportion in the face, it must be said, of
passages such as *Comm. Joh.* 5-6 (LW III, p. 7; EE, p. 124) in
which Eckhart seems explicitly to reject the analogy of
proportion.
8. LW II, p. 282 (TP, p. 178). The square brackets in this case
are mine.
9. ibid.
10. LW IV, p. 372 (quoted in Brunner [1969], p. 339).
11. The 'transcendentals' are those properties which cannot be
assumed into the category of accidents. Accidents (e.g.
hardness, roundness, roughness) have no existence apart from
the substantial being of the entity to which they are attached,
while the transcendentals are said to be 'perfections' which
are prior to entities.
12. *The Book of Divine Consolation* (DW V, p. 36: my translation).
13. Koch (1973), p. 385. It does appear that there is a parallel
here with Luther's theory of analogy as contained in his
account of justification.
14. I find myself in disagreement on this point, therefore, with
Frank Tobin who, in his excellent study of Meister Eckhart
(*Meister Eckhart: Thought and Language* [1986], pp. 44f.,
48, 53, 63) suggests that Eckhart's system of analogy serves
to stress the *transcendence* of God. When Eckhart argues that
the property of the first analogate does not reside *formaliter* in
the second, then what he means is that the property of the
first analogate, *as found in the second*, remains nevertheless a
proprium of the first. The thrust of his system of analogy, and
indeed his use of ontological terms (*esse absolutum, esse hoc
et hoc* etc.), is to emphasize the immanence of God rather than
his transcendence, for Eckhart, in his own words, is 'not
depriving things of existence or destroying their existence but
on the contrary . . . establishing it' (*Prologue to the Book of*

Propositions, LW I, p. 176; M, p. 100; see also *Comm. Wis.* p. 260, LW II, p. 591).

15. *Comm. Joh.* 6 (LW III, pp. 7ff.; EE, p. 124).
16. *Comm. Joh.* 5 (LW III, p. 7; EE, ibid.).
17. *Comm. Joh.* 16–17 (LW III, pp. 14f.; EE, p. 127).
18. In his important article, 'Eckhart's condemnation reconsidered' (1980), Bernard McGinn makes the point that it was the *inquantum* principle and the judges' failure to understand it which was 'one of the major sources of Eckhart's difficulties' (pp. 406f.).
19. *The Book of Divine Consolation* (DW V, p. 9; EE, pp. 209f.).
20. *Gen. Prol.* 10 (LW I, pp. 154ff.; M, p. 84). The phrase in quotation marks is from the twentieth proposition in the *Liber de causis* by Proclus.
21. There is an interesting discussion of the whole field of pantheism in LTK, VIII, pp. 25–9. See also Grace Jantzen, *God's World, God's Body* (London, Darton, Longman and Todd; Philadelphia, Westminster, 1984). Albert (1976) makes the point that the initial accusation of pantheism made against Meister Eckhart was determined by the condemnation of Amalric of Bene, who is supposed to have taught that God is identical with the 'formally inherent being' of things (pp. 71–3). In his *Defence* (RS III, p. 5; Théry, p. 193; Daniels, p. 10; B, p. 264) Eckhart states that he does not identify God with 'formally inherent being', and this accusation does not reoccur in *In agro dominico*.
22. Albert (1976), p. 38. 'Being is God' is therefore a statement of predication and not one of identity. Eckhart does also use the phrase *Deus autem est esse* (e.g. in RS VIII, p. 7; Daniels, p. 29), although this is rare and should probably be understood to be an emphatic inversion.
23. In the *Defence* these terms of opposition are replaced by *esse absolutum* and *esse formaliter inhaerentum*, which are the more familiar ones of Thomas Aquinas. There is no reason to think that Eckhart was unhappy with the Thomist term *esse formaliter inhaerentum*, as long as it was not taken to mean that the creature possesses being *in itself*, as distinct from its relation to God. But V. Lossky (1960), p. 322, well sums up the differences between Eckhart and Thomas when he says that analogy, for the latter, was a way of speaking about God and creatures *non secundam puram aequivocationem* while, for Eckhart, it is a way of speaking of the First Cause and its effects *non omnino univoce*.

24. *Prol Prop.* 8, 4, 25 (LW I, pp. 170, 167f., 181; M, pp. 96, 94 and 103: translation slightly adapted). Frank Tobin (1986), p. 41, rightly points out that Eckhart conceives of God's being very much in Thomas' terms, as a coincidence of *esse* and *essentia*; but see also Rudi Imbach on the differences between Thomas and Eckhart in their understanding of the relation between being and God (*Deus est intelligere*, 1976).
25. Creatures therefore have two causes. The first (*causa prima*) is God himself, who is the source of their being, while the second (*causa secondaria*) is the form of the object which is what makes it what it is. Thus God is the cause of the fact that a tree *is*, while its form is the cause of the fact that it is a *tree* (see Albert, p. 75, and *Prol Prop.* 11, LW I, pp. 171f.; M, p. 97). God alone confers being, while the form determines the specific particularity of created being.
26. For *negatio negationis*, see in particular *Comm. Wis.* 148 (LW II, pp. 485f.; TP, pp. 167f.). R. Klibansky has argued that the source of this phrase is Proclus' commentary on the Parmenides (*The Continuity of the Platonic Tradition*, London 1939, p. 26). Thomas Aquinas uses the word *puritas* with respect to God's being in *De ente et essentia*, c.6: 'Unde per ipsam suam puritatem est esse [dei] distinctum ab omni esse.'
27. TP, p. 395.
28. Here I am correcting the judgement I expressed in *God Within* (1988). The likely chronology of Eckhart's writings does not support the idea of an evolution. The relevant Parisian *Quaestio* dates from 1302/3 while the Prologues to the *Three-Part Work* are likely to have been written after the second teaching period in Paris (after 1313/14). For a recent study of the *Parisian Questions*, see E. Zum Brunn, Z. Kaluzia, A. de Libera, P. Vignaux and E. Weber, *Maître Eckhart à Paris: Une critique médiéval de l'ontothéologie, Les Questions parisiennes n. 1 et n. 2 d'Eckhart*, Paris 1984.
29. LW V, p. 40; M, p. 45.
30. LW V, p. 42; M, p. 46.
31. LW V, p. 43; M, p. 47.
32. LW V, p. 41; M, p. 45. *Liber de causis*, prop. 4.
33. LW V, p. 45; M, p. 48.
34. ibid.; M, ibid.
35. LW V, p. 50; M, p. 51. The Aristotle reference is to *De anima*, II, 7.
36. LW V, pp. 52ff.; M, p. 53.
37. DW I, 145f. (W 67). My translation.

38. *Ser.* 29 (LW IV, pp. 269f.; TP, p. 226).
39. *Comm. Ex.* 57 (LW II, pp. 62f.; TP, p. 62).
40. *Comm. Ex.* 141 (LW II, p. 128; TP, pp. 87–9).
41. *Comm. Wis.* 107 (LW II, p. 443; TP, p. 161).
42. Being then has the sense of participative being.
43. See *Comm. Wis.*, 144–57 (TP, pp. 166–71) and LW I, pp. 154f. (M, p. 84). McGinn has an excellent discussion on this in his 'Meister Eckhart on God as Absolute Unity' in D. O'Meara, ed., *Neoplatonism and Christian Thought* (Albany 1982), pp. 128–39.
44. See p. 6, n. 2 above.
45. There appears to be a point of similarity, therefore, between Eckhart's view of being and Gregory Palamas' concept of the 'powers' of God. The relation between knowledge and being in God in the work of Dietrich von Freiberg is thoroughly explored by Kurt Flasch in two articles, 'Die Intention Meister Eckharts' (1974) and 'Kennt die mittelalterliche Philosophie die konstitutive Funktion des menschlichen Denkens?' (1972). Dietrich's ideas on this theme may well have exercised an important influence upon Eckhart with respect to his linkage of intellect and purity of being in God.
46. *Comm. Ex.*, 112–18 (LW II, pp. 110ff.; TP, pp. 81f.).
47. Denzinger, *Enchiridium Symbolorum*, ed. 31, 1957, p. 202: '*quia inter creatorem et creaturam non potest tanta similitudo notari, quin inter eos maior sit dissimilitudo notanda*'.
48. As Lossky (1960) perceptively points out, a theory of analogy based on a (Thomist) analogy of attribution will, within the context of an essentialist ontology (such as Eckhart's) necessarily lead to a dialectic of opposition, as the 'non-identity' of the analogates combines with the identity of the attributes (p. 322).
49. See M. de Certeau, *La fable mystique* (Paris 1982), especially pp. 156ff.
50. Albert (1976) notes: '*Zunächst ist Eckhart kein Wahrheits-sucher. Er weiss sich immer schon in der Wahrheit. Sein Suchen geht nur dahin, der bereits gefundenen Wahrheit neue und überraschende Aspekte abzugewinnen*' (p. 152).
51. e.g. *Comm. Gen.* 7; *Comm. Joh.* 216.
52. RS III, 5 (Théry, p. 194). It is indeed strange in the light of such a passage that the accusation of having taught the existence of the world from eternity should have appeared in the first three articles of the Bull of condemnation.

53. *Confessions* I, 6, 10 (Augustine frames the sentence as a rhetorical question), transl. from M, p. 101.
54. M, p. 78.
55. *Comm. Wis.*, 45 (LW II, p. 367; TP, p. 175).
56. DW I, 69f.; *Comm. Joh.*, 206; *Comm. Joh.*, 308 (my translations).
57. *Comm. Ex.*, 40 (LW II, p. 45; TP, p. 55).
58. ibid. (my underlining). For Eckhart on the creation, see Bernard McGinn, 'Do Christian Platonists really believe in creation?' in David Burrell and Bernard McGinn, eds, *God and Creation* (Notre Dame 1990), pp. 197–225. Just as it would be wrong to think that Eckhart is actually denying the ontological validity of *creata* in his rhetorical formulations on the nothingness of creatures, so too it would be wrong to think that the virtual absence of the role of history in his system implies a denial of its validity. Eckhart consistently subordinates his ontological propositions to the kerygmatic demands of his epistemological principles. See below, pp. 199–201, for an elucidation of this point.

6 • THE IMAGERY OF UNION

In the preceding section we saw how Eckhart's vision of union with God shaped his metaphysics and his fundamental theology. In the section which follows, we shall see how this same intuition determines and informs his mystical theology. And the characteristic stratagem we will find here is what we might call conceptual poetry, which is the manipulation of abstract images, to do primarily with the soul's relation to God, for the purposes of a kerygmatic expressivity: the intention to explore and to expound the deepest areas of our *relatedness* to God. There are two principal dimensions of this relatedness with which we will be concerned. The first is Eckhart's teaching on the divine image within us, and the second is his teaching on the 'birth of God' in the soul. In both of these images Eckhart is drawing on much which belongs to tradition while, at the same time, creating his own specific emphases.

In our discussion of Eckhart's ontology we relied mainly upon his Latin works, which is where he expresses himself most clearly with regard to the important questions of the transcendentals (e.g. Being, Goodness, Unity etc.) and of analogy. But it is his German sermons which provide the greater part of the material in the following section. The reason for this is evident: it is in the sermons which he gave in the churches and convents of the Rhineland that Eckhart most attempted to communicate the vision which inspired him. And he did so not just by alerting people to the possibility of mystical union with the Godhead, or by talking about what such a thing might mean, but he did so also by seeking to *awaken* in his listeners the very possibilities of which he was speaking. Eckhart uses one device after another in order to shake his listeners free from their assumptions, in order to deliver a 'metaphysical shock'. This means of course that the kind of language which Eckhart uses in his German sermons represents in a heightened degree the type of expressive fluidity which we have already seen in his Latin treatises. They have a dynamic and flamboyant character all their own, and they teem with pointed comparisons (some we might judge extravagant and some highly effective) which seek to get Eckhart's point across about the unnameability of God, the immediacy of his presence to us and the transcendent potentialities of the human soul. Unlike the Latin texts however, there are considerable difficulties with the transmission, and so we are far less certain that the texts we read today accurately represent the actual teaching of Meister Eckhart in every case.[1] The situation is further complicated by the fact that the German sermons were not actually written down by him at all but survive in the form of *reportationes*, which is to say records made by the audience at the time the sermons were given. Although the one hundred or so sermons which have been published in the critical edition can safely be judged to be overwhelmingly accurate and authentic in their form and content, nevertheless there are clearly ruptures, and there is always the very real possibility of error.

I. IN THE IMAGE OF GOD

Tradition

The early Christian understanding of our human relatedness to God was powerfully influenced by two distinct traditions. The first of these is Hebrew and stems from the statement in the book of Genesis that men and women are made in the 'image' and 'likeness' of God (Gen. 1.26). This is a theme which is constantly taken up in both the Old and the New Testaments, and it provided a fertile stimulus to Christian thinking on what precisely there is in us which constitutes this image and likeness. Irenaeus and Clement of Alexandria, two of the earliest Greek theologians, used this passage from Genesis as the basis for a spiritual anthropology, which is to say an understanding of human nature in the light of the Christian revelation. They argued that the 'image' is our natural being while the 'likeness' is our conformity to God: that process whereby we are sanctified and drawn closer to his nature.[2] This idea was to prove particularly influential. Origen, on the other hand, argued that the statement of our creation in Gen. 1.26 referred to the creation of our spiritual self in God, while a second passage (that God 'fashioned man of dust from the soil': Gen. 2.7), referred to the creation of our worldly and material self. For other Greek Fathers the image is constituted by the formless contemplation of the higher mind or *nous* (Evagrius), by our state of *apatheia* or 'freedom from passions' (Gregory of Nyssa), or by our baptism (Diadochus of Photike).

The Latin fathers were also confronted with the problem of what really constitutes the 'image' in us. For Tertullian, writing in the third century, the image is our free will and our dominion over creatures, while, for Cyprian of Carthage, it is our capacity to exercise patience.[3] For other Fathers, it is virtue, or the immortality of the human soul. Building upon the Greek distinction between our natural relation to God (image) and our conforming to God through grace, purification and ascetical practice (likeness), St Augustine argued that the mark of the Trinity in us is to be found in the operation and constitution of the human mind itself (our memory, intelligence and will) and that the image is most fully formed in us when we remember, know and love God.

The Middle Ages saw a continuation of some of these early debates, although in general the Franciscan school (especially in the person of St Bonaventure) saw the presence of the image in us in terms of our natural love for God and responsiveness to him, while the Dominican school (especially St Thomas and Eckhart himself) liked to stress the particularity of our own capacity to *know* as being that which constitutes the image in us and makes us most like God.

The Greek patristic tradition which was at least part of Eckhart's inheritance liked also to see the character of human nature as being 'in the image' of God in relation to Christ, the Son, who is himself God's very Image. Thus we are perfected as the image of God through our own participative integration into the archetypal Image of God, which is Christ himself. This is actually an idea which originates in the Logos theology of Philo, an Alexandrian Jew, but it is also to be found in the work of Origen and Maximus the Confessor, and is powerfully present in Eckhart.

The second tradition concerning the image of God in humankind stems from Greek classical philosophy and is mediated to Eckhart largely through his Neoplatonic sources. Here we find that it is the rational or thinking capacity of human kind which constitutes our special affinity with the divine Being. The very first intimations of this idea are to be found in the work of the Presocratic philosophers (especially Anexagoras and Diogenes of Apollonia). The most important account of the Creation in the classical world was that given in Plato's *Timaeus* (a substantial part of which survived into the Christian Middle Ages) and here we find that it is the Demiurge himself (and not the lesser gods) who puts the divine 'guiding principle' (*to hegoumenon*) into humankind. The later Neoplatonic tradition retains this same basic idea and in Plotinus, for instance, the human mind (*nous*) has an undoubted affinity with the divine Mind, which is the first emanation of the supreme principle he calls the One. Another vital source for the idea that the divine image within us is our intellective nature is the work of Aristotle himself. In his *Metaphysics* (*lamda*) he describes the deity, enigmatically, as 'self-reflecting mind' (*noesis noeteos*), while according to the Aristotelian system of psychology, it is our intelligent nature which is the highest property of our being. The concept of 'Logos' (or intelligence) as both our own inner principle and the cohesive principle of the world as a whole is also strongly developed by the Stoic philosophers, who were greatly influential in the later classical period.

If the tradition which Eckhart inherits reflects both a Hebrew scriptural emphasis upon our *relatedness* to God through the idea of the 'image' and, at the same time, the Greek privileging of our capacity to think as being that in us which most reflects our affinity with the divine, then we also find a number of other concepts which play an important part in the tradition prior to Eckhart and which surface in one guise or another in his own work.

The first of these is the concept of the 'active intellect', which we have already touched on briefly in our discussion of Eckhart's Neoplatonic background. The source for this idea is a notoriously difficult passage in Book Three, chapter 5, of Aristotle's work *De anima* ('On the Soul') in which Aristotle seems to be suggesting that there is something in the mind which is wholly active and is itself the *cause* of intelligibility. Some of Aristotle's remarks, here and elsewhere, seem to suggest that this 'active intellect' is separate and immortal and, indeed, later commentators tended to stress this aspect of it to such an extent that, finally, the Arab Averroes postulated the existence of a universal and immortal active intellect, which is the source of all knowing and in which the human mind can only participate for the length of its mortal life. Although this view gained some ground in the Latin West in the twelfth and thirteenth centuries, it was strongly challenged by Thomas Aquinas, who located the active intellect firmly within the integral human individual.[4]

A second key theme is that of the 'ground of the soul', which is as it were the transcendent essence of our being. The Presocratic philosopher, Heraclitus, wrote: 'If you travel every path you will not find the limits of the soul, so deep is its account',[5] and we find the idea that there is something in us which is like the Godhead in its unfathomability in Gregory of Nyssa and John Scotus Eriugena,[6] but the immediate source of this phrase, for Eckhart, is the Latin *fundus animae* (or sometimes *abditum animae*) which Dietrich of Freiberg employs and which originates with St Augustine. In Augustine the *fundus* is the *memoria* (memory), by which Augustine means the astonishing capacity of the mind to retain knowledge of things which are not immediately present to our consciousness. The classic passage in which Augustine discusses this idea occurs in his *Confessions* (X, 8) in which it becomes clear that Augustine is, in fact, drawing our attention to certain functions of the human mind which, since Freud, we have known as the 'unconscious'. As we have already seen in our discussion of the Rhineland school in the preceding chapter, one of the prime achievements of that Dominican school was to identify the Aristotelian 'active intellect' with the 'ground of the soul', thus establishing the view that the very essence of the human soul is itself intellective. According to this theory then, we are, in our own deepest essence, mind.

There remains just one other theme which needs to be discussed at this point: the 'spark of the soul' or *synderesis*. This is an idea which originated with the fourth-century scholar St Jerome who, in his commentary on the first chapter of the Book of Ezekiel, interpreted the four creatures of Ezekiel's vision in the light of Plato's teaching on the four parts of the soul. The first three of these, what Jerome calls the *logikon* (the rational part), the *thumikon* (the willing part) and the *epithumikon* (the concupiscent part) are followed by the fourth of which Jerome says that it is called by the Greeks *synderesis*, which is 'the spark of conscience which is not extinguished even in Cain's heart'.[7] Now *synderesis* is not a word that can be found in a Greek dictionary, and it has been argued that it is a slip for *syneidesis*, which means 'conscience'. It was an influential slip, however, and the word passed into the technical discussions of the Middle Ages. It is this same synderesis, or 'spark of the conscience', which is a primary source for Eckhart's own 'spark of the soul', which blends with the theme outlined above regarding our own intellective essence, and takes on a more metaphysical than moral meaning.[8]

The ground of the soul

Eckhart's discussion of the nature of the human soul is extensive and diverse. It poses many problems, not only on account of the complexity of his ideas but also because of the fluctuation in terminology, which is so characteristic of Eckhart's method. Once again, we need first to identify the varying images and formulations which Eckhart uses and then penetrate the deeper structures of Eckhart's discussion in order to identify the underlying consistence and coherence of his position.

Let us begin with his clear statement that the human soul, as image, is created in relation to the Son, who is himself the Image of God. Eckhart follows Augustine, and ultimately the author of the Fourth Gospel, in believing that all things are created *through the Son*: 'The heavenly Father speaks one Word and speaks it eternally, and in the Word He expends all His might and utters His entire divine nature and all creatures in the Word' (W 35). And yet there is a difference between 'all creatures', as God's image, and the human soul: 'He is fecund in the soul alone, for though every creature is a vestige of God, the soul is the natural image of God' (W 2). Unlike creatures, God has made the soul 'not merely like the image in Himself, or like anything proceeding from Himself that is predicated of Him, but He has made her like *Himself*, in fact like everything that He is – like His nature, His essence and His emanating-immanent activity . . .' (W 92). At one point Eckhart directly addresses the relation between the soul as the image of God and the Son, by suggesting virtually (and of course rhetorically) that they have the same source:[9]

> The soul is created in God's image, but the masters say that the Son is God's image, and the soul is created after the image of the image. But I say further: the Son is an image of God above all images, he is an image of His concealed Godhead. And from there, where the Son is an image of God, from the imprint of the Son's image, the soul receives her image. (W 95)

Here Eckhart is speaking for effect, but in another passage we find what is perhaps his more considered position. In this instance Eckhart says that there are three forms of the 'Word' of God and he states that the human soul (here conceived of as mind), as the image of God, holds an intermediate position between creatures and the Son:

> There is one uttered word: that is the angel, man and all creatures. There is another word, thought but unuttered, through which it can come that I imagine something. There is yet another word, unuttered and unthought, which never comes forth but is rather eternally in Him who speaks it. (W 67)

As we have seen above, the question as to what exactly constitutes the divine image in humankind has received a diversity of responses over the centuries. Eckhart shows little interest in a number of the traditional answers (i.e. that the image is our virtue, goodness, baptism or free will), although the theme of the divine image is present in him in all its depth and richness. It is a theme moreover which Eckhart explores in shifting images which can be most aptly described as poetic. The key images to which he returns time and again are those of the 'ground' and the 'spark' of the soul. There is in fact a passage from one sermon in which he gives an account of the different names which he has adopted in order to express the same transcendent reality:

> I have sometimes said that there is a power in the soul which alone is free. Sometimes I have called it the guardian of the spirit, sometimes I have called it a light of the spirit, sometimes I have said that it is a little spark. But now I say that it is neither *this* nor *that*; and yet it is a *something* that is more exalted over 'this' and 'that' than are the heavens above the earth. (W 8)

In this same, very fine passage, Eckhart goes on to stress that the reality he is attempting to capture is indeed deeply mysterious and essentially beyond the reach of human concepts and words:

> So now I shall name it in a nobler fashion than I ever did before, and yet it disowns the nobler name and mode, for it transcends them. It is free of all names and void of all forms, entirely exempt and free, as God is exempt and free in Himself. It is as completely one and simple as God is one and simple, so that no man can in any way glimpse it. (ibid.)

All Eckhart's discussion on this divine element in the soul has to be seen, therefore, in the light of its mystery and on the acknowledged difficulty in finding language which is adequate to its transcendent quality. Indeed, the very plurality of names which Eckhart finds for it importantly reminds us that it is precisely something which defies all our attempts to contain and to define it. Here Eckhart is close to that tradition we referred to above which is present in Gregory of Nyssa and John Scotus Eriugena and which finds its chief expression in Augustine's amazement and wonder at the depth, the reach and the mystery of the human soul.

In the passage quoted above Eckhart seems unwilling to give precise definition to what the nature of the 'spark' might be which is the divine presence within the soul. But elsewhere he is keen to do just that, although once again his account is full of inconsistencies. At one point Eckhart speaks of two powers within the soul which together constitute the image: the intellect and the will. In the latter 'God is fiery, aglow with all His riches, with all His sweetness and all His bliss' (W 8), but generally he reserves primacy to the intellect above the will.[10] More frequently, Eckhart speaks of the intellect alone as being the image: 'The soul has something in her, a spark of *intellect* [my italics], that never dies; and in this spark, as at the apex of the mind we place the "image" of the soul' (W 7).

But here we immediately encounter another difficulty, which turns on the meaning of the word 'intellect' for Eckhart. We not only confront the undeniable gulf between his fourteenth- and our twentieth-century understanding of human psychology, but also the fact that Eckhart himself is inconsistent in his use of terms. On one occasion at least he seems to mean by 'intellect' that faculty which discerns truth when he speaks of our 'natural' understanding as something which is 'fitful' and 'changing' (W 90). This would seem to be the closest approximation to what we mean today by our 'intellect' and 'understanding'. But elsewhere he speaks of 'intellect' as being that faculty for which 'nothing is distant or external' so that objects 'beyond the sea or a thousand miles away' are fully present to it (W 24a; cf. W 11). This usage would seem to be closer to what we mean today by the visual imagination. Thirdly, we find a number of passages in which Eckhart explicitly identifies 'intellect' with the image of God in us because it alone can seek God out in his own bare essence: 'Intellect takes God bare, where He is stripped of goodness and being' (W 67). Finding modern parallels to this kind of language is a matter of some considerable difficulty, although we might call this faculty 'spiritual intuition' or 'spiritual intelligence'.[11]

On at least one occasion Eckhart shows that he is himself aware of this confusion, as he attempts to distinguish the 'natural' or 'outward' intellect from the other, more spiritual and 'inward' form of knowing (W 7). And in another passage Eckhart clearly distinguishes between three kinds of cognition, that of the senses and the two 'intellects' within us. But here, typically, Eckhart now changes the paradigm by applying the 'questing' dimension to the natural intellect and says of the spiritual intellect that it is sovereignly unmoved:

> A master says that in this light [from Heaven] all the soul's powers are lifted up and exalted: the outer senses we see and hear with, and the inner senses we call thoughts. The reach of these and their profundity is amazing. I can think as easily of a thing overseas as of something close at hand. Above thoughts is the intellect which still seeks. It goes about looking, spies out here and there, picks up and drops. But above the intellect that seeks there is another intellect which does not seek, but stays in its pure, simple being, which is embraced in that light. (W 19)

More generally however Meister Eckhart refers to the divine image in the soul as being prior to both the will and the intellect, which 'burst forth' from it as from their source (W 72, cf. W 14a):

> Some masters have said it [blessedness] lies in knowing, some say that it lies in loving: others say it lies in knowing and loving, and they say it better. But we say that it lies neither in knowing nor in loving: for there is something in the soul from which both knowledge and love flow: but it does not itself know or love in the way the powers of the soul do. (W 87)

It is clear from the quotations given above that as we approach the whole question of Eckhart's teaching on the divine image in humankind, we are confronted with a bewildering array of images, some of which appear contradictory but all of which seek to convey the same sense of a transcendental reality within us. But just as we have seen with regard to Eckhart's theology, there is an underlying consistency in them all. Eckhart wishes to stress two facts. The first is that the 'something' in the soul exists *beyond the level of specific being within the world*, and the second is that *it exists in a state of direct relationship with God*. Taken in its fulness and in its essence, the diversity of his imagery serves to express these two truths. And the extent to which the concept of the human 'intellect' (as Eckhart understands it) is an ideal vehicle for this is evident from a passage in which Eckhart speaks of the five properties, or potentialities, of 'intellect'. The first is its freedom from the 'here' and 'now':

> It [intellect] becomes detached from here and now. 'Here and now' means the same as place and time. *Now* is the minimum of time; it is not a portion of time or a part of time. It is just a taste of time, a tip of time, and end of time. Yet, small though it be, it must go. Again, it [intellect] is detached from *here*. 'Here' means the same thing as place. The place where I am standing is small, but however small, it must still go before I can see God.

The second point is the fact that the 'intellect' has nothing in common with anything else:

> It is like nothing. A master says God is a being that nothing is like and nothing can become like. Now St John says: 'We shall be called children of God' (John 3.1), and if we are God's children we must resemble God. How is it then that the master says God is a being whom *nothing* is like? This is how you must understand it: By virtue of being like nothing, this power is like God. Just as God is like nothing, this power is like God.

The third point is that the 'intellect' contains nothing which is foreign to itself:

> It is pure and uncompounded. By nature God can tolerate no mingling or admixture. Thus, too, this power has no mingling or admixture; there is nothing alien in it, nor can anything alien invade it.

Fourth, the 'intellect' reflects upon itself:

> It is ever inwardly seeking. God is a being such that He ever abides in the innermost. Therefore the intellect goes ever seeking within. But the will goes *out* to seek what it loves.

And, finally, Eckhart says that the human 'intellect' is itself the image of God and is thus in union with him:

Mark this well and remember it: here you have the whole sermon in a nutshell. Image and image are so fully one and joined, that no difference can be discerned. We can well understand fire without heat, and heat without fire. We can understand the sun without light and light without the sun. But we can understand no difference between image and image . . . if the image should perish that is formed after God, then God's image would also disappear. (W 42)

It is not difficult to see in passages such as these that Eckhart is applying to the human 'intellect' (or sometimes to what he calls the 'something' in the soul) the terms which are normally reserved for God in the tradition of apophatic theology and of which he himself makes abundant use in his discussion of the divinity. The 'intellect' is accordingly free of specific being in the 'here' and 'now', it has nothing in common with anything else, it is entirely united within itself and it reflects upon itself inwardly. *These are all precisely the terms which Eckhart has applied to God in his Latin works and which he is now using with reference to the human 'intellect'.* And in a further passage we find additional imagery which Eckhart has applied to God and which he is now using to describe the 'intellect'. These are chiefly uncreatedness, unnameability, and the concept of the divine ground and desert:

In created things – as I have said before – there is no truth. There is something that transcends the created being of the soul, not in contact with created things, which are nothing; not even an angel has it, though he has a clear being that is pure and extensive; even that does not touch it. It is akin to the nature of deity, it is one in itself, and has naught in common with anything. It is a stumbling-block to many a learned cleric. It is a strange and desert place, and is rather nameless than possessed of a name, and is more unknown than it is known. (W 17)

Summing up

If in his Parisian *Questions* Eckhart identifies God with intellect, or with knowledge (*intelligere*), then in the German sermons he applies the language normally reserved for God to what he calls the 'intellect' itself. Thus, on the one hand, Eckhart mentalizes God and, on the other, he divinizes the human mind. His purpose is to establish a deep-going reciprocity between the essence of our being and the essence of the Divine Being itself, and one which is moreover *dynamic* in character.

If to some people this formula might seem to come dangerously close to obscuring the distinction between creature and Creator, then it needs to be reiterated that Eckhart is careful to defend himself against this charge through the use of the *inquantum* principle in his theory of analogy (in so far as we are 'good', our 'goodness' is the 'goodness' of God etc.). Essentially he applies the same principle with regard to the divine 'ground' or 'spark' of the soul. Thus in so far as we are 'intellect', we are one with God; but there is much in us which is not 'intellect', as Eckhart well knows. This is the meaning of the line: 'There is a power in the soul, of which I have spoken before. If the whole soul were like it, she would be uncreated and uncreatable, but this is not so' (W 24a).[12] All Eckhart's comments on our union with God, which can at times seem exuberantly extravagant, have to be seen in the light of his clear teaching on the analogical relations which govern the identity and distinction between God and his creatures.

But the second point to note is that although Eckhart does evolve this system of apparent identity between God as intellect and the human 'intellect', we should not place too much emphasis upon this particular imagery. Eckhart, as we have seen, is sometimes just as happy to call God the 'One' or indeed to call the divine image a 'citadel', a 'spark', the 'soul', a 'light', a 'guardian' or a 'something'. In the first instance Eckhart wishes to stress the fundamental transcendence of God above and beyond any form of existence within the world and, in the second, he wants to emphasize that this transcendent Godhead can be *immediately present to us*, despite our createdness and contingency. The particular terms in which Eckhart conveys that dialectical message are determined by the concepts and imagery which are at hand. But, having said that, it is above all to the idea of God as 'intellect' and of our own highest mystical potential as 'intellect' that Eckhart turns. For according to the Aristotelian tradition which Eckhart inherited, the 'higher' intellect is something which is untouched by anything and yet is free of the restrictions of time and place. Intellect is immaterial and is pure activity. It is mixed with nothing but is pure, sovereign and remote, yet penetrates everywhere and is capable of knowing all things. It is not surprising, therefore, that it is in the concept of intellect which he inherits that Eckhart found the dynamic image which proved most adequate to his needs.

II. SANCTIFICATION

Eckhart's teaching on the nature of the divine image within us has to be seen in the context of other types of patristic and medieval theology of the image, which together formed his intellectual inheritance. This is no less true of Eckhart's understanding of the process of sanctification and, once again, it is important that we cast a side-long glance at the different ways in which the Church has sought to understand this theme in the centuries prior to Meister Eckhart. Only in this way will we be able to appreciate his indebtedness to other thinkers, and gain an idea of where his originality lies.

Tradition

Over the centuries the Christian Church has conceived of the process of our sanctification in a whole variety of different ways. These are often technical, though seemingly unsystematic, and we may well be forgiven for thinking that the whole matter is one which is too profound for theological reflection and would have been best left well alone. The intention in what follows is only to give the reader some taste of the different ways in which medieval and patristic theologians sought to come to terms with this issue.

The idea that the righteous believer can in some way actually in a sense become God, or participate in his nature is to be found in a number of passages from Scripture (e.g. 1 Cor. 13.12; 1 John 3.2; 1 Cor. 15.52; 2 Pet. 1.4). Though we do not find a systematic theology of *divinization* (or *deification*) here, the Greek Fathers nevertheless found sufficient hints in this direction for them to take up and develop this theme. One of the problems they encountered was that their Greek language and culture was already permeated by Platonic, Stoic and Gnostic ideas of deification, as well as those of the mystery cults, which sat uneasily with critical aspects of the Christian revelation. In the early Alexandrian theologians, for instance, we find a markedly speculative understanding of union with God, based (in the case of Clement) on the idea of Christ as Illuminator and (in that of Origen) on the idea of a divinizing contemplation. Other of the Greek Fathers (Irenaeus and Athanasius) sought to establish the principle of our divinization more firmly within the context of the Incarnation: 'God became man so that man might become God.' According to this, deeply influential, patristic idea, our sanctification becomes possible because Christ, through his incarnation, assumed to himself our human nature. The idea of our divinization was also to play an important role within the context of Basil the Great's teaching on the Holy Spirit. Basil argued that if the function of the Spirit is to make us divine, then the Spirit must itself be divine, and hence belong equally with the Father and the Son within the Blessed Trinity. Yet other Greek Fathers took the theme of divinization and established it within the developing sacramental theology of the day. Thus Cyril of Alexandria, Pseudo-Dionysius and Maximus the Confessor stressed the role of the sacraments in our divinization, especially that of baptism and the Eucharist.

The thought of Greek-speaking theologians remained powerfully influenced by the idea of our divinization, and a figure such as Gregory Palamas (roughly a contemporary of

Eckhart) founded his bold spiritual theology on the concept
of a union between the human soul and God's 'powers' or
'energies'. The Latin West, however, was more cautious and
less speculatively inclined. Although Tertullian, Ambrose
and Augustine made use of the theme of divinization, they
laid much greater stress upon its moral connotations and its
ecclesial context. The term *deificatio* never takes root within
the Western tradition as *theosis* (and *theopoiein*) do among
the Greeks.[13]

More important for the West was the concept of *grace*. Once
again the ultimate source for this is an abundance of
scriptural passages, but as theologians came to reflect upon
sanctification and, in particular, upon the experience of
conversion, the theme of grace emerged as being a key
element within the Church's self-understanding. This trend
received its greatest impetus from the work of Augustine.
Known as the 'doctor of grace', Augustine thought long and
deeply on its nature, in part as a result of his own experience
of conversion from Manichaeism and in part on account of
his confrontation with the thought of Pelagius, who reserved
a greater part in the process of sanctification to our own
efforts than Augustine deemed right. The thinking in the
West in later centuries can be seen largely to represent the
development and systematization (under the influence of
the new Aristotelianism) of positions which are already
present in Augustine.

The chief opportunity for the scholastic theologians to
express their views on grace came when they had to
comment on Peter Lombard's *Sentences*, the textbook of
medieval theology. Peter Lombard did two, seemingly
contradictory, things. He equated grace with the Holy Spirit
within us and he denied that our nature can be divinized.[14]
Later commentators on his work sought to avoid a blunt
equation of grace with the indwelling Holy Spirit and they
stressed the created character of sanctifying grace. The
Franciscan theologian Alexander of Hales and his school
defined grace as that which makes us pleasing to God and
thus makes possible our assimilation into him. These early

Franciscans also stressed that grace is not a 'power' of the soul but is commensurate with its very essence. St Bonaventure, the greatest of the Franciscan theologians, developed the theology of grace into a highly sophisticated system. In his hands grace shows God's ultimate condescension towards us and it is the infusion of his own nature into us, the gift which he bestows on us in order to conform us to himself. Bonaventure places the characteristically Franciscan stress upon the role of the will in the process of our sanctification worked through grace. And here, once again, the language of divinization emerges, for grace makes us 'deiform'. But in order to ward off the charge of pantheism, the Western theologians emphasize throughout that even transforming and deifying grace is *created*, even if it is the highest of all created things.[15]

A sophisticated theology of grace was developed also by the Dominicans, who added their own characteristically intellective emphases. Thus, for Albert the Great, grace is an emanation from God which transforms us from within (like a light) but it indwells us as a *habitus*, or enduring propensity. Being a reflection of God's own nature, it makes us aware of our own essential nothingness.[16] For Thomas Aquinas, created grace is the *similitude* of God which attaches to our soul and enables us to *participate* in the divinity. It is in Thomas also that we find the distinctions most clearly stated between the different 'kinds' of grace (i.e. prevenient, habitual, actual), or the different ways in which we experience grace in our lives.

It can appear that medieval discussion on the role of grace in our sanctification tended to eclipse that of the *Holy Spirit*. Nevertheless, the theme of the indwelling of the Holy Spirit is constantly present in the scholastic writers, who take up the patristic tradition, itself based on the Pentecost experience which animated the Early Church. For Basil the Great, it is the Holy Spirit which divinizes us and, for Augustine, the Spirit is the enlivening principle of love between the Father and the Son which is at the same time the foundation for our own integration into the mystery of the Trinity and our establishment in the Church. In the Middle Ages, it is particularly amongst those mystical theologians whose experience has a Trinitarian flavour, such as William of St Thierry and Jan van Ruusbroec, that we find a special stress on the role of the Spirit as the spirit of love which binds us into the Trinity itself.[17]

But of great importance during the Middle Ages were the *seven gifts of the Spirit*. These were the particular gifts of the Spirit which allowed us to live a righteous life. The Vulgate translation of Isaiah 11.2–3 spoke of 'the spirit of wisdom and understanding, the spirit of counsel and might, the spirit of knowledge and piety and a spirit of fear of the Lord'. The gifts feature large in much medieval hagiography, but it was not until 1235 that Phillip the Chancellor first made a distinction between the gifts of the Spirit and the virtues as such.[18] In the work of Thomas Aquinas the gifts have the special role of making the soul responsive to the influence of the Holy Spirit.[19]

A central position is also given in medieval mystical theology to the place of the so-called *theological virtues* (faith, hope and love). This name is first used at the beginning of the thirteenth century by William of Auxerre in order to stress the primacy of these qualities as the foundation of our life of grace. Thomas Aquinas believed that faith, hope and love differ from the other virtues in that 1) their object is God 2) we are orientated to God through them 3) God alone infuses them into us and 4) their source is in scriptural revelation.[20]

In addition to these conceptual forms of reflecting on sanctification, we find others which are more imagistic. For the scholastics, one of the primary functions of grace, for instance, is to make us sons and daughters of God *by adoption*. This is called *filiation* and it reflects the spirituality of St Paul and St John. If Christ is God's Son by nature, then we are united with him through grace and become the adopted sons and daughters of God. This is one of the most enduring and influential of themes in Christian mystical writings of all ages. It has to be seen as a (less controversial)

variant on the theme of divinization, and it finds an echo in
the Greek formula which was popularized in the West by
John Damascene in his *On the Orthodox Faith*: 'We become
by grace what God is by nature'.[21]

We should mention also the theme of the *inhabitation* or
indwelling of the Blessed Trinity. According to this teaching,
grace prepares the soul in such a way that the Trinity itself
enters into us and becomes the sanctifying principle.[22] The
scholastics were intrigued (unwisely we may feel) by the
mechanics of this phenomenon.

And finally there is one further mystical image which was
to exercise a great influence upon Eckhart himself: *the birth
of God in the soul* (essentially a variation upon the theme of
filiation). The concept of the divine birth within us is to be
found in the earliest Christian theology and it can be seen,
for instance, in both Clement of Alexandria and Irenaeus.
But it is Origen, another Alexandrian theologian, who
develops this theme and with whom it is most associated in
the patristic period. From Origen it passes on to the
Cappadocian theologians, and to Maximus the Confessor.

The theme of the birth is present also in Augustine and it
was widely known in the medieval West, through theologians
such as John Scotus Eriugena, Richard of St Victor and
Bernard of Clairvaux, while Bonaventure himself wrote a
treatise on it.[23]

As we can see, therefore, the ways in which the Christian
Church had conceived of the mysterious process of
sanctification prior to Eckhart are many and varied. And
the list of themes we have above is a foolishly brief overview
of what is a markedly complex field. In particular, we have
made no mention of the sacramental theology of the Catholic
Church, East and West, according to which the sacraments
are powerful 'instruments of grace' (Council of Trent) and
are the chief, or even normative, way in which the individual
Christian encounters Christ.[24] Nor have we made mention
of the field of spiritual visions, more widespread in the
Middle Ages than today, or of their concomitants, the
spiritual senses. And it would be futile to attempt to

synthesize these different models of sanctification, for the relations between the action of the Holy Spirit in us and of grace, created and uncreated, between assimilation into and inhabitation by the Trinity, are notoriously difficult to establish. It is perhaps wiser to realize that sanctification is in itself a united phenomenon, a single or simple act, while the pluralism of our attempts to reflect upon it prove rather the diversity of our own nature.

The birth of God in the soul

Even those who know little about the work of Meister Eckhart are often aware of the connection between this particular theme and his name. The 'birth of God in the soul' is, as it were, Eckhart's trademark. And yet it would be quite wrong to suggest that this is the only mystical theme which he explores in his theology of sanctification. The ways in which Eckhart speaks of this mystery are in fact many and diverse.

Let us begin with the theme of divinization, for instance, to which Eckhart repeatedly refers, sometimes explicitly linking our own divinization with the incarnation of the Son: 'the reason why He [God] became man was that He might bear you as his only-begotten Son' (W 18). Eckhart also speaks of Christ having assumed our human nature (e.g. W 47 and 92).

There are a number of passages in which it is the Holy Spirit which is the divinizing principle. Here we must distinguish between those places in which Eckhart's Logos mysticism shows a trinitarian dimension (to be considered below) and those in which it is the Holy Spirit itself which sanctifies us and draws us up into the Godhead. In accordance with Christian tradition, the Holy Spirit is linked with the principle of love. It 'continually blossoms forth from the Son to the Father as their mutual love' (W 88), 'It is the heat, the effulgence of the Holy Ghost, wherein the soul loves God' (W 66) and the Holy Spirit is the active principle of love which draws the soul up to the Father:

Just as truly does the power of the Holy Ghost take the purest and the subtlest and the highest, the spark of the soul, and bear it all aloft in the brand of love, in the same way as I now say of a tree: the power of the sun seizes on the purest and subtlest in the root of the tree and draws it right up into the branch, where it begins to blossom. Thus in every way the spark of the soul is borne up in the light and in the Holy Ghost and carried right up into the primal source. . . . (W 32b; cf. W 54)

The theme of sanctifying grace is also a strong element in Eckhart's thinking. In the following passage he stresses that grace touches the very essence of the soul:

God's chief aim is giving birth. He is never content till He begets His Son in us. And the soul, too, is in no way content until the Son of God is born in her. And from that there springs forth grace. Grace is thereby infused. Grace does not work: its work is its becoming. It flows out of God's essence and flows into the essence of the soul and not into her powers. (W 68)

Eckhart emphasizes that the function of grace is to make us receptive to God and to form us in his likeness:

It is impossible for any soul to be without sin, unless God's grace enters into her. The work of grace is to make the soul quick and amenable to all divine works, for grace flows from the divine spring and is a likeness of God and tastes of God and makes the soul like God. (W 81)

Yet, elsewhere, Eckhart restricts the scope of grace in our sanctification, and he does so because grace is created. In the following passage Eckhart suggests that our ultimate union with God, through the soul's 'spark', is something which is beyond the reach of (created) grace:

One master says that this thing [the 'spark'] is so present to God that it can never turn away from God and God is always present and within it. I say that God has always been in it, eternally and uninterruptedly, and for man to be one with God in this requires no grace, for grace is a created thing, and no creature has any business there. . . . (W 92)

Although medieval scholasticism had defined grace as the highest of all creatures, Eckhart is clearly disturbed by its created nature. To be created, for Eckhart, is to be bound by time and place, and he has always stressed that the 'intellect', which is the image of God, transcends these dimensions. And, as far as it does so, it can be said to be 'uncreated'. Eckhart has to find some other image, therefore, for the highest unitive levels, and in the following passage he turns to that of light:

> We must ascend and grow great in grace. As long as we are growing in grace, it is grace and it is little, and in it we see grace from afar. But when grace is perfected in the highest, it is not grace: it is divine light in which one sees God. (W 41)

When Eckhart discusses divinization, the work of the Holy Spirit or the nature of sanctifying grace, then he is drawing on what are the central mystical concepts of theological discussion. But on other occasions Eckhart speaks more imagistically of our sanctification, as when he discusses the theme touched on above, for instance, that of transforming light:

> Light streams out and lights up what it falls on. When we sometimes say a man is illumined, that means little. But when it bursts forth, that is far better: it breaks through into the soul and makes her like God and divine, as far as may be, and illumines her within. In this interior illumination she soars above herself in the divine light. (W 48)

We may think of light in this case as being the light of grace, although it may also be the light of 'intellect' (and, therefore, ultimately the light of God). And yet in the former passage quoted above Eckhart makes a clear distinction between grace and the light of the 'intellect', and there is another passage in which he clearly speaks of the light of 'intellect' as distinct from transforming grace: 'In this inflowing of grace the light of intellect climbs up straightway, and there God shines with unquenchable light' (W 20). But, in a further passage, Eckhart explicitly identifies light with both grace and the Second Person of the Trinity: 'If we are to enter there [into God's heart] we must climb from the natural light into the light of grace, and grow therein into the light that is the Son Himself' (W 88). Ultimately therefore light is an image to which Eckhart turns in order to explore the deepest realms of our union with God, but it is one which appears to have no precise referent.

Other images of union we find include that of the *Brautmystik* ('nuptial mysticism') which the writings of St Bernard of Clairvaux did so much to popularize during the Middle Ages. This identifies the soul as the Bride, and Christ as the Bridegroom, and it is a form of mystical imagery which draws its inspiration from the Song of Songs:

> When God created the soul, He created her according to His own most perfect nature, so that she might be the bride of his only-begotten Son, who, knowing this full well, decided to go forth out of the private chamber of his eternal Fatherhood in which he eternally slept, remaining unspoken within . . . For this reason he went forth and came leaping like a young stag, and suffered the pangs of love: and he did not come out except with the wish to return to the chamber with his bride. This chamber is the silent darkness of the mysterious Fatherhood. When he went forth from the Most High, he wanted to show her the hidden mystery of his secret Godhead, where he is at rest with himself and all creatures. (W 53)

The 'kiss' to which Eckhart occasionally refers also belongs to this same bridal imagery:

> The soul's mouth is the highest part of the soul, and she means this when she says: 'He has put His word into my mouth'; that is the kiss of the soul, where mouth has come to mouth; there the Father bears His Son in the soul. . . . (W 23 and cf. 51)

And the passages in which Eckhart speaks of the 'touch' of God, which inspires us to ever greater love, also owe something to the atmosphere of the Song of Songs, although this image is essentially founded in a theology of the Third Person: 'In the first touch with which God touched the soul and continues to touch her as uncreated and uncreatable, there, through God's touch, the soul is as noble as God Himself is.' (W 66)[25]

Meister Eckhart uses a whole series of different themes

and images therefore for exploring the process of our growth towards and into God. But a good number of the passages we have quoted above contain references to the one overriding image which dominates all Eckhart's thinking on this subject: that of the birth of God in the soul.

The birth of God in the soul results essentially from two factors: the nature of God and the nature of the 'ground' or 'spark' of the soul, which is God's image in us. Eckhart stresses in many places that it is fundamental to the fertile nature of God that he should seek always to give birth: 'All that is in God moves Him to beget: His whole ground, His essence and His being move the Father to generation' (W 59). Indeed, so great is the fertility of the Father that Eckhart links his generation of the Son within the Trinity to his generation of the Son in us:[26]

> The word 'father' implies pure begetting and means the life of all things. The Father begets His Son in the eternal intellect, and thus the Father begets His Son in the soul just as He does in His own nature, and begets him in the soul as her own, and His being depends on His bringing His Son to birth in the soul, whether He would or no. (W 40)

The birth in the Godhead and that in us is *one* birth: 'Now I say as I have often said before, that this eternal birth occurs in the soul precisely as it does in eternity, no more and no less, for it is one birth, and this birth occurs in the essence and ground of the soul' (W 2). But if it is the nature of God to be fertile in the soul, then it is the nature and desire of the soul to receive the birth: 'God's chief aim is giving birth. He is never content until He begets His Son in us. And the soul, too, is in no way content until the Son of God is born in her' (W 68). That same fertility which we find in the Godhead is reflected in the ground of the soul, and it is here, in the divine image, that the birth takes place:

> Elsewhere I have declared that there is a power in the soul which touches neither time nor flesh, flowing from the spirit, remaining in the spirit, altogether spiritual. In this power, God is ever verdant and flowering in all the joy and all the glory that He is in Himself. There is such heartfelt delight, such

inconceivably deep joy as none can fully tell of, for in this power
the eternal Father is ever begetting His eternal Son without
pause, in such wise that this power jointly begets the Father's
Son and itself, this self-same Son, in the sole power of the
Father. (W 8)

In further passages Eckhart points out that it is the
imageless character of the soul's essence which makes it a
place which God can inhabit:

This [the birth] cannot be received by creatures in which God's
image is not found, for the soul's image appertains especially to
this eternal birth, which happens truly and especially in the
soul, being begotten of the Father in the soul's ground and
innermost recesses, into which no image ever shone or (soul-)
power peeped. (W 2)

Images are created and they point to that of which they are
the image, and so God can only work where we are free of
all images:

Therefore you have to be and dwell in the essence and in the
ground, and there God will touch you with His simple essence
without the intervention of any image. No image represents and
signifies itself: it always aims and points to that of which it is
the image . . . And therefore there must be a silence and a
stillness, and the Father must speak in that, and give birth to
His Son, and perform His works free from all images. (W 1)

The birth, too, takes place beyond the created dimensions of
time and place:

All time must be gone when this birth begins, for there is
nothing that hinders this birth so much as time and creatures. It
is an assured truth that time cannot affect God or the soul by
her nature. If the soul could be touched by time, she would not
be the soul, and if God could be touched by time, He would not
be God. But if it were possible for the soul to be touched by
time, then God could never be born in her, and she could never
be born in God. For God to be born in the soul, all time must
have dropped away from her, or she must have dropped away
from time with will or desire. (W 29)

Just as the act of Creation itself is eternal, since it occurs
outside time, so too the birth is eternal: 'This birth does not

take place once a year or once a month or once a day, but all the time, that is, above time in the expanse where there is no here or now, nor nature nor thought' (W 31).

Since the birth can only happen when we are free of images, it follows naturally for Eckhart to stress that if this birth is to come about, then we must prepare ourselves inwardly. Above all, we must withdraw from our diversified powers into the central unity of our transcendent being:

> Therefore the soul in which this birth is to take place must keep absolutely pure and must live in noble fashion, quite collected and turned entirely inward; not running out through the five senses into the multiplicity of creatures, but all inturned and collected and in the purest part. (W 1)

Sometimes Eckhart tells us that the various functions of the soul must cease, allowing us to become still:

> And so in truth, if you would find this noble birth, you must leave the crowd and return to the source and the ground from which you came. All the powers of the soul, and all their works – these are the crowd. Memory, understanding and will, they all diversify you, and therefore you must leave them all: sense-perceptions, imagination, or whatever it may be in which you find or seek to find yourself. After that, you may find this birth but not otherwise – believe me! (W 4)

In particular, Eckhart stresses that our role in the birth is an entirely passive one, founded upon the embracing of our essential nothingness and emptiness:

> This above all else is needful: you must lay claim to nothing! Let go of yourself and let God act with you and in you as He will. This work is His, this Word is His, this birth is His, in fact every single thing that you are. For you have abandoned self and gone out of your (soul's) powers and their activities, and your personal nature. Therefore God must enter into your being and powers, because you have bereft yourself of all possessions, and become as a desert, as it is written: 'The voice of one crying in the wilderness' (Matt. 3.3). Let this eternal voice cry out in you as it listeth, and be as a desert in respect of yourself and all things. (W 3)

As soon as the soul is prepared by becoming empty of all creatures and images, then God *must* enter its ground and be born there. This is a theme in which Eckhart particularly delights:

> I declare in all truth, by the eternal and everlasting truth, that into any man who has abandoned self right down to his ground, God must pour out His whole self in all His might, so utterly that neither of His life, nor His being, nor His nature, nor of His entire Godhead does He keep anything back, but must pour out the whole of it as fruitfulness into that man who in abandonment to God has assumed the lowest place. (W 60)

Sometimes Eckhart states this central idea in striking and rhetorical imagery:

> Do not imagine that God is like a human carpenter, who works or not as he likes, who can do or leave undone as he wishes. It is different with God: as and when God finds you ready, He has to act, to overflow into you, just as when the air is clear and pure the sun has to burst forth and cannot refrain. (W 4)

And again:

> The earth can never flee so low but heaven flows into her and impresses his power on her and fructifies her, whether she wishes it or not. It is just the same with a man: he thinks he can get away from God, but he cannot escape Him, for every nook and cranny reveals Him. He thinks he is fleeing from God, and runs into His arms. God gives birth to His only-begotten Son in you whether you like it or not; whether you are asleep or awake, God does His work. (W 53)

Although Eckhart conceives of the birth of God in the soul very much in metaphysical terms, it would be wrong to suggest that it is something which occurs in a vacuum with respect to our moral lives. In the following passage Eckhart stresses that the birth is known only to those who walk 'in the ways of God':

> We shall therefore speak of this birth, of how it may take place in us and be consummated in the virtuous soul, whenever God the Father speaks His eternal Word in the perfect soul. For what I say here is to be understood of the good and perfected

man who has walked and is still walking in the ways of God; not of the natural, undisciplined man, for he is entirely remote from, and totally ignorant of this birth. (W 1)

Elsewhere Eckhart says that in this birth we 'will share in the divine influx and all its gifts' (W 2) and in one passage he speaks of what some of those gifts might be: 'God bears the Word in the soul, and the soul conceives it and passes it on to her powers in varied guise: now as desire, now as good intent, now as charity, now as gratitude, or however it may affect you' (W 3). And in another birth is the foundation for every just act: 'The Father begets His Son the just and the just His Son: for every virtue of the just, and every act performed by the virtue of the just is nothing but the Son begotten by the Father' (W 59).

The chief consequence of the birth is detachment (an idea we will explore more fully in the next chapter), but in one passage Eckhart enumerates three chief ways in which we can know whether the birth has occurred in us: the presence of love in us, our passivity to God's will and our devout filial relationship with him. There can be no doubt, therefore, that although Eckhart does conceive of the birth throughout in metaphysical terms, it remains nevertheless something of deeply moral significance:

> First, if we are to be the Son, we must have a Father, for none can say he is a son unless he has a father, and no one is a father unless he has a son . . . and that man is truly a son whose every work is done for love. The second thing that most makes a man a son is equanimity. If he is sick, he would as lief be sick as well, well as sick . . . The third thing a son should possess is that he can bow his head to none but the Father. (W 11)

Summing up

The relations between the 'birth of God in the soul' and other aspects of our sanctification are not always consistent in Eckhart's work, but one principle does nevertheless clearly emerge, which is that God imparts his very life and very essence when he is born in the soul of the individual believer (W 89). This is an important point, for it reminds us of the affinity between the image of God in us and the birth of God in us. Both, for Eckhart, entail a degree of identity between ourselves and God which, in the case of the image, is permanent though generally potential, and in the case of the birth, is generally actual though realized to a varying degree. In other words, it makes sense to think of the image/birth distinction as being Eckhart's version of the image/likeness distinction of the classical Christian tradition. The birth then (or the 'likeness') represents the extent to which the original divine image in us has been retrieved and actualized.[27]

From the stress upon *identity* with God which is implied by Eckhart in the doctrine of the birth (as it is in that of the image), there emerges a further point, which is the dependence of his teaching concerning the image and the birth on his understanding of the analogical relation between the creature and the Creator. In the latter, as we have seen, it is the Nicene Creed which provides the relational formula with its language of *generation* and *identity of being,*[28] and it is this same principle of identity of essence which prevails in Eckhart's teaching on the image of God within us and on the birth of God in us. The latter is a form of divine self-giving that is grounded in the infinite fertility of God in the former, and the principle which must be evoked in order to safeguard against the total assimilation of the creature into the Creator is once again that of the *inquantum.*

If Eckhart's teaching on the birth of God in the soul can be thought of as the 'likeness' dimension in an image/likeness opposition, then it is also the case that, for all his originality of expression, Eckhart seems to be presenting in his doctrine of the divine birth a conventional scholastic theology of grace. We find all the necessary ingredients. The birth is entirely sovereign and free; it is the self-communication of God (the imparting of his essence); it is that which sanctifies us and makes us like him, and it establishes the order of moral virtue within us. And yet, though Eckhart is essentially presenting a theology of grace here, he finds it difficult to employ the conventional terms. There are occasions when he speaks of grace as a 'likeness' to God which makes us 'like God' (W 81), which is wholly orthodox scholasticism, but he can also be emphatically dismissive of the role of grace. The reason for this is that it is *created* (W 92), while Eckhart's theology of God, his divine metaphysics, is based upon the view that anything which is created has local being and it is precisely this local being which we transcend as we become united with God (who is himself supremely non-localized Being). In the light of this, it would seem that Eckhart had no choice but to find another 'likeness' to God which would in this instance be 'uncreated', and which he found ideally in the image of God's birth in the soul.

THE IMAGERY OF UNION: CONCLUSION

It becomes increasingly apparent, as we enter more deeply into the German writings of Meister Eckhart, that the use he makes of some of his central imagery is not 'scientific' and descriptive so much as 'poetical' and evocative. Certainly he can adopt contradictory positions. Thus he tells us that the 'ground' of the soul is to be identified with the *synderesis* (W 32a) and that it is not to be identified with the *synderesis* (W 32b). It is both intellect (W 42) and not intellect (W 72). The ultimate paradigm for our union with God is not love but knowledge (W 72), not knowledge but love (W 77). The 'birth' is to be identified with grace in one passage (W 68), but not in another (W 41). Also Eckhart tells us at one point that the 'birth' is something which happens only in those whose 'ground' is properly prepared (e.g. W 1) and, at another, that it is something which happens in all of us all the time (and inward preparation means that we receive its benefits: W 2). And yet it would be wrong to dismiss Eckhart as a 'muddled thinker'.[29]

As we have persistently sought to show, the underlying structures of his thought remain remarkably sound despite the surface fluctuations in its expression. Eckhart is a highly eclectic thinker, who likes to build themes and ideas from other thinkers into his own system. In the case of his speaking of God, this leads, as we have seen, to the compounding of images and ideas in such a way that what we might want to say about God is subverted in the interests of his total transcendence. Eckhart is keen to remind us by this method that whatever we might want to say of him is utterly inadequate. Something of this same technique can be seen in the accumulation of images for the divine element within us ('spark', 'fortress', 'crown' and so forth), but in his use of the image of the 'ground' of the soul and the 'birth of God in the soul' a different characteristic can be noted. Here Eckhart is not so much concerned to articulate the transcendence of God through a pluralism of names but rather to anchor certain ideas firmly within the world of human experience *by compounding those aspects of our lives to which such themes can be said to refer*. Thus the two central images of the 'ground' and the 'birth' serve as a 'hold-all' in which Eckhart is able to contain diverse areas of human experience. In the case of the former, these are those elements within us which have been privileged by patristic and medieval theology as being the 'image of God' within us, and in the case of the latter they are the diverse forms of the operation of sanctifying grace. The pluralism no longer functions at the level of the signifier then, in order to draw out the transcendence of the signified, but is now a pluralism of the signified, in order to make of the signifier a highly fertile, flexible and expansive image which begins to function precisely with the hauntingly expressive power which we associate normally with the evocative character of an image in a poem.

It would be wrong, therefore, to think that Eckhart is saying something radically new in his theology of grace and the divine life within us. His message is in fact very close to that of other scholastics of his age. What is certainly new and distinctive, however, is the power of his verbal and imagistic expressivity: his capacity to grip the mind with free-floating dynamic images which convey, in turn, the sense of a personal spiritual vision of immense energy. These images are more a form of conceptual poetry than they are scientific theology, and they set up resonances throughout the whole field of medieval mystical theology while remaining simple and evocative enough to engage the imagination of Eckhart's unlettered listeners. If the 'ground' and the 'spark' convey the unfathomable mystery of the human soul and its transcendence, then the 'birth' captures the infinite fertility and dynamism of God. It is a remarkable and memorable image which holds before us the immediacy of our union with God together with our total passivity before his transforming grace.

NOTES TO CHAPTER 6

1. In his *Defence* Eckhart, for instance, says: 'In the sermon presented to me some time ago, I have found many things which I never said. Many things, too, are written there without understanding, obscure and confused like dreams . . .' (Théry, p. 258; Daniels, p. 60; B, p. 301). The final Bull of condemnation also records that Eckhart denied that he had taught the last two articles, although in fact there is considerable textual evidence that he had. See Colledge and McGinn (p. 42), for some remarks on this. The problems surrounding the transmission of Eckhart's work are well summarized in Steer (1988).
2. There is a good article on the theme of the divine image within us in the DS (Vol VII², cols. 1401–72). See also Caird, *The Image of God in Man*, London 1953.
3. St Cyprian of Carthage, *De bono patientiae*, 3. The positions of the other theologians mentioned here are well known and can be found in any detailed discussion of the theology of the Image.
4. There is a good account of the fortunes of this passage in the introduction to the translation by Hugh Lawson-Tancred (Harmondsworth, Penguin, 1986). Franz Brentano, *The Psychology of Aristotle* (ET, Berkley 1977), can also be consulted.
5. J. Barnes, *Early Greek Philosophy* (Harmondsworth, Penguin, 1987), p. 106.
6. e.g. *De hominis opificio*, xi, and *Periphyseon*, II, 572 c–d.
7. PL 25, 22. It is worth noting also that Jerome's Greek terms do not exactly correspond to those of Plato. The best history of this word is to be found in the New Catholic Encyclopaedia ('synderesis'), but see also H. Hof, *Scintilla animae* (Lund and Bonn 1952).

8. In one sermon (W 32a) Eckhart repeats the traditional view that the 'spark' is our inclination to the good, while more generally he equates the 'spark' with the transcendent 'ground' of the soul (e.g. W 17).

9. This same idea is more technically presented in the *Comm. Joh.* (LW III, 10–12) where Eckhart speaks of our eternal being in God (the *ratio*) in terms specifically of the *verbum*. There are also passages in which he says that the human intellect contains all creatures (W 53). The immediate source for this idea may well be Dietrich of Freiberg who argues in his *De intellectu* that when we know something in the world, the image which we actually perceive originates is the mind itself.

10. e.g. in W 11. In this, of course, Eckhart is expressing the Dominican privileging of the intellect above the will in opposition to the inverse relation advocated by their Franciscan opponents.

11. This question is well discussed in Smith (1988), pp. 14ff.

12. This is also why Eckhart, in the defence he himself delivered in the Dominican Church in Cologne on 13 February 1327, stresses that we should not think of the 'spark' as something divine which has been added or 'attached' to the human soul.

13. There is an extensive article on 'divinization' in the DS (III, cols. 1370–1459) and there are a good number of studies of this theme in individual fathers. See also V. Lossky, *The Mystical Tradition of the Eastern Church* (ET, Cambridge and London 1957).

14. *Sententiae* I, 17.

15. Gérard Philips, *L'Union Personelle avec le Dieu Vivant* (Gembloux 1974), is a useful study of historical understandings of grace.

16. ibid., pp. 123–35.

17. In general we don't find in the medieval Church the same kind of emphasis on the role of the Holy Spirit which we find in modern Pentecostalist and charismatic movements. These trace their origins largely to the seventeenth-century Pietists and, in the English-speaking world, to the great Methodist revivals of the nineteenth century.

18. See Y. Congar, *I Believe in the Holy Spirit* I (ET, New York and London 1983), pp. 117–20 and J. Aumann, *Spiritual Theology* (London 1980), pp. 247–75.

19. For Thomas on the gifts of the Spirit, see *Summa Theologiae* 1, 11, q.62 and 2, II, qq.1–45.
20. Aumann, pp. 247–75 and LTK, X, cols. 76–80.
21. See *Gotteskindschaft* in LTK, IV, cols. 1114–17.
22. See E. Ancilli and M. Paparozzi, eds., *La Mistica*, II (Rome 1984), pp. 113–38 and Aumann, pp. 75–8.
23. See H. Rahner, *Symbole der Kirche* (Salzburg 1964), pp. 13–87, for an exhaustive account of this teaching. There are also interesting remarks on it in Hans Urs von Balthasar, *Theodramatik* II, 1 (Einsiedeln 1976), pp. 275–84.
24. We have made no mention of the phrase 'infused contemplation' either. This important theme first becomes significant in the mystical theology of the sixteenth and seventeenth centuries.
25. There is a long tradition of linking the image of the divine 'touch' with the Holy Spirit which goes back to a number of scriptural passages. As a mystical topos, it enjoyed special favour among the Flemish mystics, especially Hadewijch of Brabant and Jan van Ruusbroec (see my *God Within*, p. 208).
26. Eckhart generally conflates the immanent and ecumenical Trinity by identifying the generation of the Son, the Incarnation and the birth of God within us, but he does so for reasons of rhetorical effect.
27. Typically, Eckhart rejects the term 'likeness' as a description of his 'birth' on the grounds that 'likeness' is not 'union' (W 7), although he affirms it elsewhere (W 63).
28. See *Comm. Joh.*, 5–8 and p. 105 above.
29. This was the view of Denifle, and even of Koch, who wrote in a letter to Herbert Grundmann (4 January 1945): 'Basically the judgement of Denifle, whom I respect more and more, was correct: he was a muddled thinker' (Degenhardt, p. 285). The study of hermeneutics has led to a number of recent studies on the role of metaphor in theology. See for instance P. Ricoeur and E. Jüngel, eds, *Metaphor: Zur Hermeneutik religiöser Sprache*, Munich 1974, J. M. Soskice, *Metaphor and Religious Language*, Oxford 1985 and C. E. Gunton, *The Actuality of Atonement: A Study of Metaphor, Rationality and the Christian Tradition*, Edinburgh 1988.

7 • THE SPIRITUALITY OF UNION

We have considered the way in which Eckhart's sense of union with the divine penetrates his metaphysical theology, making it something which is both mystical and existential. We have also seen how this same vision informs Eckhart's theology of mystical union, according to which God becomes an immediate presence to the soul in its very depths. The third area of the Eckhartian 'system' which we need now to discuss is that of his spirituality. In this chapter we will examine the way in which Eckhart's theology of union and imagery of union lead to a specific way of living within the world. The accent here then is upon human existence, and our multiple experience of the world in which we live.

Tradition

In the discussion of the background to Eckhart's 'birth of God in the soul', we touched on the medieval and patristic understanding of the divinizing action of grace and the Holy Spirit within us. In the Middle Ages great emphasis was laid upon the seven gifts of the Holy Spirit (i.e. wisdom, understanding, counsel, might, knowledge, piety and fear of the Lord). To these we may add the 'theological' or transcendental virtues which ground our life in God: faith, hope and love.

But it is the monastic authors who were in the main Eckhart's spiritual ancestors, for it is the monks who throughout the Middle Ages were most concerned with the practicalities of spiritual living. Even to be a monk was to adopt a particular way of life with particular spiritual values, and it is these values which are discussed and expounded in the spiritual literature of the Middle Ages, which comes overwhelmingly from the pens of monastic writers.

The early monks laid great stress upon the principle of ordering the passions through asceticism and the sovereign power of our rational nature (which distinguishes us from the animals), and so the spiritual life is frequently presented as a continual struggle against the desires of the flesh. In addition, love and humility emerge as the chief ways in which we enact our spiritual calling in this life, both of which, for instance, are given special emphasis in chapter 7 of the Rule of St Benedict. Benedict is writing here under the influence of John Cassian, who mediates to the western world much of early Greek monastic thought and whose *Institutions* (chapter 11) contains an extended discussion of these same themes of humility and love. Later monastic authors, such as Bernard of Clairvaux, or William of St Thierry, follow Benedict in their sophisticated spiritual systems based almost entirely on the ascending degrees of love and humility, and Bernard, in his *On the Degrees of Humility and Pride* (which is actually a commentary on the Benedictine Rule), shows the centrality of both in his vision of the spiritual life. The twelfth-century Carthusian writer, Guigo II, dedicated the first of his *Twelve Meditations* to humility and, in the following century, Francis of Assisi picked up the themes of poverty, humility and love and brought them, through the exemplary quality of his life, to new heights. Richard of St Victor, who is one of the most influential spiritual theologians of the West, gives classic theological expression to the ascent of the soul to God through love in his *Benjamin Minor*.[1]

The spiritual values of the Christian West were naturally close to those of the East, but we can discern characteristic differences. Among the Greeks, for instance, the concept of spiritual living in the world remained more metaphysical, and ideal, and the virtuous life was seen more in terms of a human participation in the qualities of God. An influential concept from the earliest times was that of *apatheia*, or 'passionlessness', and it is this to which the Greek Fathers constantly return. The word originates with the Stoics, for whom it signified a desired state of internal equilibrium, but it was soon taken up by Christian thinkers. Ignatius of Antioch applied the term to the glorified Christ, and Athenagoras used it of God. For Clement of Alexandria it came to mean the state of impassibility which we achieve at the end of our spiritual journey and which constitutes our 'equality' to God. Thus, for Clement, the perfected Christian dwells in a God-like state of serenity, undisturbed by any passion or sentiment. And for the monastic writer, Evagrius, *apatheia* is the end of contemplation, which comes to us when we transcend all passions, all images and all thought, thus entering the vision of the formless Godhead. But other of the Fathers took a more pragmatic view of 'passionlessness', and they set it in the context of the other outstanding virtues of the Christian life and the struggle of the spirit with the flesh. For Athanasius it is a great gift of God to us which is merited by the incarnation of his Son while, for Gregory of Nyssa, *apatheia* was the original human state before the Fall and it is thus the condition which is restored to us through baptism and a life of penance within the Church. For Maximus the Confessor, the great seventh-century Father who exercised considerable influence in the West, *apatheia* is the foundation of the spiritual life and is the fruit of both temperance and love. While the term *apatheia* is widely used by the Greek Fathers, therefore, it appears in varying contexts and can be said to embrace a number of divergent meanings.[2] Much the same could be said of Eckhart's use of the term *abegescheidenheit* or 'detachment'.[3] As is the case with 'passionlessness', 'detachment' is a concept which covers a wide range of meanings. Essentially moreover, it is an idea which spans both the metaphysical and the moral/ascetical dimensions. Eckhart's use of this term therefore serves to distinguish him from the greater part of western writers, for whom the metaphysical dimension of morality is implicit rather than explicit. But it can be shown that Eckhart's *abegescheidenheit* embraces also the traditional emphasis upon humility, obedience and love, which are the foundation of the monastic ascetical ideal.

Detachment and metaphysics

There is a clear connection in Eckhart's mind between our own 'detached' being in the world and the metaphysical birth of God in the soul. In the following passage we read of the way in which the birth of God in us is simultaneously our birth back into him:

> If a soul stands in this present now, the Father bears in her His only-begotten Son, and in that same birth the soul is born back into God. It is one birth: as often as she is born back into God, the Father begets His only-begotten Son in her. (W 66; cf. 79)

This illumines the condensed formulation: 'God bears Himself out of Himself into Himself, and bears Himself again back into Himself' (W 79), and it leads to a yet further idea, that of the birth of the soul *out of the world*: 'Man has a twofold birth: one into the world, and one out of the world, which is spiritual and into God' (W 7).

Eckhart is clear that true detachment means the spirit should transcend the created dimension: 'all our perfection and all our bliss depend on our traversing and transcending all creatureliness, all being, and getting into the ground that is groundless' (W 80), and at one point Eckhart specifies the three things which prevent the soul from attaining true detachment:

> The first is that she is too scattered, that she is not unitary, for when the soul is inclined towards creatures, she is not unitary. The second is when she is involved with temporal things. The third is when she is turned towards the body, for then she cannot unite with God. (W 85)

The above passage well shows the extent to which Eckhart conceives of detachment in deeply metaphysical terms. All three of the points made in the above quotation refer to the specific physicality of human existence as that from which we must escape. Through the body and the sentient powers of the body, the spirit is held at the level of created things and is not free to realize its own potential. The true nature of the soul is imageless and – hence – divine, and it is restrained and contained by its connectedness, through images, with the world. The soul is thus filled with (created) images when it should be free to realize its own imageless (and therefore 'uncreated') nature. Thus, in becoming 'detached' we emulate the Godhead itself, and the process of 'detachment' is simultaneously the process of our divinization: 'Therefore a man must be slain and wholly dead, devoid of self and wholly without likeness, like to none, and then he is really God-like. For it is God's character, his nature, to be peerless and like no man' (W 16). This same theme of divinization is also made explicit in the treatise *On detachment*:[4]

> Now you might ask, what is detachment, since it is so noble in itself? Here you should know that true detachment is nothing other than this: the spirit stands as immovable in all the assaults of joy or sorrow, honour, disgrace or shame, as a mountain of lead stands immovable against a small wind. This immovable detachment brings about in man the greatest similarity with God. For if God is God, he has it from his immovable detachment, and from this detachment he has his purity, his simplicity and his immutability. (DW V, pp. 411f.)

According to this view, therefore, the 'powers' of the soul represent her connectedness with the world, and they are contrasted with the soul's God-like 'essence' which is beyond all activity and beyond all created imagery:

> Whatever the soul effects, she effects with her powers. What she understands, she understands with the intellect. What she remembers, she does with memory; if she would love, she does that with the will, and thus she works with her powers and not with her essence. Every external act is linked with some *means*. The power of sight works only through the eyes; otherwise it can neither employ nor bestow vision, and so it is with all the other senses. The soul's every external act is effected by some means. But in the soul's essence there is no activity, for the powers she works with emanate from the ground of being. Yet in that ground is the silent 'middle': here nothing but rest and celebration for this birth, this act, that God the Father may speak His word there, for this part is by nature receptive to nothing save only the divine essence, without mediation. (W 1)

Having established this dichotomy between the ground and the powers, Eckhart goes on to stress that our sentient life, the perception of the world or creatures through our senses, is counter to the transcendence of the ground:

None can touch the ground of the soul but God alone. No creature can enter the soul's ground, but must stop outside, in the 'powers'. Within, the soul sees clearly the image whereby the creature has been drawn in and taken lodging. For whenever the powers of the soul make contact with a creature, they set to work and make an image and likeness of the creature, which they absorb. That is how they know the creature. No creature can come closer to the soul than this, and the soul never approaches a creature without having first voluntarily taken an image of it into herself. (W 1)

The spirituality of the 'ground' therefore is founded upon a withdrawal of the centre of consciousness away from sentience, imagery, and into that part of the soul which transcends the world. It is this, the spirituality of transcendence, which is at the heart of Eckhartian mysticism:

When the powers have been completely withdrawn from all their works and images, *then* the Word is spoken . . . And so, the more completely you are able to draw in your powers to a unity and forget all those things and their images which you have absorbed, and the further you can get from creatures and their images, the nearer you are to this and the readier to receive it. (W 1)

There are in addition a number of passages in which Eckhart urges us to become 'nothing', as God himself is nothing: 'Since it is God's nature not to be *like* anyone, we have to come to the state of being *nothing* in order to enter in to the same nature that He is' (W 7). We must leave the dimensions of time and place, which determine our specific being and which are foreign to God in his transcendence:

Nothing hinders the soul so much from knowing God as time and place. Time and place are fractions, and God is *one*. Therefore if the soul is to know God, she must know Him above time and place: for God is neither this nor that as these manifold things are: God is one. (W 69)

Elsewhere Eckhart tells us that we must withdraw from our *specific* being (i.e. being 'this or that') into the bareness of our *universal* human nature:

I say humanity and man are different. Humanity in itself is so noble that the highest peak of humanity is equal to the angels and akin to God. The closest union that Christ had with the Father, that is possible for me to win, could I but slough off what there is of *this* and *that*, and realise my humanity. (W 10)

It is this universal human nature which was assumed (and so divinized) by Christ, and thus, by withdrawing into it from what is 'accidental' or secondary in our nature, we are united with Christ:

Therefore, in order to be one Son, you must discard and depart from whatever makes for distinction in you. For man is an 'accident' of nature: so, do away with whatever is an accident in you and take yourselves in the freedom of your indivisible human nature. But since this very nature wherein you take yourselves has become the Son of the eternal Father by the assumption of the eternal Word, thus you, with Christ, become the Son of the eternal Father by reason of taking yourselves by that same nature which has there become God. Beware therefore, lest you take yourselves as being either this man or that, but take yourselves according to your free, indivisible human nature. (W 47)

Through breaking down the determinacy of our own specific nature, we attain a kind of universal consciousness:

This or that thing is not all things, for, as long as I am this and that or have this and that, I am not all things and have not all things. Cease to be this and that, and to have this and that, then you are all things and have all things and so, being neither here nor there, you are everywhere. Therefore, being neither this nor that, you are everything. (W 49)

Detachment and the virtues

The passages quoted show that Eckhart thinks of detachment as being essentially a metaphysical category, and yet there are many other passages in which he speaks of its decidedly moral character. In the following extract, the idea of our universal being leads to a particular moral position:

I say something else and even harder. Whoever would exist in the nakedness of this nature, free from all mediation, must have left behind all distinction of person, so that he is as well disposed to a man who is across the sea, whom he never set eyes on, as to the man who is with him and is his close friend. As long as you favour your own person more than that man you have never seen, you are assuredly not right and have never for a single instant looked into this simple ground. (W 13b; cf. 74)

Here Eckhart uses the non-particularity of our conscious-ness, the shedding of our specific being (which he calls 'accidental' in the Aristotelian sense), as a basis for urging that we love others as ourselves: 'If I detach myself fully from my own and have one equal love, then I shall love all things equally . . .' (W 74). Not to do this is a sure sign that something is wrong:

Whoever loves God as he ought and must (whether he would or not), and as all creatures love Him, he *must* love his fellow-man as himself, rejoicing in his joys as his own joys, and desiring his honour as much as his own honour, and loving a stranger as one of his own . . . And you should know in truth that if you take more pleasure in your own honour than in that of another, that is wrong. (W 40)

We need to love others as ourselves moreover because we seek to imitate God who is equally generous towards all:

God as being pours himself out into all creatures, to each as much as it can take. This is a good lesson to us to love all creatures equally with all that we have received from God, and if some are by nature nearer to us by kinship or friendship, then we should still favour them equally out of divine love in regard to the same good . . . Thus God loves all creatures equally and fills them with his being. And thus, too, we should pour forth ourselves in love over all creatures. (W 88)

If, firstly, detachment brings us to love all others equally, then, second, it leads us also to practise humility. We find a number of passages in which Eckhart speaks of our self-emptying less in terms of a metaphysical detachment as such but rather in the more moral terms of a classical humility:

Just as the power of heaven works never so effectively, and in no element, as in the ground of earth, although it is the lowest, for here it has the greatest opportunity to work, so too God works most in a humble heart, for He has the greatest opportunity to work therein, and finds His like most therein. He thus teaches us to enter into the ground of true humility and true nakedness, to cast off everything that we do not have by nature (which is sin and defect), and also whatever we have by nature that is born of attachment. (W 46)

But in other passages Eckhart plays upon the image of the emptiness of humility as an anticipation of the fulness of God's presence:

And it is just the same with a truly humble person who has subjected all creatures to himself and subjects himself to God: God in His goodness does not hold back, but pours Himself out fully into that man: He is compelled to do this and must needs do it.

In the continuation of this passage, Eckhart establishes humility as the basis for our union with God. Thus humility here becomes, in essence, synonymous with detachment:

I said in the schools of Paris that all things shall be accomplished in the truly humble man. The sun represents God: the All-Highest in its unfathomable Godhead corresponds to the all-lowest in the depth of humility. The truly humble man has no need to pray to God for anything: he can command God, for the height of the Godhead seeks nothing but the depth of humility, as I said at St Maccabees. The humble man and God are one, the humble man has as much power over God as He has over Himself, and whatever is in the angels, that the humble man has for his own. What God performs, the humble man performs, and what God is, he is: one life and one being. (W 50)

The pre-eminence of humility among the virtues, and its proximity to the Eckhartian detachment, is made clear in the lines: 'For that virtue which is called humility is a root in the ground of the Godhead, where it is so implanted that it has its being solely in the eternal One, and nowhere else' (W 51). But third, and finally, we also find a passage in which Eckhart makes explicit the fact that a metaphysical transcendence of our 'created' dimension is at the same time an overcoming of our physical appetites:

That man's animal passions and desires must be herded up into the highest power of the soul. For unless the soul is raised and lifted above created things, the Holy Ghost cannot enter in or operate in her. For all the divine work done by God he must do in the spirit, above time and place, for corporeal things corrupt the divine influx. Divine light shed on spiritual creatures engenders life, but if it falls on material things, it is extinguished and perishes altogether. (W 75)

Detachment and human experience

At the level of ordinary living, the process of detachment begins with the giving up of our own will. In the *Talks of Instruction*, where Eckhart is writing for his fellow-Dominicans, he speaks of religious obedience in the following terms:

When someone leaves what is theirs in obedience, God must of necessity enter in again, for if someone does not want anything for themselves, God must will for them in the same manner as he does for himself. For I have surrendered my will into the hands of my superior and want nothing for myself, therefore God must will for me, and if he neglects me in this matter, then he neglects himself. (DW V, p. 187)[5]

Indeed, it is only through giving up our own will that we can be sure that we possess God and are possessed by him:

He who makes his will over wholly to God, to him God gives his will in return, so wholly and so genuinely that God's will becomes that man's own, and God has sworn by himself to do nothing but what that man wills, for God will never be anyone's own who has not first become God's own. (W 10)

To abandon our human will, however, is to give up the sense of being in possession of things, which flows from the ego:

We must learn to remove from all God's gifts to us the sense of our own self, to possess nothing of our own and to seek nothing, neither advantage nor pleasure nor inwardness nor sweetness nor reward nor heaven itself nor our own will. God never has entered, nor ever does enter someone through their will but only through his own will. And so whenever he finds his own will, there he gives himself and enters in with all that is his. The more we strip ourselves of ourselves, the more we become him. (DW V, p. 281)

Eckhart warns us accordingly that we should never feel that anything is permanently our possession:

> We should rather possess things as if they had been lent to us, and not given: whether it be body or soul, the senses, faculties, outer goods or honour, friends, relatives, house, land or anything.
>   What does God intend by this, and why is he so keen that it should be so? Now he wishes to be himself our sole possession. This is his whole meaning and desire. In this lies all his yearning and delight. And the more fully and completely he can accomplish this, the greater his bliss and joy; for the more we possess other things, the less we possess him, and the less love we have for other things, the more we possess him with all that he brings us. (DW V, pp. 295f.)

The Eckhartian state of detachment in the world is one of complete self-abandonment, in which the giving up of the ego, of the sense of self, and the giving up of the sense of possession, are one:

> This above all else is needful: you must lay claim to nothing! Let go of yourself and let God act with you and in you as he will. This work is his, this word is his, this birth is his, in fact every single thing that you are. For you have abandoned self and have gone out of your (soul's) powers and activities, and your personal nature. Therefore God must enter into your being and powers, because you have bereft yourself of all possessions, and become as a desert. . . . (W 3)

Eckhart's intense belief in the nothingness of the creature and of the necessity of detachment leads him to espouse a radical critique of works, which can themselves all too easily become the objects of possession:

> The just man seeks nothing in his works: for those who seek anything in their works or work for any 'why' are thralls and hirelings. Therefore, if you would be informed with and

transformed into justice, have no ulterior purpose in your work, allow no 'why' to take shape in you, as regards either time or eternity, reward or blessedness or this or that: for in truth *such* works are dead. (W 59)

Works, Eckhart tells us, belong to the specificity of time and space; they perish, therefore, as soon as they are born. There is nothing in works as such that can endure:

> The work has no being, nor has the time in which it occurred, since it perishes in itself. Therefore it is neither good nor holy nor blessed, but rather the man is blessed in whom the fruit of the work remains, neither as time nor as work, but as a good disposition which is eternal with the spirit as the spirit is eternal in itself, and it is the spirit itself. (W 15)

Elsewhere Eckhart makes the same point more simply:

> People should not worry so much about what they should do; rather about what they should be. If we and our ways are good, then what we do will be radiant. If we are just, then our works will be just. We should not expect to be able to ground sanctity on what we do, but on what we are, for it is not works which sanctify us, but we who sanctify our works. (DW V, pp. 197f.)

In the same way he cautions us against mistaking a way to God for God himself. Here he is warning against the pride of spiritual or ascetical achievement:

> If a man thinks he will get more of God by meditation, by devotion, by ecstasies or by special infusion of grace than by the fireside or in the stable – that is nothing but taking God, wrapping a cloak around his head and shoving him under a bench. For whoever seeks God in a special way gets the way but misses God, who lies hidden in it. But whoever seeks God without any special way gets him as he is in himself, and that man lives with the Son, and he is life itself. (W 13b)

It is not surprising, therefore, that Eckhart advocates the dropping of particular devotional practices, if these are felt to obstruct our union with God. External practices are superseded by the inner reality: 'If a man knows himself to be well trained in true inwardness, then let him boldly drop all outward disciplines' (W 3). But if Eckhart points here to the ultimate inward character of all spiritual practice, he is equally at pains to stress that works remain integral to the spiritual life:

> Some people hope to reach a point where they are free of works. I say this cannot be. After the disciples had received the Holy Ghost, they began to do good works. And so, when Mary sat at the feet of our Lord, she was learning, for she had just gone to school to learn how to live. But later on, when Christ had gone to Heaven and she received the Holy Ghost, she began to serve: she travelled overseas and preached and taught. (W 9)

Eckhart stresses also that we should not turn our prayer into the idol of a 'work' by telling God what he should give us: 'As soon as you pray to God for creatures, you pray for your own harm, for creature is no sooner creature than it bears within itself bitterness and trouble, evil and distress' (W 11). Rather, Eckhart says: 'I declare that I will not pray to God to give to me, nor praise him for what he has given me, but I will pray to him to make me worthy to receive, and I will praise him because he is of such nature and essence that he must give' (ibid.).

The chief area, however, in which Eckhart sees the principle of detachment at work in us in our daily living is the way in which we respond to suffering. Here he is adamant that we need to attain a place of serenity which is beyond the vicissitudes of life:

> The whole of human perfection therefore is to become distant from creatures and free from them, to respond in the same way to all things, not to be broken by adversity nor carried away by prosperity, not to rejoice more in one thing than in another, not to be frightened or grieved by one thing more than another (LW IV, p. 694).

We need to 'love God equally in all things', for only in this way will we be like God himself who is 'immutable, imperturbable and eternal stability' (W 49): 'Love God as much in poverty as in riches, love him as much in sickness as in health; love him as much in temptation as without temptation, love him as much in suffering as without suffering' (W 18).

Above all, however, Eckhart identifies in suffering the opportunity to discover and to deepen our detachment. In a memorable passage he speaks first of how we should respond to the physical or external suffering which comes our way:

> For that man who wishes to cast his soul, the grain of wheat, into the field of Jesus Christ's humanity that it may perish therein and so become fruitful, the manner of his perishing must also be of two kinds. The first way must be physical, and the second spiritual. The physical side is to be understood like this: whatever he suffers from hunger, thirst, from cold or heat, or from being scorned and suffering unjustly, in whatever way God sends it, he must accept it willingly and gladly, just as if God had never created him except to endure suffering, discomfort and travail, not seeking anything for himself therein nor desiring anything in heaven or earth, and he should consider all his suffering as trifling, as a mere drop of water compared to the raging sea. That is how you should regard all your suffering compared to the great suffering of Jesus Christ. Then the grain of corn, your soul, will become fruitful in the noble field of Jesus Christ's humanity and will perish there so as to abandon self completely.

But this same thorough-going acceptance of the will of God is necessary also in the inner sphere, where we encounter more subtle forms of suffering:

> Now observe the second manner of the fruitfulness of the spirit, of the grain of wheat. It is this: all the spiritual hunger and bitterness that God permits to invade him, he shall patiently endure: and even then, having done all he can both inwardly and outwardly, he shall desire nothing. Even if God wanted to annihilate him or cast him into hell, he should neither wish nor desire that God should preserve him in existence or save him from hell. You should let God do what he will with you, what he will – just as if you did not exist: God's power should be as absolute in all that you are as it is within his own uncreated nature.

In a way that closely parallels the teaching of St John of the Cross two centuries later, Eckhart goes on to warn us against lingering on our journey towards God with the sweet consolations of spiritual union, which can hinder us and hold us back:

> There is another thing you should have. It is this: if God were to take you away from inner poverty and invest you inwardly with riches and with grace and were to unite you with himself as far as ever your soul could endure this, you should hold yourself free of these riches and give the glory to God alone, just as your soul remained empty when God created it from nothing into something. (W 89)

Conclusion

If Eckhart's concept of the 'spark in the soul' and of the 'birth of God in the soul' are expressive metaphors which convey a range of metaphysical and spiritual meanings, then much the same is true of Eckhart's use of the term *abegescheidenheit*. We have identified above a whole range of themes and matters which are included in this same semantic field: detachment is at once our likeness to God, it is the state of our creaturely nothingness, it is our resignation to God's will, it is our equal love for all human beings, and it is our humility. Above all, it is a term which straddles both the metaphysical and the moral dimension, and it is here that we find a very distinctive note in Eckhart's teaching.[6] Prior to Eckhart and after him, western thinkers have in general not cared too much for metaphysics in their ascetical theology; and yet we find in Eckhart a determinedly and uncompromisingly metaphysical view of the structures of moral life. Detachment, for Eckhart, is the kind of living in the world which results from the birth of God in the soul and the actualization of the God-like essence within us. To live in a 'detached' manner is thus, in a very real sense, to be in the world but not of it (cf. John 17). But both categories of experience, the transcendent and the existential (or 'everyday'), need to be held in balance. Although some of Eckhart's statements on detached living are impossibly ideal (and to these we will later return), the metaphysical dimension is constantly held in check by actual forms of human living. We would be quite wrong to think of Eckhart as teaching that we can become so united with God, in our essence, as to be free from a life of struggle and virtue lived out in the real world. Although he does not dwell on this struggle, most of what he writes implies it. At the same time, Eckhart is keen to challenge the idea that our sanctification is an external matter or one which we bring about through our own energies and powers. There are few teachers of the Church who have so systematically and unequivocally asserted the view that all moral and ascetical advance is rooted in a sovereign and grace-filled intervention of God in the depths of our being: the 'birth of God in the soul'. Eckhart reminds us of this at all points in his ascetical teaching, but he can remind us too that works are there 'to catch a man and restrain him from things alien and ungodly' (W 3).

NOTES TO CHAPTER 7

1. There is a fascinating article on 'Humility' in the DS, vol. VII i, cols. 1136–87.
2. See DS, vol. I, cols. 727–46 on 'Apatheia'.
3. Eckhart does not restrict himself to the word *abegescheidenheit* alone in order to express this concept, but he speaks also of *gelâzenheit* (serenity), *demuot* (humility) and *geistliche armuot* (spiritual poverty). These are all broadly synonyms, but it is the word *abegescheidenheit* which Eckhart mostly uses in order to convey the sense of detachment in its full metaphysical sense.
4. The authenticity of *On detachment* has been and is still disputed. In his article 'Das Echtheitsproblem des Traktats "Von abegescheidenheit"' (in *La Mystique rhénane*, pp. 39–57; also DW V, pp. 392–7) Josef Quint argued for its authenticity, with which view Alois Haas is in agreement (1989, p. 400). Kurt Ruh, on the other hand, has expressed reservations (see his review of Eduard Schäfer's 'Meister Eckharts Traktat "Von abegescheidenheit"' in *Zeitschrift für deutsche Philologie*, 78

[1959], pp. 100–5; also 1985, pp. 165ff.). There is a consensus, however, that the substance of the treatise is Eckhartian, even if the form sometimes seems to suggest another hand. The quotation here is from Clark and Skinner, pp. 163f.

5. The passages quoted from the *Talks of Instruction* are taken from my forthcoming translation of the selected works of Meister Eckhart (Penguin Classics, Harmondsworth).

6. Dietmar Mieth (1969) in particular has traced the ultimate unity of the ethical and ontological dimensions in Eckhart's work. See also his 'Meister Eckhart: Authentische Erfahrung als Einheit von Denken, Sein und Leben' in A. Haas and H. Stirnimann, eds (1980), pp. 11–61.

PART THREE

UNDERSTANDING MEISTER ECKHART

8 • MEISTER ECKHART'S LANGUAGE

It is usual for histories of Christian spirituality to concentrate largely upon the evolution of ideas within the Christian spiritual tradition. Rarely, if ever, will questions of imagery and style be given the prominence they deserve. This results from a preoccupation with the principles represented by the main body of theological debate, which centre upon the definition of doctrine, disputation and scientific analysis. While this idea-centred approach is appropriate for the history of theology as such, it can prove seriously inadequate when applied to the field of spiritual theology. The reason for this is evident. If theology is concerned with the articulation and systematization of faith, then spiritual theology addresses the innermost experiences of human consciousness. The spiritual theologian is attempting to bring order and form to the most subtle and elusive areas of human experience. He or she will be confronted with the seemingly impossible task of articulating an encounter with the uncreated divinity, who is beyond all categories of created knowledge and experience. 'God', as Eckhart observed, 'is beyond the reach of words'. It is no wonder, therefore, that argument gives way here to metaphor and science to poetry.

It is not only because of the wisdom which their words convey to us that we select certain mystics from the past, dub them 'great' and read their works in profusion, but also, and fundamentally, because they possessed literary gifts of a high order which allowed them to *make present* for us, their readers, something of that very experience which inspired them and their lives. The experiences of those from the past who were equally gifted in a mystical but not in a creative way are lost to us, except through the communion of the saints. We must speak of a double gift therefore, when referring to those mystical writers from the past who are widely read today in religious circles and yet whose work is justly considered to be (and is studied as being) an integral part of the literatures of their respective national traditions.

If we are to understand Meister Eckhart in depth, therefore, we must also consider his nature as a stylist.[1] This is not to apply to him a purely academic lens which will be of concern only to students of language, rather it is to analyse why Eckhart's writing stirs us as it does and communicates to us something of his transcendental vision; for Eckhart believed, after all, that 'words also have great power; we could work wonders with words. All words have their power from the first Word' (W 36). Through tracing Eckhart's achievement as a rhetorician, we will come closer to understanding the character of his greatness as a mystical theologian.

Meister Eckhart's conceptual poetry

The theological analysis contained in the central chapters of this book sought to show that Eckhart proceeds by picking up specific thematic elements from tradition and investing them with a new and expressive significance. We are justified in calling this process the 'poeticization' of theological language because it involves the loosening of the relation between the signifier and signified, and thus the foregrounding of language, as bearer of meaning, rather than meaning itself – a phenomenon which is usually judged to be a prime characteristic of poetic texts. Thus at his hands, the 'spark of the soul' (and its partners), the 'birth of God in the soul' and 'detachment' become cyphers which represent a whole complex of theological positions. These themes lose specific meaning, and move evocatively within the sphere either of the theology of the Divine Image within us, of the operation of grace or, finally, that of traditional spiritual or ascetical theology. Thus, rather than being distinct ideas with a specific significance, they take on the evocative properties of an *image* and a *metaphor*.

The definition of these two terms within the literary field has generated a body of theoretical rumination which is as complex as it is extensive. For our present purposes, therefore, I shall restrict myself to a working definition of what we mean by these terms which is simple rather than comprehensive. But we shall not go far wrong if we define the *image* as being an abstract figure (within a poem or work of literature) whose origins lie nevertheless in an act of sense perception.[2] An image, by this definition, therefore, must be reducible to our experience of something within the world. C. Day Lewis defines 'imagery' as 'a picture made out of words' and Fogle calls it 'the sensuous element within poetry'.[3] Even if the 'image' is used within an entirely abstract context, traces of its origin in the life of the senses will remain. An 'idea', on the other hand, may be an entirely formal entity which stands within a chain of reasoned argument, or whose origins lie in the abstract order rather in that of physical sensation.

By this definition, therefore, the 'spark (or 'crown' or 'summit') of the soul', the 'birth of God in the soul' and 'detachment' can all be seen to be images. This is self-evidently the case with the 'spark' (and its partners), but is no less so with the 'birth' and 'detachment'. After all, Eckhart uses the term 'birth' in a very concrete sense, with a clear reference to the actual birth of Jesus, and he is happy to speak of the 'motherhood' of God (W 90) and of the 'child' who is the product of this birth. The concept of 'detachment' is also one which derives from our observation of the world. Eckhart's Middle High German word *abegescheidenheit* is constructed from the verb *abescheiden*, which means 'to cut off' and which is thus very much a term of *physical* relation. However metaphysical the significance which Eckhart attaches to such figures, they remain empirical in origin and therefore qualify as 'images'.

But they are, at the same time, *metaphors*. Here we have a definition to hand, which is that a metaphor is a 'condensed verbal relation in which an idea, image, or symbol may, by the presence of one or more other ideas, images, or symbols, be enhanced in vividness, complexity, or breadth of implication'. Put another way, the metaphor is a figure of speech 'in which an unknown or imperfectly known is clarified, defined, described in terms of a known'.[4] In the case of Eckhart's 'conceptual poetry', the attendant images are those of (1) a 'spark', (2) a 'birth' and (3) 'cutting off' and the abstract realities which they metaphorically illumine are (1) the divine image in the soul, (2) the action of grace and process of sanctification and (3) the state of being 'in' the world while not being 'of' it. And the juxtaposition of these two dimensions of reality, the one originating in the natural order of sense-perceptions and the other based in the supernatural order of transcendence and grace, lends to otherwise elusive and ethereal abstractions a startlingly vivid actuality. The 'spark' and the 'birth' and the 'cutting off' convey to us more of the spiritual worlds which they reflect than any amount of discursive argument, description and reasoning could do.

In addition to the three major areas of theological imagery discussed above, there are numerous instances in Eckhart's work, particularly in his German sermons, in which he coins figures of speech which brilliantly capture the whole variety of spiritual nuance. It would be a grave oversight in a book of this kind not to highlight at least some of these configurations which arouse and provoke us today as much as they did the original audiences who gathered in church and cloister to hear the celebrated Dominican preach.

When talking of the God who is beyond all images and words and who is himself formless, Eckhart enjoys making use of intensely vital and physical imagery. At one point, therefore, he states that 'all creatures are green in God' (i.e. the green-ness of creatures is where they exist as an idea in the Divine Mind); elsewhere that God pours himself into creatures with the delight of a horse galloping in a meadow:

> God delights so in this likeness that he pours out his whole nature and being in this equality with himself. He rejoices in it, just as if one were to turn a horse loose in a green meadow that was entirely smooth and level, and it would be the horse's nature to let himself go with all his strength in galloping about the meadow – he would enjoy it for it is his nature. (W 57)

Sometimes Eckhart uses boldly physical language of God himself, as when he tells us that we should 'strip God of all his clothing – seize him naked in his robing-room, where he is uncovered and bare in himself' (W 63) or that 'if a man thinks he will get more of God by meditation, by devotion, by ecstasies or by special infusion of grace than by the fireside or in the stable – that is nothing but taking God, wrapping a cloak round his head and shoving him under a bench' (W 13b). In one sermon (W 90) Eckhart speaks of 'motherhood' in God, and in another of 'childbed' in God (W 16). And in a third, Eckhart speaks of God 'clearing his throat': 'Where is this God? It is just as if a man were to hide himself and then to give himself away by clearing his throat: God has done the same. No man could ever have found God, but he has revealed his presence' (W 91).

In describing our experience of God, who is ineffable, Eckhart also makes extensive use of graphic language which is strongly evocative of the life of the senses. Thus he speaks of the 'touch of God' (W 66) and, in a memorable passage, of 'tasting God': 'The soul that God loves and to whom he communicates himself must be so wholly stripped of time and from all creaturely flavour that God in her tastes only of his own flavour' (W 73). The paradoxical nature of applying the language of the senses to the knowledge of God is summed up in a passage in which Eckhart speaks of our ascent to the third heaven. This, he says, 'is purely spiritual knowledge, therein the soul is rapt away from all objective, bodily things. There we hear without any sound and see without matter' (W 76).

In one of his most virtuosic images Eckhart captures the multiplicity of human experience through constructing a three-dimensional metaphysical metaphor. There are a number of points at which he speaks of the inwardness of the human soul, of the depths of humility (which is detachment) and indeed of that depth which is simultaneously height (since, in the words of the Magnificat, God 'raises the lowly'). In one classic passage however all three dimensions are brought together in an image which brilliantly captures a sense of metaphysical space:

Just as the power of heaven works never so effectively, and in no element, as in the ground of the earth, although it is the lowest, for here it has the greatest opportunity to work, so too God works most in a humble heart, for he has the greatest opportunity to work therein, and finds his like most therein. He thus teaches us to enter into the ground of true humility and true nakedness, to cast off everything that we do not have by nature (which is sin and defect), and also whatever we have by nature that is born of attachment. For whoever would enter God's ground, his inmost part, must first enter his own ground, his inmost part, for none can know God who does not first know himself. He must enter into his lowest and into God's inmost part, and must enter into his first and his highest, for there everything comes together that God can perform. Whatever is highest in the soul is in the lowest, for it is the innermost. . . . (W 46)

Meister Eckhart's language

There is something deeply paradoxical about applying sensual imagery which, in Joseph Quint's phrase is redolent of the smell of earth,[5] to the formless Godhead who is the 'negation of negation' (i.e. transcends the created order) and is beyond all images. But, as we have seen, Eckhart's work is as a whole shot through with paradox which, in the opening chapter of this book, we interpreted as being a reflex of the fundamentally Christian paradox of our transformative encounter with God. It is this, we have argued, which inspires Eckhart's thinking and writing, leading him to seek to *enact* this vision through theological and literary means in a way that both gives *expression* to it and *communicates* it for other people. The parallel with a poem has been cited. This is both a personal expression of the poet's experience and sensibilities and yet at the same time is always a dialogue with the reader; it exists, therefore, both 'for' the poet and 'for' the reader. In the same way Eckhart's work serves to *make present* his dialectical vision of God both in order to body forth his own inner experience and to cause it to be shared by others. He achieves this, in any case, not just through the use of subtle and daring imagery, but also through the very fabric of his language. It is to the characteristic stylistic devices of Eckhart's prose that we shall now turn.

Antithesis

There are many and varied forms of opposition (or antithesis) to be found in Eckhart's works, and they function at different levels. One such type is his frequent use of paradoxical formulations with reference to the nature of God. Here, of course, Eckhart is seeking to remind us that God transcends the created level and yet is immanent within it. And so these kinds of paradox, generally in the form of an oxymoron (in which two contradictory ideas are combined) closely parallel Eckhart's teaching on analogy in so far as God is simultaneously within creation and beyond it. Formulations of this type include the phrase that God is both 'spoken and unspoken' (W 22), that he is a 'changing without change' (W 93),[6] a 'newness without renewal' (W 93), that God 'is pure nothing' (W 54), a 'desert' (W 16) and a 'beingless being' (W 62), and that the intellect (which is, of course, in God's image) is an 'expanseless expanse' (W 29) which, when it unites with God, is reformed into its 'imageless image'. Of a similar kind are the statements that 'God is not good' (W 96) and that 'whoever sees anything of God, sees nothing of him' (W 55).[7]

If Eckhart likes to use paradoxical language when speaking of God, then this is no less true of those passages in which he speaks of our union with the transcendent divine. We have already seen something of this in the reference above to depth, which is at the same time height and inwardness (W 46), but there is another passage in which this paradox is even more powerfully drawn out:

> The highest height of elevation lies in the deepest depth of humility. For the deeper and lower the ground, the higher and more immense the height and the exaltation. The deeper the well, the higher it is. Height and depth are the same thing. Therefore the more anyone can humble himself, the higher he is. (DW V, pp. 293f.)

The same sense of paradox is conveyed in Eckhart's metaphor of love, the love between ourselves and God, as a fisherman's hook:

> Whoever is caught in this net, whoever walks in this way, whatever he does is all one: whether he does anything or nothing is of no account. And yet the least action or practice of such a man is more profitable and fruitful to himself and all men, and more pleasing to God, than all the works of others who, though free from mortal sin, are inferior to him in love. His rest is more useful than another's labour. Therefore, just watch for this hook, so as to be blessedly caught: for the more you are caught, the more you are free. (W 4)

Paradoxical antithesis is used also in the area of *possession*: 'He who wishes to receive all things must also give up all things' (DW V, p. 295). Eckhart reminds us that absorption with the self and being taken up into God are clean contraries:

> The more we have of our own, the less we have him; the less we have of our own, the more we have of him, with everything that he can offer . . .
>
>   If I forsake myself for his sake, in return God will be absolutely my own, with everything that he is and that he can offer, mine just as it is his, neither more nor less. He will be a thousand times more mine than anything that anyone ever obtained that he has in his chest . . . (DW V, pp. 297f.)

Elsewhere Eckhart describes our 'finding' God again in highly paradoxical terms: 'The more we seek thee, the less we find thee. You must seek him in such wise that you never find him. If you do not seek him, you will find him' (W 51). And he speaks of following the 'way', which is 'really being at home' and through which we attain a state of union in which the subject and object fuse: 'How marvellous to be without and within, to embrace and be embraced, to see and be the seen, to hold and be held – that is the goal, where the spirit is ever at rest, united in joyous eternity' (W 9). Finally, the dialectic of encounter with God is expressed in its fulness in Eckhart's remarks on our 'knowing' of God which is at the same time an 'unknowing':

But here we must come to a transformed knowledge, and this unknowing must not come from ignorance, but rather from knowing we must get to this unknowing. Then we shall become knowing with divine knowing, and our unknowing will be ennobled and adorned with supernatural knowing. (W 2)

Style

If the content of Eckhart's writings is often searchingly paradoxical, then this is a characteristic which is sustained and strengthened by his use of a number of purely stylistic devices. We find many instances of chiasmus, for instance (a form of inverted repetition: a + b, b + a), as in Eckhart's comment on the transcendence/immanence dialectic of God and the world: 'The more he is in things, the more he is out of things: the more in, the more out, and the more out, the more in' (W 18). It is a device which Eckhart uses also in order to enhance the rhetorical effect of his words: 'See, thus we have proved the truth of my assertion, as it truly is. And all those who contradict it, I contradict them and care not a jot for them, for what I have said is true, and truth itself declares it' (W 15). Frank Tobin has also isolated further statements in which the principle of chiasmus is linked with parallelism, as in the statement that God is 'a speaking work' (*'ein sprechende werk'*) while the Son is 'speech working' (*'ein spruch würkende'*: W 22).[8] Here, as Tobin observes, a formal chiasmus is contrasted with a parallelism (or opposition) of meaning: the Father's work is to speak – while the Son, who is spoken, works. But there are also many instances in which Eckhart uses simple forms of chiasmus which are nevertheless highly effective, as when he speaks of our union with God in the innermost recesses of the spirit: 'Here God's ground is my ground and my ground is God's ground' (W 13b),[9] or when he refers to the mutual possession of God and the soul: 'But if I am to know God without means, then I must really become he, and he I' (W 96).

Constructions of proportion are a further figure much beloved of Eckhart, and these enhance his analogical theory of the *inquantum*, or 'in so far as'. Numerous examples of this kind of syntactical construction can be found in any of Eckhart's works, but many of them refer specifically to the extent that we can be said to be one with God: 'And the extent that he has freed himself with good works while he was in mortal sin, just so far does he leap forward to unite with God' (W 15), 'As far as you depart from all things, thus far, no less and no more, does God enter into you' (DW V, p. 197), 'as far as you are outside God, you will be outside peace' (DW V, p. 308). This construction also commonly occurs in the form of the comparative: 'For the more naked and empty the heart is when it falls on God and is supported by him, the deeper we are placed in God and the more we become receptive . . .' (DW V, p. 262), 'A true and perfect will means to tread absolutely in the will of God and to do without self-will. The more one has of this, the more and more truly one is placed in God' (DW V, p. 227), 'the more man is transformed into his likeness, the more all sins and the suffering of sin will fall off from him' (DW V, p. 246), 'the more anyone can humble himself, the higher he is' (DW V, pp. 293f.), 'the more we have of our own, the less we have of him' (DW V, p. 297), 'the more a man lays himself bare, the more like he becomes to God, and the more like he becomes to God, the more he is made one with him' (W 63).

Another typical device is that of the conditional (or 'if') clause. Here Eckhart seems to be suggesting that we are as close to God as we *want* to be: 'If you want God to be your own, you must be his own like my tongue or hand' (W 50), 'if we keep ourselves free from the things that are outside us, God will give us in exchange everything that is in heaven' (DW V, p. 298). This also takes the form of 'whoever would', as in: 'whoever would exist in the nakedness of this nature, free from all mediation, must have left behind all distinction of person' (W 13b). 'For whoever would enter God's ground, his inmost part, must first enter his own ground, his inmost part' (W 46).

Eckhart also makes free use of the hypothetical conditional in order to drive a point home through hyperbole (or exaggeration), as when he says: 'Even if all creatures denied him, and swore hostility against him, indeed if God himself denied him, he would not lose confidence' (DW V, p. 241), and 'Truly, if there were a person who suffered for God's sake and for God's sake alone, and if there came upon him all the suffering which mankind has ever known and all that the world knows, then that would cause him no pain and would not weigh upon him' (W 8). The frequent occasions when Eckhart speaks of God *having* to act in a particular way can also be regarded as hyperbole. God, as Eckhart well knows, is entirely free in all that he does, and yet it is in accordance with his nature to answer our needs when the ground is properly prepared. Eckhart plays on this rhetorically by insisting that God *must* pour himself into the emptied soul: 'The Father gives birth to the Son in the soul in the very same way as he gives birth to him in eternity, and no differently. He must do it, whether he likes to or not' (W 65), and again; 'The Father gives birth to his Son, and thereby feels such delight and peace that it consumes his whole nature. For whatever is in God drives him to give birth; indeed, God is compelled to give birth by his Ground, his Essence and his Being' (W 59).

Vocabulary

Just as Eckhart seeks in his theology to stress that we must always transcend the particular, it is a striking feature of his vocabulary that he moves strongly in the direction of the abstract. This happens in a number of ways. The first is his use of abstract nouns (often of his own composition) which generally end in *-heit* and which derive from more specific nouns (e.g. *gotheit*/godhead, *wesenheit*/essentiality, *nihtheit*/nothingness, *zîtheit*/temporality). Another category derive from adjectives and often end in *-keit* (e.g. *innikeit*/inwardness, *lûterkeit*/pureness, *grundelosikeit*/groundlessness, *wesenlicheit*/essentialness, *unwandelberkeit*/unchangingness); while still another group of words end in *-ung* and, according to Quint, generally 'designate the mystical act of cognitive union' (e.g. *begrifunge*/comprehensions, *beruerunge*/caresses, *inliuhtunge*/enlightenings, *indrukunge*/impressions, *infliezunge*/influxes).[10] As Quint points out, these words are more often than not German translations of abstract Latin words ending in *-tas* and *-tio*. Linguistic scholars used to stress the extent to which Eckhart was coining a new vocabulary more than they do today for Eckhart is now seen to be part of a general movement towards stating in German what had previously only been said in Latin. His originality in this has to be balanced by the achievements of his contemporaries.[11]

What is distinctive in Eckhart's work, however, is the sheer abundance of words whose meaning is either abstract *per se* or which seem to force abstraction upon words which are otherwise specific, and therefore concrete, in their application. Indeed, Quint speaks of the *Entkonkretisierung* (the 'de-concretization') of experience as being a paramount characteristic of Eckhart's language.[12] One way in which this is achieved is through the use of the German substantival infinitive (cf. English gerund: i.e. 'being', 'doing', 'going'): 'One does not think of basing holiness on doing (*uf ein tuon*), one should base holiness on being' (*uf ein sîn*: DW V, p. 198). The use of the infinitive, of course, removes the possibility of gender, tense and number.[13] More important, however, is the technique of creating nouns in an abstract form for things normally rendered in more concrete ways. A fine example of this is a passage in which Eckhart marshals and combines a whole series of what we might call abstract 'possessive nouns'. In each case these words refer to what is most immediate and of this world, that is the very sense of personal identity itself, even of personal existence. And yet, through the addition of *-heit* and *-keit* (i.e. English: '-ness'), the substance of the passage becomes abstract and conceptual:

> You should wholly sink from your youness (*dîner dînesheit*) and dissolve into his hisness (*sîne sînesheit*), and your 'yours' (*dîn dîn*) and his 'his' (*sîn sîn*) should become so completely one 'mine' (*ein mîn*) that with him you understand his unbecome isness (*istikeit*) and his nameless nothingness. (W 96)

Something of this same 'de-concretization' is achieved through Eckhart's abundant use of negative forms. Indeed, this is one of the principal areas in which he shows his astonishing ability to make language register the very transcendence which he is striving to communicate. We have already seen some instances of this (e.g. God is *ungesprochen*/unspoken in W 22, *weselos*/beingless in W 62), but in one sermon (W 96) we find a remarkable series of lexical negatives which endeavour to convey the fact that God is beyond any conception we might have of him. We are to love God 'as he is: a non-God (*ein nihtgot*), a non-Spirit (*ein nihtgeist*), a non-Person (*ein nihtpersône*), a non-Image (*ein nihtbilde*). And our knowing of him is, of course, more 'an unknowing' (*ein unwizzen*) and 'an unfamiliarity' (*ein unbekantheit*). The word which perhaps typifies Eckhart's skill with negation more than any other is *entwirt* (DP, p. 273). The inseparable prefix *ent-* denotes the English 'de-' and indicates the removal of something. What is being removed in this case is the process of *werden*, which means 'becoming' and which is an experience which belongs wholly to the domain of time, in which things begin and have their end. The significance of the word, therefore, which can be rendered in English as 'to cease to become', is the process of transcending particular being, based in or constituted by time, in favour of a timeless and eternal state beyond particularity.

Before concluding this brief overview of Eckhart's extensive linguistic gifts, we need to turn to one further area of vocabulary which conveys a vital element in his vision. This is the sense of fusing or of union which underlies his unitive experience of God, and it is expressed first and foremost in a whole series of verbs of movement, such as 'flying', 'going', 'falling', 'sinking', 'drifting', 'running', 'bubbling', 'pushing', 'pulling'. The inherently dynamic quality of such verbs is further enhanced by the addition of prefixes of movement such as 'in', 'out', 'through' and 'over'.[14]

Conclusion

Questions of imagery and style are fundamental to the nature of mystical writing. It is these that give life, and form, to intuitive experience which is otherwise locked away in individual subjectivity, and cannot be shared, except, of course, by direct personal contact. The use of the written word allows some gifted individuals from the past to speak to us today with an undiminished clarity and vigour. The particular use which a mystic makes of words will express and convey the particular quality of their vision. In this sense, close linguistic analysis of a mystic's work reveals the wealth of their inner world.

We have seen in Eckhart's work a predominance of paradox, both at the level of thought and that of expression. Now paradox is based on opposition, and it is engendered when two seemingly conflicting ideas, or words, are brought into collision. Eckhart's extensive use of paradox follows from his concern with communicating a transcendent truth. In order to do this, he has to break down the conventional parameters of thinking. He has to take opposites and thrust them together in such a way that his audience is forced to draw near to the deeply paradoxical realities of transcendence and immanence, of the divine and human made one, which for Eckhart are the foundations of Christian truth.

The fact that this density and compression is achieved largely through the use of *abstract* words, powerfully enhanced by the nominal endings *-heit*, *-keit* and *-ung*, lends the whole of his writing an intensely noetic or cognitive colour. This means that we feel we are overwhelmingly in the presence of a *mind* which is seeking to express to us an experience of *knowing*, a free interpenetration of the Mind of God with the mind of a man. Eckhart's 'music of abstraction' (in Karl Jaspers' phrase)[15] springs from Eckhart's acute sense of the need to transcend all that is created and of the world. We need, in his judgement, to shed the forms of ordinary knowing (of knowing objects, that is), which determines our everyday being. We need to activate the 'intellect' which alone is undefined and unlimited and whose proper object is the undefined and unlimited being of God. In order to bring this change of cognition about in his audience, Eckhart firstly chooses numerous stylistic devices which are founded on paradox and which serve to rupture the ordinary level of cognition in favour of a transcendent one. Secondly, he employs a particular form of lexis, or vocabulary, which evokes the level of the mind rather than that of the world, and which will serve once again to draw the audience away from their ordinary level of cognition to a new, transcendent and wholly abstract dimension of divine knowing and divine being.

NOTES TO CHAPTER 8

1. Much work has been done on the language of Meister Eckhart. A full bibliography on this theme can be found in Schaller (1969), p. 32, and more recent works are noted in the bibliography to Tobin's important study *Meister Eckhart: Thought and Language* (1986). There are also a number of influential articles by Alois Haas on the theme of language and mysticism, including 'Mystische Erfahrung und Sprache' (in *Sermo mysticus*, pp. 19–36), 'Die Problematik von Sprache und Erfahrung in der deutschen Mystik' (in *Grundfragen der Mystik*, pp. 75–104) and 'Meister Eckhart und die Sprache' (in *Geistliches Mittelalter*, 1984). In his 'Das Ereignis des Wortes' (in *Gott Leiden, Gott Lieben*, pp. 201–40) Haas compares Eckhart's use of language with parallels in Zen Buddhism. Walter Haug has also made an important contribution on the question of mysticism and language ('Zur Grundlegung einer Theorie des mystischen Sprechens' in Kurt Ruh, ed., *Abendländische Mystik im Mittelalter*, pp. 494–508).
2. See *Princeton Encyclopedia of Poetry and Poetics* (1965) under 'Imagery' for a bibliography.
3. ibid., p. 363.
4. ibid., p. 490.
5. Quint (1928), p. 687.
6. Quoted from Tobin (1986), p. 164, with his translation.
7. Quoted from Tobin (1986), p. 165, with his translation which seems preferable to that of Walshe (DW III, 66, 4: '*Swer iht sihet an gote, der ensihet gotes niht*').
8. Tobin (1986), p. 169.
9. ibid.

10. Quint (1928), pp. 685f. I have borrowed the preceding examples also from Quint's article.
11. This is the conclusion which Georg Steer draws in his extensive study of the Middle High German translations of Thomas' *Summa Theologica*. See his 'Germanistische Scholastikforschung' in *Theologie und Philosophie* 1970, 1971 and 1973.
12. Quint (1928), p. 685.
13. See Georg Stötzel's article 'Zum Nominalstil Meister Eckharts', p. 294, in *Wirkendes Wort* 16 (1966), pp. 289–309.
14. I am quoting these two lists from Quint (1928), p. 701.
15. *Von der Wahrheit* (Munich 1947), p. 897.

9 • MEISTER ECKHART AND CHRISTIAN ORTHODOXY

To anyone who is acquainted with the broad outlines of the
Christian mystical tradition, as it extends from St Paul and
St John to Augustine of Hippo and Maximus the Confessor,
from Bernard of Clairvaux and Hildegard of Bingen to John
of the Cross and Teresa of Avila, from Francis de Sales to
Charles de Foucauld, will realize that Meister Eckhart in
this context is a bit of a queer fish.[1] Indeed, it is his
singularity as a Christian mystic which has led some to
revere him as being a western Buddhist *avant le mot* and
others to denigrate him for precisely the same thing. In the
present book we have attempted to show that Eckhart is
deeply rooted within his own medieval scholastic tradition
and that themes such as the divine 'ground' of the soul and
'birth' of God are devices with which to present scholastic
theological material in an imaginative and provocative way.
We have tried to show also that in his Latin works, where
Eckhart is generally eschewing the rhetorical devices of his
German sermons, his systematic theology is deeply impreg-
nated with a personal sense of an immediate union with the
living God which finds expression in a thorough-going
immanence/transcendence dialectic. Eckhart's theology,
ultimately, is the systematization of what essentially remains
a wholly mystical moment. We have also sought to stress
the extent to which Eckhart was integrated into the Catholic
Church, in terms both of his service to the Church in his life,
his debt to other Catholic theologians in his thinking, the
evident support of his Dominican brethren in his time of
trial and his own submission to the judgement of the Holy
See. But the question still remains to be asked: to what
extent is Eckhart's mystical theology Christian?

In order to answer this question, we must first address
those propositions in his work which, at first glance, would

appear to be outrightly heretical and of which by no means all appear in the Bull of condemnation. But here, once again, we must point to the *intentional* character of much of Eckhart's writing, which we have continually sought to stress. This intentionality is constituted by his deliberate attempt to use language and imagery not in a descriptive manner but primarily in an expressive way in order to effect a cognitive transformation within his audience. This means that the literal meaning of Eckhart's words is not always the correct one. Rather, any proposition extracted from his work must be seen in the context of his entire thinking if we are not to mistake expressive, imagistic language for the discourse of scientific reflection.

The case for this view is strongly supported by the fact that Eckhart's 'heretical' statements are easily paralleled by passages in which he presents a contrary and entirely orthodox position. There are sermons, for instance, in which Eckhart speaks of the *total union* of the soul with God, which is 'one and not united' (W 57, 78), which is not mere 'likeness' (W 24a) but an identity of *essence* (W 7, 49) in which the soul 'loses her being and her life' (W 5). All these would appear to contradict the principle that a distinction between God and his creature must always be upheld if pantheism is to be avoided. Pope Benedict XII's Bull *Benedictus Deus* of 1336 reaffirmed *inter alia* the orthodox position that the soul cannot attain full union with God (i.e. enjoy the Beatific Vision) in this life but only in the life to come. These statements of Eckhart must be compared, however, with a passage from Sermon 94 in which he speaks of the survival of the soul's individuality: 'Thus it is with the soul: when she imbibes God she is turned into God, so that the soul becomes divine but God does not become the soul. Then the soul loses her name and her power, *but not her will and her existence*' (my italics). This is repeated in Sermon 63 where we find: 'So, when we talk of man being one with God, and being God according to that unity, we refer to that part of the image in which he is Godlike, and not his created nature.' And again, in Sermon 75, Eckhart expresses the view that full knowledge of God's 'works' is reserved for the next life: 'The third thing is that man can see and know God's works, but while he is in this life he cannot attain to them perfectly, just as Moses saw the burning bush but could not go right up to it.'

A second area of difficulty is Eckhart's comments on suffering. On a number of occasions he tells us that, if we are truly detached, not only our own suffering but that of people who are close to us should leave us unmoved (W 11). Grieving at the suffering of others is a sign that the birth is not yet complete in us (W 7). Such cool detachment is founded, of course, upon the ultimate impassivity of God, who is beyond all fluctuation. But passages of this kind clash with the contrary view clearly stated in Sermon 9: 'You may think that as long as words can move you to joy or sorrow you are imperfect. That is not so. Christ was not so, as he showed when he cried, 'My soul is sorrowful unto death . . .' (Matt. 26.38).

Therefore I declare that no saint ever lived or ever will attain to the state where pain cannot hurt him nor pleasure please.' And in a number of fine passages on suffering, Eckhart speaks of the fact that God himself suffers with us and for us, 'and bears the load' (W 8).

Thirdly, we find passages in which Eckhart speaks of Christ as having assumed universal human nature but not specific human nature. Orthodox teaching is that he assumed both. The view that Christ did not become an individual man was condemned by Pope Alexander III in 1170 and 1177 as 'nihilianism'.[2] And yet, in Sermon 92, we read:

The masters declare that (essential) human nature has nothing to do with time, being wholly unshakable and much more inward and close to a man than he is to himself. That is why God took on human nature and united it with his own Person. Then human nature became God, for he put on essential human nature as such and not that of a specific man. Therefore, if you want to be the same Christ and God, go out of all that which *the Eternal Word did not assume*.[3]

This same view is repeated in Sermon 47: 'The Eternal Word did not take upon itself this man or that, but it took upon itself one free, indivisible human nature, bare and without image, for the impartible form of humanity is imageless.' These passages must be balanced, however, by others in which Eckhart declares that God in Jesus took on both specific and essential human nature, which must be his meaning when he says: 'God not only became man, but he took on human nature' (W 13b).

A further area of difficulty (and one which does appear in the Bull of condemnation, unlike the above) is Eckhart's teaching on the existence of something uncreated within the soul. This 'spark' is for Eckhart 'something that transcends the created being of the soul' and is 'not in contact with created things' (W 17). It is 'free of all names and void of all forms, entirely exempt and free, as God is free in himself' and is 'completely one and simple as God is one and simple' (W 8). And yet, elsewhere, Eckhart states:

> There is a power in the soul, of which I have spoken before. If the whole soul were like it, she would be uncreated and uncreatable, but this is not so. In its other part it has a regard and a dependence on time, and there it touches on creation and is created. (W 24a)

It would be wrong to conclude however that Eckhart is saying here that the soul has two (or more) 'parts', one of which is created and the other uncreated. He clearly rejected this view, with good reason, in the defence which he gave in the Dominican Church in Cologne and which was read out for him in a German version by his fellow Dominican Conrad of Halberstadt. In this piece Eckhart protested that he had never taught that the 'spark' was something 'added' to the soul.[4] Indeed, Eckhart's teaching had consistently been that we are united with God through an act of *knowing*. This is the tradition which he inherits from Albert the Great and the German Dominican School and which he has in common with Thomas Aquinas. The 'spark' therefore, which is as it were the faculty whereby we 'know' God in a unitive vision, must be thought of as a *potentiality* within the soul and not as a 'part' of it. The image of the 'spark' represents our capacity to 'know' God which is exercised in this life variously but which, in this life, can never be exercised to perfection. This is the meaning of Eckhart's repeated reference to the 'spark' or 'ground' of the soul: it is the claim that we are able to 'know' God in a real and unmediated way at the very depths of our being and it must not be taken as the belief that there are no other, quite ordinary and created ways of 'knowing' – and therefore of being – which are similarly constitutive of the human mind and person.

This point is of radical importance in our evaluation of Meister Eckhart, and it is in fact summed up in one passage from Sermon 63 in which Eckhart clearly acknowledges the existence of both created and transcendental potentialities within us: 'So, when we talk of man being one with God, and being God according to that unity, we refer to that part of the image in which he is Godlike, and not his created nature.' Eckhart then goes on to explain that to concentrate on the one aspect (here the 'divine') is at the same time to neglect the other (the 'created'):

> For when we consider him as God, we do not regard him according to creaturehood: in taking him as God, we do not deny his creaturehood in the sense that such a denial would imply a negation of his creaturehood, but it implies an assertion about God, by denying it of God.

Finally, Eckhart refers to the example of Christ, who is both human and divine and whose divinity is *for the moment* left out of view when we concentrate our attention on his humanity: 'Thus Christ is God and man: when we consider his humanity, in so doing we deny his Godhead; not that we really deny his Godhead, but we deny it *for the moment*.'[5] Accordingly, Eckhart states that that to which we turn our mind (or love) itself determines our own nature, and the passage continues with a quotation from Augustine:

> This is how we should understand St Augustine's words: 'What a man loves, a man is. If he loves a stone, he is a stone, if he loves a man, he is a man. If he loves God – now I dare say no more: if I were to say that then he is God, you might stone me.'

This, it seems, reveals the foundational principle of Eckhart's rhetorical mannerisms. He wishes to hold up before his audience the transcendental potentialities within themselves, and he seeks to do this by rigorously omitting from his sermons any elements which will activate their natural, 'created' or non-transcendental cognitive capacities. And he wishes to do this because, if they turn their minds to God rather than to any objects in the world, they will themselves become divinized, and united with God on the principle of a union of knowing which, as we have seen, was fundamental to the spirituality of the Dominican Order. In other words, by holding before them their own transcendental potential, he wishes his audience to activate their 'uncreated' and to extinguish their 'created' forms of knowing. It is this which will lead them into an immediate, albeit imperfect, union with God.

The several instances of 'heretical' statements which we have analysed above are excellent examples of this kind of rhetorical device which seeks to hold before the minds of the listener the state of oneness with God through transcendental knowledge. They all have one common factor, which is the rhetorical eradication of the created element: thus our union with God is 'perfect', we cannot suffer (for only created things suffer), Christ assumed only non-specific 'human nature', we are in our own essence 'uncreated'. And to these we might add other similar comments, such as the view that the 'just have no will at all' (W 65), that we must shed what there is in us 'of this and that' (W 10), and some of Eckhart's difficult comments on prayer whereby we should not pray 'for creatures' (e.g. W 5).

A sermon which sums up this technique of removing the 'created' dimension for the purposes of awakening the audience's transcendental (i.e. 'divine' or 'uncreated') potential is *Beati pauperes spiritu* (W 87). Here Eckhart asks what it is that makes someone 'poor in spirit', and he decides that there are three things. Firstly, 'we say that a poor man is one who wants nothing.' Eckhart goes on to explain that the 'poor man' can want nothing because he no longer possesses a will: 'For a man to possess true poverty he must be as free of his created will as he was when he was not.' The important word here is 'created'. Secondly, 'he is a poor man who knows nothing.' Now a 'poor man must live so that he is unaware that he does not live for himself, or for truth or for God'. He 'should be as free from his own knowledge as he was when he was not'. Once again, therefore, Eckhart is saying that the 'poor' man must transcend the created dimension, leaving behind all that belongs to createdness. Eckhart continues: 'Thirdly, he is a poor man who has nothing' and adds that he means by this not material poverty but poverty of the will: 'I have said before, the poor man is not he who wants to fulfil the will of God but he who lives in such a way as to be free of his own will and of God's will, as he was when he was not.' The three injunctions of *Beati pauperes spiritu*, therefore, are all essentially the same: they present us with ideal formulations which imply the eradication of the created dimension, couched in terms of a return to the state of nothingness prior to our creation. *Beati pauperes spiritu* is an extraordinary sermon, full of startlingly original language and imagery. But essentially it is a *tour de force* of rhetoric. If we were to take Eckhart literally, then he would seem to be saying that a total and essential union with the Godhead is possible for us now, in this present life, in which all that is distinctive in us disappears and we are left wholly one and wholly identified with the Godhead. We can become God, fully, now. But Eckhart knows full well that we live in bodies and are human beings who inhabit a world. What the preacher is doing here is holding an extreme and (impossibly) idealized form of union with God before the minds of his listeners in order to shake them from their complacencies and fill their minds with the excitement and inspiration of what can be. The statement at the end of the sermon, to the effect that 'this is a naked truth which has come direct from the heart of God' is a final rhetorical flourish which sums up the whole spirit of the sermon; it is a touch of spice for what is already a piquant meal.

The final point on which Eckhart's orthodoxy has been questioned is his trinitarian theology, which also appears in the Bull of condemnation. The thrust of the objection here is that in certain passages from his German sermons Eckhart appears to be suggesting that the state of unicity within the Trinity is prior or superior to the state of multiplicity. What this means is that Eckhart may have believed that the Persons (Father, Son and Holy Spirit) can be transcended as we enter the 'ground' of the Godhead which is entirely unified and as one. Christian orthodoxy believes that God is both Three and One, and that neither the Threeness nor the Oneness is superior or prior to the other.

Let us begin with two passages in which Eckhart appears to be putting the former, suspect view:

> This spark is opposed to all creatures: it wants nothing but God, naked, just as he is. It is not satisfied with the Father or the Son or the Holy Ghost, or all three Persons so far as they preserve their several properties. I declare in truth, this light would not be satisfied with the unity of the whole fertility of the divine nature. In fact I will say still more, which sounds even stranger: I declare in all truth, by the eternal and everlasting truth, that this light is not content with the simple changeless divine being which neither gives nor takes: rather it seeks to know whence this being comes, it wants to get into its simple ground, into the silent desert into which no distinction ever peeped, of Father, Son or Holy Ghost. (W 60)

The second passage reads as follows:

> So one and simple is this citadel in the soul, elevated above all modes, of which I speak and which I mean, that the noble power I mentioned is not worthy even for an instant to cast a single glance into this citadel; nor is that other power I spoke of, in which God burns and glows with all his riches and all his joy, able to cast a single glance inside; so truly one and simple is this citadel, so mode- and power-transcending is this solitary One, that neither power nor mode can gaze into it, nor even God himself! In very truth and as God lives! God himself never looks in there for an instant, in so far as he exists in modes and in the properties of his Persons. This should be well noted: this One Alone lacks all mode and property. And therefore, for God to see inside it would cost him all his divine names and personal properties: all these he must leave outside, should he ever look in there. But only in so far as he is one and indivisible, without mode or properties (can he do this): in that sense he is neither Father, Son nor Holy Ghost, and yet is a Something which is neither this nor that. (W 8)

In both these passages Eckhart is speaking of a faculty within us which corresponds to a divine 'ground' which is beyond the Persons of the Trinity (although in another passage Eckhart actually identifies the 'ground' with the Father: W 11). This ultimate divine 'ground' cannot be entered by either distinctions or names. Taken at face value, therefore, these passages suggest that Eckhart did indeed subordinate traditional Christian teaching on the Trinity of the Persons to a Neoplatonic metaphysic of the 'One'. In the *Commentary on Exodus*, we find a similar position when Eckhart speaks of the distinctions between the Persons of the Trinity as being 'as it were' outside the substance: 'For this reason relation is the only kind of category that is not absorbed into substance in the Godhead, but it remains *as it were standing on the outside*' (my italics).[6] Eckhart is in fact following Thomas here, but as P. L. Reynolds remarks in his illuminating article on this theme: 'Where Thomas considers why the relations, while one with the essence, remain distinct from each other, Eckhart asks why they are not drawn into the unity of the essence'.[7] Although Eckhart does not suggest that there is a distinction between the Persons and the essence (except, of course, for their relations), it might be argued that they are *less securely located* within the essence than is the case in Thomas, and thus the way is left open for a theory of the transcendence of the Persons as the soul advances through knowledge into the unified 'ground' of the Godhead where Persons and their distinctions yield to a total oneness.

There is a case for arguing, however, that this is not what Eckhart intends. I believe it can be shown that when Eckhart speaks of 'going beyond' the Persons to some prior 'ground', what he is doing is rejecting the traditional terms of the Christian Trinity and not the trinitarian principle itself. There is some evidence of this in the second of the two passages quoted above, in which he talks of 'going beyond' the Persons. If God is to enter our own 'citadel' or divine 'ground', Eckhart tells us, then he must leave behind 'all his divine names and personal properties'. Eckhart never tires of telling us that the 'spark of the soul', which is the image of God within us, is beyond names; it is 'rather nameless than possessed of a name' (W 17). Within the context of Eckhart's metaphysical system, moreover, this reluctance to apply names to that which is of God is very understandable. Eckhart frequently emphasizes the principle that what bears a name has specific, or 'created' being: it is 'this or that', while God is as far above all specific being as 'Heaven is above Earth' (W 8). Only creatures can have names therefore. In other passages Eckhart speaks out even more vehemently against the use of names with respect to God:

> And in the same ground, where he has his own rest, we too shall have our rest and possess it with him. The place has no name, and no one can utter a word concerning it that is appropriate. Every word that we can say of it is more a denial of what God is *not* than a declaration of what he is. (W 39)

This is repeated in Sermon 72, where we find: 'I say, if one knows anything in God and affixes any name to it, that is not God. God is above names and above nature'. And again in Sermon 11:

> It [the peak of the soul] does not want God as the Holy Ghost nor as the Son: it flees the Son. Nor does it want God, as he is God. Why? *There he has a name*, and if there were a thousand Gods it would go on breaking through, it wants to have him there where he has no name: it wants a nobler, better thing than God having a name (my italics).

In this same passage Eckhart goes on to say that the peak of the soul wants 'God' where he is Father, but he immediately subverts this name by adding to it a whole series of metaphors (i.e. 'the marrow from which goodness comes', 'the kernel from which goodness flows', 'a root', 'a vein'), thus implicitly reminding us that the term 'Father' is no less a metaphor despite its venerable history.

Finally, in a passage from the Latin works, Eckhart states his views quite clearly when he says: 'note that everything that is said or written about the Holy Trinity is in no way really so or true . . . since God is inexpressible in and of his nature, what we say he is, surely is not in him. Hence the Psalm text "Every man is a liar" (Ps. 115.11). [But] it is true, of course, that there is something in God which corresponds to the Trinity we speak of and to other similar things.'[8]

Eckhart quite clearly rejects the idea, therefore, that names, and the multiplicity which pertains to names, can be found in the Godhead itself, which is entirely One and is as opposed to number 'as God is to creatures'.[9] And yet I do not think that he is denying the principle of the Trinity as such. The reason for this is Eckhart's identification of the unified essence of God with the act of *intelligere* or 'knowing'. If Eckhart tells us that God is beyond names, then he also tells us that God's being 'is itself to know',[10] and that: 'God alone has unity. Unity is the special characteristic of God; it is on account of his unity that God *understands* that he is God, and without it God would not be.'[11] This is a point of great consequence. Through the principle of understanding or knowledge, Eckhart admits into the oneness of the Godhead the element of diversity. And, I would submit, it holds both these ideas together in perfect accord.

In order to trace this dimension of Eckhart's thinking, let us first consider the God of the Parisian Questions, in which Eckhart states: 'God is an intellect and understanding, and his understanding itself is the ground of his existence'.[12] What precisely is the meaning of the terms 'intellect' and 'understanding' here? In order to answer this question, we need to recall the definition of intellect as we find it in the Dominican School of Albert the Great, particularly in Meister Dietrich von Freiberg. There it is tantamount to 'consciousness', which is knowledge reflecting upon itself. Dietrich states:

> Within an intellect which is intellect by essence there is no place to distinguish the substance and the act itself by which the intellect receives within itself its own intellection. All this is in effect one and the same: the substance of the intellect, the act of the intellect and the object, itself interior, of the intellectual act.[13]

What Dietrich means here is that in human consciousness, the subject (that which knows) is the same as the act by which it knows and the object of its knowing (which is itself). These three principles form a perfect unity. Bernard Mojsisch, in his study of Dietrich, makes a similar point:

> In that the intellect knows itself, it knows its object, and in that it knows its object, it is itself known as object; as intellectual being (*intellectualiter ens*) it is simultaneously that which knows (*intelligens*) and that which is known (*intellectum*) and it relates in the same way both to itself and to the Other, to the Other as to the Other of itself, and to itself as to the Other of itself.[14]

The keynote here is that the idea of 'understanding', in the tradition which Eckhart inherited, contains the idea of a trinity within unity, and unity within trinity. 'Understanding' in this sense is a wholly dynamic yet wholly unified image, which centres upon the notion of mind, intellect or consciousness as being constituted by an identity of the subject which knows, the object which is known and the act of knowing which is its own substance. Although Eckhart nowhere makes explicit and succinct reference to Dietrich's theory, his metaphysics of the Word is founded upon *precisely the same sense of a fertile diversity being perfectly contained within a single unified act.* God, we recall, is 'a word that utters itself'. He is a 'speaking work'. The word makes known 'but it remains within'. God's 'outgoing is his ingoing' (W 22). And in another sermon (W 80), we read:

> Now take note! The divine Father himself hears nothing but this Word, he knows nothing but this Word, he utters nothing but this same Word, he gives birth to nothing but this same Word. In this Word the Father hears and the Father knows and the Father gives birth to you yourself and to this same Word, to all things and to the whole of his divinity, to himself according to his Nature and to this Word with the same Nature in another Person.

Passages such as the above show beyond any doubt that Eckhart's thinking is deeply and incontrovertibly trinitarian. For him the principle of diversity within the Godhead (the 'knowing') not only contains within it absolute unity, but it is also infinitely fertile and is the origin of the Creation (or of Being), as well as the 'birth of God' in the human soul. If he expresses reservations about the Father, Son and Holy Spirit, then he does so because of his belief in the inappropriateness of names with regard to the uncreated order. To speak of the Word is, of course, also to use a name, but we have already seen in the preceding chapter how Eckhart likes systematically to make concrete things abstract. This exactly accords with his theory of knowing, and he attempts within his imagery and language to reduce concrete entities to abstractions as far as this is possible. The apparent rejection of the classical trinitarian names, therefore, is the removal of something which, for Eckhart, smacks of the created order and is thus wholly inappropriate. And his intense and extensive Logos-mysticism must be seen as an attempt to capture the same essential truth of the Christian Trinity (i.e. unity within diversity, and diversity within unity) in terms which are more abstract, more suited to the Eckhartian system, and which reflect not only the truth that God is wholly Three and wholly One but also the truth that he is entirely beyond the realm of things and creatures and cannot be thought of in terms which derive from the created order.

There seem to be no grounds, therefore, for holding the view that Eckhart taught propositions of a heretical kind. On those occasions when he might appear to do so, he is in fact motivated by rhetorical aims which prompt him to make statements that point to an ultimate and *ideal* state of union with God. And where he speaks of the Trinity, the instability in some of his writings derives from the fact that we find in his work a critique of the classical terms of the Christian Trinity and the partial creation of alternative terms. The character of these, while equally metaphorical, is deemed more appropriate on account of their greater abstraction.

But if we are no longer concerned with the question of Eckhart's orthodoxy, we need still to enquire into his status and quality as a specifically Christian spiritual thinker.

Christian spirituality must in some way be founded upon the call to discipleship experienced by the Apostles in their encounter with Jesus. According to the received biblical account of this process, it was one which involved a radical conversion of heart which found expression at all levels of the human person, and it was a manner of transformation which centred upon the reception of the particular and unique presence of God in Jesus Christ. This experience led to an attitude of faith which was founded upon love and structured towards an open-ended obedience to Christ himself. Above all, this was a response of loving obedience which included all dimensions of the human person, which is to say the bodily, emotional and intellectual life of the disciples, which was itself a reflection of the total obedience of body, heart, mind and spirit visible in the Son's relationship with the Father.[15] Judged from this perspective then, some Christian spiritual systems will seem to explore the fundamental Christian themes in greater depth than others, and the quality of Christian spiritual thinking can be gauged by the extent to which a particular approach resonates within the depths, both visible and invisible, of the Christian revelation with its crucial emphasis on discipleship and a loving, obedient assent to God.

In the case of Eckhart, we find that there are two primary principles at work in his thinking: the understanding of God as fertile intellect, or mind, and the dialectic of divine transcendence and immanence. The former, as we have seen, can be said to incorporate the principle of unity within diversity which underlies the Christian doctrine of the Trinity, while the second touches on themes foundational to the doctrines of incarnation and the Christian life.

Eckhart's transcendence/immanence dialectic is most fully and systematically expressed in his theory of analogy. As we have seen, Eckhart is exercised by the conviction, on the one hand, that God wholly and absolutely transcends the created dimension. He is the 'negation of negation' and 'pure nothingness'. And yet, at the same time, God exists at the heart of his creation, whose being, in so far as it has being, is his being, whose goodness, in so far as it has goodness, is his goodness, and so forth. It is this dialectic which underlies some of Eckhart's most pointed – and most easily misunderstood – formulations, especially those which address the 'nothingness' of created being. We have sought to argue, moreover, that this paradox, which takes both theological and literary form in Eckhart's work, is a reflection of his own mystical experience. That experience is, of course, irretrievable to us today, and yet its life and reality can be felt at all points in Eckhart's thinking, which systematically accommodates this dialectic and is fundamentally structured towards it.

But dialectic, as we have seen, is no novelty in Christian theology. Indeed, it is most strongly present in the creeds, which tell us of the hypostatic union when 'God became Man'. And the God-Man himself passed on to his disciples a deeply dialectical kind of teaching. He told them that 'the meek shall inherit the earth' (Matt. 5.4), that 'the first shall be last and the last shall be first' (Matt. 20.16) and that 'those who lose their lives for me shall gain them' (Matt. 16.25). And so, as with his belief in the intellectual character of God's being, Eckhart's transcendence/immanence dialectic is reducible to a core Christian experience, that of the interpenetration of the human and the divine, consumately occurring within history in Jesus Christ for all time, but also enacted, inwardly, in the souls of the faithful who conform themselves to him and who build up his Church.

At the first level of Eckhart's work, therefore, which is that of his deepest intuitions, it can be argued that these are profoundly Christian in origin and that they spring from the Trinity and the Incarnation, which are the two primary doctrines of the Christian Revelation. But concerning the second level, which is to say the working out of these principles within Eckhart's own particular scheme of theology with its emphasis upon the intellective nature of our sanctification, there are a number of questions which need to be asked.

On account of his age and education, Meister Eckhart was, after all, powerfully under the influence of Neo-platonism. The term 'Neoplatonism' represents a rich and diverse body of thought but it is one which is, broadly, founded upon certain common philosophical principles. Among these we may count the view that the physical world is a shadow-land whose origins lie within a remote, transcendent reality which, at least in thinkers such as Plotinus and Proclus, is conceived of as absolute unicity. Although trapped at a point far removed from this original source of things, the human soul bears an affinity with the supreme principle within its faculty of *mind*. The process of sanctification for the Neoplatonists, therefore, was one of ascent back to the source which is expressed in terms (generally) of intellective contemplation. The physical dimension, and the human body, while not in themselves evil, represent the lowest point (or one of the lowest points) of emanation away from the supreme principle, and are thus entirely to be overcome and left behind as the soul ascends back to its source.

The key point at which Eckhart's thinking is moulded by Neoplatonic principles, and is reduced in its Christian resonance, is his belief that the human body, and indeed the world, is *contained within* the higher principles of mind or intellect. 'The body is more truly in the soul than the soul in the body', Eckhart writes and thus gives exact expression to this theme. And if this is the case, if the physical world needs to be subsumed into the world of mind, then there is little scope for developing a spiritual responsivity of body and emotions.

Eckhart's architectonic vision of essential and intellective union with God cannot, therefore, be said to be incarnational in the fullest sense. This is not to deny that the incarnation is deeply meaningful to Eckhart, for the belief in a God who incarnates is foundational to Eckhart's thought. It is the admission rather that in the evolution of his spiritual *responsorium*, Eckhart bypasses the dimension of everyday human reality with its physical and emotional components. Believing that this dimension is truly contained within the higher one of mind, Eckhart feels that he is addressing human reality in its entirety by addressing the level of the mind alone. This is his Neoplatonism, and it is a trend which prevents him from exploring in fullest depth the concept of a God who incarnates not only at the level of essence and intellect, but also, and crucially, at the level of ordinary, everyday human existence. Eckhart did not doubt the historical incarnation of the Word, but neither did he adequately incorporate the phenomena of empirical existence into the spiritual form of his responsivity to the incarnational God.

The originality of Meister Eckhart

But if Meister Eckhart is to some extent limited as a spiritual theologian, then we also find in his work spiritual themes of great originality. We have noted the place of detachment in his work, which spans both the moral and the metaphysical field, and which surely has a unique place in western mystical theology. But paramountly it is the theme of our own essential nothingness which Eckhart takes up and develops in a radically new way.

'Nothingness' is a theme which is intrinsic to Christianity, but it is one which has too often been neglected. It is present in the *kenosis*, or self-emptying of Christ, who 'came down from Heaven' and 'was born of the Virgin Mary', as it is present in the reciprocal self-emptying of the Father and the Son in the Holy Spirit, which is the ground of the Trinity. We find it, too, in the self-emptying of the believing individual, who seeks to conform their life to Christ so that, with Paul, they can say: 'It is not I who live but Christ who lives in me' (Gal. 2.20), and it is the theme of a spiritual nothingness which animates much Marian piety, whereby she becomes a 'vessel' or a 'window' or an 'empty space'. 'Nothingness', then, is not foreign to Christianity, rather the concept of negation, transparency or self-denial is fundamental both to its doctrinal truths and lived experience of faith.

When he says that we are 'nothing', Eckhart does not, of course, believe that we do not exist in an empirical sense.

His call to 'nothingness' must rather be seen in the light of his professed technique of holding before his audience the deepest truths of their natures. Before God, we are indeed nothing, and the life of faith is indeed, in a sense, an ever greater participation in the divine nothingness, which is the fertile life of the Trinity. Eckhart is right, then, to stress this theme time and again, and he does so with a clarity and a vigour which surpasses the efforts of those who came before him and those who have come after.

Meister Eckhart and eastern religions

This is a topic which has generated a considerable literature from the nineteenth century to the present day.[16] It is, however, also a field which is fraught with difficulty, and Eckhart has found few commentators who are as familiar with the subtleties of late medieval scholasticism as they are with the intricacies of Vedantic Hinduism or Zen Buddhism. And yet clear parallels emerge: in Eckhart's advocacy of a principle within the Godhead of absolute unicity, in his teaching on the divine spark in the soul, as well as his belief that we realize our union with God through transcendental knowledge and, not least, his dynamic and transformational use of language. It is easy to understand, therefore, why some interpreters have read Eckhart as teaching essentially Eastern truths.

But the matter is, all too often, not as simple as it might seem. First of all, the task of textual comparison presents linguistic difficulties of considerable proportions. We must beware of immediately thinking that we are dealing with the same concepts in two texts when one is an English translation from Middle High German (itself a 'translation' from scholastic Latin) and the other a translation from Pali into an equally bland form of the vernacular, which is – as all translators know – woefully inadequate for the trans-mission of subtle speculations. Secondly, as we have seen, not all that Eckhart says is to be taken at face value. Thirdly, there are elements and emphases which are fundamental to Eckhart's thinking and which reflect the Christian roots of his speculative theology. Amongst these we may count firstly his tempering of the principle of unicity by his elucidation of it as *intelligere*, or *knowing*, which guarantees a form of dynamic multiplicity within the unicity. Secondly, Eckhart's remarks on the idea of the divine spark in the soul show that it is to be seen as a *potentiality* within the human person and moreover one which shall be fully realized only at a point in the future. Thirdly, the sense of the human person, although neglected in Eckhart, still remains intact, and it grounds his residual theology of altruism and works which we find, for instance, in his classic exposition of the Mary and Martha theme (W 9).[17] Finally, and perhaps most importantly, Eckhartian 'nothingness' and 'detachment' are to be thought of as gifts bestowed by the activity of God himself within us, who self-communicates and incarnates as the Birth of God in the soul. Union with God, therefore, is for Eckhart brought about by God himself, who is conceived of in incarnational terms, even if the manner of that incarnation within the soul of the individual believer is understood and presented by Eckhart in the wholly abstract terms of speech and cognition.

The question of Eckhart's affinity with schools of Eastern religion is thus a complex and fascinating one, which is as yet far from resolution. If Eckhart is indeed to be a bridge figure between East and West, then he must not be used in a simplistic and reductionist manner which tears him from his own Christian origins. It has been the intention of this book, in part, to show that the grand speculative themes we find in Eckhart actually derive from the Christian world which formed him. These are not, therefore, to be seen as a form of superstructure imposed upon Christianity and which can then be easily detached for the purposes of convenient comparison with other religious systems. Indeed, Eckhart can only begin to function as a bridge figure when it is understood that his speculation is rooted in Christian doctrine and thinking which will thus always serve to co-define their parameters of meaning. It is only then that the undoubted affinity in terms of spiritual *timbre* and atmosphere which exists between Eckhart and some Eastern forms of religious thought and experience may prove to be the richly fertile ground it promises to be.

NOTES TO CHAPTER 9

1. For a detailed discussion of the theological content of the Bull *In agro* including the *inquantum* principle which was a major source of difficulty, see B. McGinn (1980).
2. For a discussion of Nihilianism, see LTK VII, p. 962.
3. I have adapted Walshe's translation a little, also adding brackets and italics, in order to make Eckhart's meaning more clear.
4. See Laurent, pp. 344f.
5. Here I am adapting Walshe slightly and providing italics. I translate the phrase *nâch dem nemen* as 'for the moment' rather than 'in this case'.
6. *Comm. Ex.*, 65 (LW II, pp. 69f.; TP, p. 65).
7. '*Bullitio* and the God beyond God: Meister Eckhart's Trinitarian Theology' in *New Blackfriars* (April 1989), pp. 169–81 and May 1989, pp. 235–44. The quotation is taken from the May issue, p. 236.
8. Sermon 29 (LW IV, pp. 269ff.; TP, pp. 210ff.).
9. Paraphrase from *Comm. Wis.* 154 (LW II, pp. 481–94; TP, p. 169).
10. e.g. 'sibi esse est intelligere', *Comm. Gen.*, 11 (LW I, p. 195).
11. DW I, p. 368 (my italics).
12. LW V, p. 40 (M, p. 45).
13. *De vis. beat.*, 1.1.3., 4 (quoted in de Libera [1984], p. 184).
14. *Die Theorie des Intellekts bei Dietrich von Freiberg* (Beihefte zum *CPTMA*, Beiheft 1), Hamburg, 1977, p. 65.
15. These are broadly the terms of Hans Urs von Balthasar's analysis in his seminal article, 'Zur Ortsbestimmung christlicher Mystik' in W. Beierwaltes, ed., *Grundfragen der Mystik* (Einsiedeln 1974), pp. 37–71.
16. There is a bibliography of this literature by Niklaus Largier in Haas (1989), pp. 428–31.
17. The second and third points are made by Alois Haas in his stimulating studies *Meister Eckhart als Gesprächspartner östlicher Religionen* (pp. 199f.) and *Das Ereignis des Wortes: sprachliche Verfahren bei Meister Eckhart und im Zen-Buddhismus* (p. 238) in Haas (1989), pp. 189–200 and pp. 201–40.

10 • THE INFLUENCE OF MEISTER ECKHART

In 1575 Everard Mercurian, the General of the Jesuit Order in Spain, put a number of mystical writings upon the index of books prohibited to members of the Order. These included the works of Tauler, Ruusbroec, Harphius, Suso, Mechthild and Gertrude. He did so on account of the attacks by the Dominicans, who accused the newly founded Jesuit Order of encouraging quietism.[1] What is interesting about this list is that it does not include the name of Eckhart, though not on account of Mercurian's sympathy for him, for no one was reading his works (or at least not consciously) in Spain at this time. Indeed, it even seems questionable whether Everard Mercurian would have known Eckhart's name. But the omission of Eckhart from this list is an indication of the complexities involved in an analysis of his posthumous influence.

Although the Bull *In agro* was published only in the diocese of Cologne, its effects were far-reaching. The Latin works of Eckhart survive in only some four major manuscripts and, while there are many more manuscripts in which his German sermons have been preserved, these are generally clustered around the places where Eckhart himself preached and taught, and where his memory remained alive.[2] Before examining those who may have been influenced by the writings of Eckhart more indirectly, we will begin by discussing the work of two men who knew him personally and who came under his sway as pupils or disciples.

1. John Tauler

Tauler was born in Strasburg around the year 1300, where he entered the Dominican Order as a youth.[3] It is not known whether he studied at the Dominican *studium generale* in Cologne, where he may have coincided with Eckhart's presence there, but Tauler is very likely to have come under his influence during Eckhart's residence in Strasburg from 1313 to 1323/4.

John Tauler developed into one of the most popular preachers of his day, and some 84 of his sermons, which were collected into a unified corpus at an early stage, were translated into Latin by Laurentius Surius in the sixteenth century and were read extensively outside his native Rhineland. Very interestingly, a number of sermons which are judged today to be the work rather of Eckhart were included in the Surius translation, and thus gained a wider currency than would otherwise have been possible.[4] Tauler, both as a disciple of Eckhart and occasionally as his pseudonym, was thus a key channel of influence for Eckhartian thought.

We find in Tauler's sermons a considerable number of lexical and thematic borrowings from Eckhart, including the images of the birth of God in the soul, the spark of the soul, the nothingness of creatures, *gelâzenheit* and *abege-scheidenheit*. Indeed, there are passages in Tauler which have a very authentically Eckhartian feel, as when he speaks of the 'birth of God in the soul':

> Truly, in this ground the heavenly Father gives birth to his only begotten Son a hundred times more quickly than is a single moment in our reckoning, and in the sight of eternity. It is always completed anew and in its own inexpressible radiance. If we wish to experience this, then we should turn within ourselves, far beyond the activity of our outer and inner faculties and images and beyond all that has its origin in the world, and we should sink into and become one with the ground. Then the power of the Father will come and call us into himself through his only begotten Son, and as the Son is born from the Father and returns to the Father, thus we too are born from the Father in the Son and return with the Son to the Father and become one with him. (H, p. 202)

But, in general, Tauler subtly adapts Eckhartian themes by adding his own emphases. This is evident for instance in his use of the term 'ground' of the soul, Whereas the 'ground' in Eckhart is generally one of the several synonyms for the transcendent potentiality of the soul, in Tauler it can take on its own ontological weight and thus communicates a sense of inwardness, which is not simply divine but is the soul's own inner reality.[5] Something of this distinction can be discerned in the following passage:

> No created light can penetrate this ground, for God alone dwells there. The whole of creation could not fill this abyss, nor reach its innermost depths. It could not satisfy us, for no one can do that but God alone in his infinity. Only the Divine Ground corresponds to this ground of our soul. 'Deep calls upon deep.' If we are attentive to it, then this ground acts upon the faculties of the soul. It seizes and draws the higher and lower powers back to their beginning, their origin, if only we are attentive to it, keep our own company and listen to the precious voice that calls out in the solitude, in this ground, drawing more and more into it. (H, pp. 336f.)

This greater stress upon human reality, with its experience of battle and moral struggle, can be felt throughout Tauler's work. Thus *abegescheidenheit* loses much of its metaphysical significance, and takes on a more explicitly moral character:

> Now what does 'true detachment' mean . . . ? It means that we should turn and detach ourselves from all that is not God alone, that we should examine with the light of reason all our works, words and thoughts to see whether there is not something in the ground of our soul which is other than God and which does not hunger for God in all things, in activity as in passivity. And should we find something which is directed at something other than God, then we should cut it off and cast it out. (H, p. 154)

This same trend also occurs in Tauler's discussion of the 'nothingness of creatures', as when he says: 'he who looks upon his nothingness, his non-being, his helplessness, in him truly the grace of God is born' (H, p. 324), or again, 'If you hold your pious actions or exercises to be of importance, then it would be far better if you were to do nothing at all but turn inwards to your own pure nothingness, to your good-for-nothingness, your helplessness' (H, p. 390). Here the inner meaning of this quintessentially Eckhartian term has almost completely vanished in so far as the metaphysical character of the word has been absorbed into the categories of a purely moral condition.

Tauler introduces a more explicitly sacramental dimension also by fusing the terms of a *Wesensmystik*, or mysticism of essence, with eucharistic devotion:

> If you wish to be transformed into God, then you must strip yourself of yourself. For our Lord said: 'Whoever eats this bread will have eternal life.' Nothing is more profitable to this end than going to the most sacred sacrament. For that frees you from yourself, and to such an extent that both inwardly and outwardly the old man in you completely dies away. Transforming and dissolving our human nature, and sending its own power coursing through our veins, so that it has one life and one being with us, this divine food frees us from ourselves. (H, p. 211)

In one sermon (H, p. 104) John Tauler speaks of a 'noble master' who advocated a path to sanctity which was 'without guidance on uncharted paths'. This, he tells us, led to misunderstanding, whereby certain people became 'poisoned'. Accordingly, Tauler tells us that it is a hundred times better that people should follow the well-trodden path with guidance. The 'noble master' here is clearly Meister Eckhart, and this passage seems to sum up the admiration which Tauler feels for him, coupled with a certain caution regarding his message. It is this caution which impels Tauler subtly to adapt Eckhartian themes and terminology by drawing them back into the mainstream of spiritual guidance with its traditional emphasis upon ascetical struggle and devotional practice.[6]

Henry Suso

Henry Suso, or Heinrich Seuse to give him his German name, is another mystic of the Rhineland school who came under the personal influence of Meister Eckhart. He was born around the year 1295 in Constance or nearby Überlingen, and entered the Dominican Order at the unusually early age of thirteen. Suso may have studied for a while in Strasburg, but he certainly did study at the

Dominican *studium generale* in Cologne around the year 1325. Suso is a strong supporter of the cause of Meister Eckhart, which may well have been the reason for the reprimand he received at the general chapter of the Dominican Order held at Maastricht in 1330. Suso certainly knew Eckhart personally, for he gives an account of a pastoral visit to him when Suso was troubled by the fact of his having been accepted into the Dominican Order two years early because of a donation by his parents to the Order.[7]

In his *Book of Truth* Suso presents a defence of Eckhart's teaching in the form of a dialogue between the Disciple and Truth. Truth elucidates various aspects of Eckhart's teaching in such a way as to clarify any misunderstanding. Thus Truth explains Eckhart's distinction between God and the Godhead in these terms:

> Truth: Yes, God and Godhead are one, though the Godhead does not act or give birth, only God does that. But this difference only follows from the names which our reason applies. In essence they are one. . . . (BM, p. 330)

Like Tauler, Suso is also concerned to place Eckhartian themes within a more traditional context. Here Truth explains the meaning of the 'breakthrough':

> The Disciple: I would like to hear something about the breakthrough by which, through Christ, we return to God and attain his blessedness.
> Truth: You must remember that Christ, the Son of God, had something in common with all men as well as being quite different. What he has in common with all men and women is his human nature, so that he was also truly man. He did not just become a person, but took on human nature . . . and whoever therefore seeks a true return to God and to be themselves a son of God in Christ, must turn from themselves to him; then they will attain their goal. (BM, pp. 335f.)

Suso also injects a note of caution into our expectations regarding the spiritual life, and here he seems to consider union with God to be a phenomenon far rarer than do either Eckhart or Tauler:

One teacher says that there is a kind of select person who is experienced in the spiritual life and who is so pure and Godlike that their virtue appears divine, for they have been destroyed and recreated in the unity of the first model and, somehow forgetful of transient and earthly life, they are transformed into a divine image and are made one with it. But it must be added that this state is only possible for those who possess this blessedness in high degree, and for the few and most pious people in this life. (BM, p. 338)

In chapter 6 of the *Book of Truth* Suso introduces a new figure, whom he calls the 'Wild Man' and who represents those individuals in Eckhart's own day who misappropriated his teaching in the service of a form of moral licence.[8] Suso is keen to defend Eckhart against just such a form of misinterpretation, and to show that his teaching is entirely wholesome. He counters the Wild Man's claim that the nothingness of God and of the human spirit allows him total moral licence by stressing that 'nothingness' as applied to God is a term for superabundant being and that the human spirit in union with God remains always itself. Secondly, he answers the Wild Man's claim that a certain 'master' had taught that we become indistinguishable from Christ by quoting a passage from Eckhart in which he specifically denies this. The heretic finally submits and asks the Disciple for instruction in the truth.

It would be wrong to think of Tauler and Suso as disciples of Eckhart in the narrow sense. While both are strongly supportive of his cause, neither is slow to adapt and change his teaching in order to make it conform to more traditional forms of piety. Indeed, in the case of Suso, it is only in the *Book of Truth* (of which there are few surviving manuscripts) that we find Eckhartian material; the spirituality of his hugely popular *Book of Eternal Wisdom* (and its Latin counterpart, the *Horologium sapientiae*) contains imagery as lush as any in medieval works of piety and is thus very different in kind from the abstractions of the Eckhartian system and sensibility. The warmth of Tauler's allusion to Eckhart and the strength of Suso's defence of his positions are thus all the more impressive since, though being of different temperament from Eckhart, they nevertheless chose to stand by him and at a time when it was difficult so to do.[9]

2. **Ruusbroec, the** *Theologia deutsch* **and the** *Book of* *Spiritual Poverty*

Both Tauler and Suso speak about Eckhart from the perspective of a personal knowledge of him. There are a number of other authors however who, though they did not personally know Eckhart, use certain of his themes. These form, broadly, the Rhineland school of spirituality.

Jan van Ruusbroec is a case in point. This great mystical writer truly belongs to a Flemish spiritual tradition, which is indebted to the love-based, trinitarian mysticism of the Cistercians and Beguines, and which is well represented by figures such as William of St Thierry, Beatrice of Nazareth and Hadewijch of Brabant. Nevertheless, the cultural and linguistic proximity of medieval Brabant with the German Rhineland has led to a tendency to see Ruusbroec in the context of the great German mystics of his age, as well as in that of his own native brabantine tradition. There is some justification for this in that in 1350 Ruusbroec despatched a copy of his *Spiritual Espousals* to the Rhineland and Tauler may well himself have visited Ruusbroec in Groenendaal. The Low Countries was also one of the few areas in which vernacular translations of some of Eckhart's sermons were circulating.[10]

Ruusbroec was born in 1293 and died in 1381 at Groenendaal, to the south-east of the city of Brussels, where he had founded a community of like-minded souls in 1343. He began writing in his thirties, and his many spiritual works won him a considerable reputation. Ruusbroec's spirituality is generally markedly different from that of Eckhart in that his point of departure is both a three-fold division of the human person and a profound emphasis upon the mystery of the Trinity. His vocabulary and imagery incline in the direction of love mysticism, as we find it in the tradition which extends from Gregory of Nyssa to Thomas Gallus, Bernard of Clairvaux and William of St Thierry. Nevertheless, there are a number of Eckhartian elements which surface in the more speculative side of Ruusbroec's thinking. Among these we may note phrases such as the 'spark' in the soul (which for Ruusbroec has the traditional meaning of an inextinguishable inclination towards the good), the transcendence of creatures and images and the entrance into an 'imageless' state, the 'ground' of the soul and even occasionally the birth of God in the soul.[11] Above all, Ruusbroec likes to speak of 'essential' (*weselec*) or 'naked' (*bloet*) being.

None of the above, however, are necessarily borrowings specifically from Eckhart in that some would have been available from common sources, all would have been available in Tauler and some certainly occur in Hadewijch of whose work (including the corpus of poems attributed to Hadewijch II) Ruusbroec had an intimate knowledge. But there is incontrovertible evidence that Ruusbroec at least knew the sermon *Beati pauperes spiritu* for in the second book of his *The Twelve Beguines*, he mounts a fierce attack against the sermon, associating it with the presence of the heresy of the Free Spirit in the Low Countries. It is striking, however, that at no point does Ruusbroec name Eckhart (unlike his follower Jan van Leeuwen, who believed him to have been a crazed heretic), although he knows of the Bull *In agro dominico*. It is tempting to speculate that if Tauler did indeed visit Ruusbroec in Groenendaal, then he may have caused Ruusbroec to refrain from lambasting the name of Eckhart as was the custom in the Low Countries at this time.[12]

The *Theologia deutsch* is a later work, dating from around the year 1430. Its author, whose name is unknown to us, was a priest and warden of the Knights of the Teutonic Order at Sachsenhausen, near Frankfurt am Main. The character of this work is rather different from that of Tauler, Suso or Ruusbroec in that it belongs in part to a later age. It has much in common, in fact, with Thomas à Kempis'

Imitation of Christ in that it presents a strongly moral view of our union with God and generally shuns speculative elements. The key notion in the *Theologia deutsch* is that of *gehôrsam*, or obedience, which counters *eigenwille* or self-will:

> This means that we should apply ourselves and accustom ourselves to such obedience to God and his commandments at all times and in all things that there is no longer any resistance to him in nature or spirit, but body and soul and all their members are ready and willing to do the will of their Creator as a person's hand is ready and willing to perform their will. For their hand is in their power, and they can turn it and use it at will. And where we find that things are not so, then we should set about putting them right, out of love and not from fear, and we should set our heart on God in all things, seeking his honour and praise.[13]

Nevertheless, although the character of the spirituality in the *Theologia deutsch* is uncompromisingly practical, we still find residual elements of the speculative side of the Rhineland tradition here, including a brief allusion to the distinction between God and Godhead, a stress upon the unity of God, upon 'spiritual poverty' and apophaticism.[14] The author speaks of the latter in these terms:

> But this perfection is beyond the grasp and recognition of creatures and they cannot express it, in accordance with their nature as creatures. Therefore this perfection is called 'nothing-ness', as it is not of their kind, which is why the creature as creature cannot recognize or understand it, cannot name or comprehend it in its thoughts.[15]

But he does not like to dwell on such matters, and prefers to stress the practical and moral dimensions of spirituality. This is evident for instance in his comments on 'spiritual poverty':

> But where there is spiritual poverty and true humility, things are very different. And this comes from the fact that we discover and recognize in truth that we are nothing in ourselves and in what we possess and that we can do nothing and serve nothing

but transgression, wickedness and evil. Thus it follows that we find we are unworthy of all that God and his creatures have done or might do for us.[16]

The *Theologia deutsch* proved to be a very popular work among the Reformers. Indeed, it was first published, in truncated form, by Martin Luther himself in 1516. Luther then published a complete manuscript, which he found in the Carthusian library at Erfurt, in 1518. Luther believed it to be a work of Tauler, or of one of Tauler's disciples, and he proclaimed it to be 'the equal of the ancients'.[17] In a later period the *Theologia deutsch* was greatly influential among German Pietist and Anabaptist circles on account of its advocacy of a simple, direct, interior and personal religion.[18]

We know as little about the author of the *Book of Spiritual Poverty* as we do of the man of Frankfurt who wrote the *Theologia deutsch*. It similarly dates from the beginning of the fifteenth century, and was long thought to be the work of Johannes Tauler, under whose name it was published by the Protestant Daniel Sudermann in Frankfurt in 1621 (under the title *The Imitation of the Poor Life of Christ*).[19] The *Book of Spiritual Poverty* is a fascinating work in that it harmonizes two of the great spiritual themes in this period, which is to say poverty of spirit, understood as a condition of inner renewal, and poverty of life, understood as the expression of renewal in the embrace of a life of material poverty. In his edition of the book in 1877, H. S. Denifle argued persuasively that the author must have been a Franciscan.[20]

Once again we find residual elements of the Eckhartian tradition, though these again largely take the form of terminology and themes which are adapted for more conventional usage. Nevertheless, there is something of Eckhart's inspiration in the following quotation in which the author asks the question: what is spiritual poverty? The words 'detached' and 'detachment' translate the Eckhartian word *abegescheiden* in the original text:

> To have spiritual poverty is to become like God. But what is God? God is a being who is detached from all creatures. He is a

free power and a pure act. Thus spiritual poverty is also a detachment from creatures. But what does detachment mean? That person is detached who clings to nothing. Spiritual poverty clings to nothing, and nothing clings to it.[21]

There are in fact a number of passages in which we seem to hear an authentically Eckhartian note, although the 'mysticism of essence' is seen in the context of a life of material poverty. The following passage speaks to us of the birth of God in the innermost part of the soul, although the word 'birth' does not actually occur. God is described also as being 'active' within the soul:

> The first way in which God speaks to us is in the essence of the soul, which no creature can penetrate nor in which any creature can speak, for God alone dwells there and he alone can speak there. And when God speaks there, the soul takes leave of all things, all its faculties fall silent and it glimpses the ground of its bare essence. And in this bareness and silence God speaks his word and the soul hears it. And this voice of God is nothing other than an inward sense of God within us, which springs forth from God into the essence of our soul and overflows all its faculties, causing such joy that we would gladly be free of all our own activity and allow God alone to work in the essence of our soul. And the more we leave our own activity, the more active God is in us.[22]

3. The Reformers, Angelus Silesius, Nicholas of Cusa, the Spanish and English mystics

In the final section of this chapter we will look at other figures in the Christian past whose names have at some time or other been associated with that of Eckhart. Here we will be dealing largely with the question of the availability of Eckhart's works, or of those of his closest followers, as well as with matters of interpretation.

We have already met the name of *Martin Luther* in the context of Rhineland spirituality since it was he who published the *Theologia deutsch* in 1516 and 1518. Also Luther undoubtedly knew the work of Tauler, whose sermons he read in the Augsburg edition of 1508. This edition also included three sermons which today are attributed to Eckhart (W 1, 2 and 4).[23] This Augsburg edition is markedly different from that made by Peter Canisius in 1543, which formed the basis for the Latin translation of 1548 by the Cologne Carthusian Laurentius Surius, in which form Tauler's work became best known outside his native Germany. Luther greatly admired Tauler and was much impressed by 'such sterling theology', although his enthusiasm for mystical writing later evolved and changed as it became integrated into his mature theology of faith.[24]

There can be no doubt that there is a deep disparity between the world of Eckhart and Tauler and that of Martin Luther. It seems that Luther liked the dimension of the *Anfechtung*, or 'assaults of spiritual temptation', which he found in Tauler's work, as well as the deep sense of our passivity before God and resignation. It was the speculative dimension with its talk of *deus nudus* ('God in himself') and strong emphasis on a *theologia gloriae* which, Luther felt, bypassed a proper faith in Christ's saving action for us in history, the *Christus pro nobis*, as well as a sound *theologia crucis*. In addition, Luther was critical of the belief in a point of contiguity between the soul and God, and in the margin of one of Tauler's sermons he substituted the word 'faith' for Tauler's 'spark of the soul'.[25] In view of that fact, therefore, that the elements which Luther liked in Tauler are generally those which Tauler does not have in common with Eckhart, we may conclude that had the whole corpus of Eckhart's sermons been available to him, he would not have been greatly impressed. He would have found in Eckhart a more marked sense of our intrinsic affinity with God than in Tauler, a less personalist view of our passivity before God and, above all, a philosophical orientation which was very different from that of Luther's nominalism. It is this latter distinction which leads to such a different atmosphere between Eckhart and Luther, the one paramountly concerned with a theology of glory, founded on a noetic essentialism, and the other with a theology of the cross. What Luther would have admired in Eckhart, however, is the internal reality of his religion, his critique of works, his understanding of the imputation of justice (so close to Luther's own theory of justification) and the stress upon the nothingness of the human being, since, for Luther, humanity only attains to its own reality through the process of faith.[26]

Jacob Boehme, who belongs broadly to the Lutheran tradition, is a figure whose complex theory of God and the world has fascinated some commentators and dismayed others. Boehme was born in 1575 near the town of Görlitz in the Silesian province of Lusatia. He lived and worked as a shoemaker. In his writings we find three themes which recall Eckhart's work. The first of these is that of the *Ungrund* which expresses the absolute transcendence and incomprehensibility of the divinity in its state of eternal rest. This is the area of potentiality from which, by an act of divine self-willing and self-knowing, all things emerge. The remaining themes are those of the birth of God in the soul and the divine spark. The source for these ideas is likely to have been the works of Tauler and the *Theologia deutsch*, familiar to close friends of Boehme, if not to Boehme himself.[27]

The writings of Jacob Boehme, which were a mix of cabbalistic, alchemical and mystical themes, had a considerable influence far beyond his native Silesia, and were of interest to prominent idealist philosophers such as Schelling and Hegel. They were read also by Johannes Scheffler (*Angelus Silesius*), who is regarded as one of the foremost German Baroque poets. Scheffler was born in the very same year of 1624 in which Boehme died, also in Silesia. He came from a noble Lutheran family but later converted to Catholicism. Scheffler studied at the University of Leiden, where he read Boehme, and he discovered the works of Tauler, Ruusbroec and the *Theologia deutsch* through his friendship with Abraham von Franckenberg, Boehme's friend and first biographer, when he later returned to his native city of Breslau in order to work as a doctor there.[28] The body of epigrammatic poetry, the *Cherubinic Wanderer*, for which Scheffler is best known, contains verses which undoubtedly reflect an Eckhartian type of spirituality. Here he speaks implicitly of the God beyond God:

Where is my dwelling place? Where I can never stand.
Where is my final goal, toward which I should ascend?
It is beyond all place. What should my quest then be?
I must, transcending God, into a desert flee.[29]

Elsewhere Scheffler stresses the idea of God as a kind of
nothingness which for ever evades our grasp:

'God is the purest naught, untouched by time or space.
The more you reach for him, the more he will escape.'[30]

And we find in Scheffler the theme of the birth of God in the
soul:

In you God must be born
If Christ is born a thousand times in Bethlehem
And not in you, then you are for ever lost.[31]

as well as that of the divine spark in the soul:

Who is it who can tell the spark within the fire?
And who, once within God, can perceive what I am?[32]

Scheffler knows from his reading in particular of Tauler
and the *Theologia deutsch* of Eckhart's detachment (for
which he uses the word *Gelassenheit*):

The more my I decreases in me and fades
The more God's I grows strong in me.[33]

And he seems at times truly to capture something of
Eckhart's exuberant delight in paradox, as in the following
passage on divinization:

I am like God and God is like me.
I am as great as God, and he as small as me;
He cannot above, nor I below him be.[34]

We cannot leave our discussion of the influence of Eckhart
within the German-speaking world without considering also
the case of Nicholas of Cusa. Cusanus, as he is sometimes
called, was a leading figure in the fifteenth-century church.
He was a highly educated man who played an important
role at the Council of Basle in 1433. He originally favoured
the Conciliar Movement, but later came to support the

papacy in whose service he was engaged in the attempts to effect reconciliation with the Church of the East. Nicholas V appointed him a cardinal.[35]

Nicholas wrote a number of works, but the one for which he is best known is *On Learned Ignorance*.[36] In this treatise Nicholas argued that our highest knowledge of God is of a special intuitive kind in which all contradictions are transcended. He was to this extent deeply involved in the current debate on the primacy of the will and of intellect in our knowledge of God.[37] In arguing his position, Cusanus drew upon a number of sources, one of which was certainly Meister Eckhart, whose ideas on the absolute unicity of God, as well as the place of intellect in our knowledge of him, had an undoubted influence.[38]

It has been a matter of debate as to whether it is legitimate to consider Nicholas of Cusa a mystic or not. There can be no doubt, however, that he was concerned with questions of mystical theology, and the extent to which we regard him as a mystic will depend largely on our definition of mysticism.[39] But his knowledge of Eckhart was certainly an immediate one since he had in his possession one of the principal codices of the Latin works of Eckhart at his own library in Cues, on the river Moselle. It was this same manuscript which was discovered by H. S. Denifle and which he described in a publication in 1886.[40] Nicholas of Cusa was in a unique position with respect to Meister Eckhart, therefore, in that prior to the modern period he alone seems to have had access to Eckhart's scholastic works, and was thus able to read him virtually as we do today. He strongly defended the cause of Eckhart against the accusations of the Heidelberg professor, Johannes Wenck.[41]

The situation in Spain regarding the availability of Eckhartian texts and material was not greatly different from that in the German-speaking countries. Eckhart himself was unknown, and the two chief channels for his thought were the Latin translation of Tauler's sermons, which also included a number of Eckhart's own sermons, and the

Theologia deutsch. Surius was rewarded by King Phillip II
of Spain for this translation of Tauler, and it has been
argued that Juan de los Angeles knew Tauler's work.[42] The
question is disputed as to whether either Teresa of Avila or
John of the Cross may have known Tauler in Surius'
translation, but it is known that the Carmelites around
Teresa were familiar with the *Theologia deutsch*.[43] There
are considerable difficulties in establishing literary influence
in the case of Teresa and John of the Cross however, and
there seems little point in attempting to show a dependence
of their own distinctive achievement on the spirituality of
the Rhineland in any way.

There is scant evidence also for the significant presence of
Rhineland material in England during the great fourteenth-
century flowering of English spiritual writing. There may
have been texts of Suso's *Horologium sapientiae* available in
England in the fourteenth century, but this is a work which,
as we have seen, is far from the spirit of Eckhart.[44] The
spiritual atmosphere in England does not in any case seem
to have been particularly congenial to the speculative
mysticism of the Continent, and it is striking that an early
English translation of extracts from Book Two of Ruusbroec's
Spiritual Espousals, entitled the *Chastizing of God's
Children,* shows a preference for the pastoral and practical
dimension in Ruusbroec's writing.[45] Any thought, therefore,
of a possible influence of Meister Eckhart on the spiritual
classics of the English fourteenth century must be entirely
discounted, not least on manuscript grounds.

Conclusion

An exploration of Eckhart's influence prior to the rediscovery
first of his German and then of his Latin works in the
nineteenth century reveals that there was little direct
assimilation of his thinking. Eckhart, even when he was
alive, was never easy to understand. The fact of the
condemnation, which severely restricted the dissemination
of his manuscripts, made his reception even more difficult.
What we do not find with Eckhart, lamentably, is the

formation of a corpus of his work at an early stage, such as we have in the case of Tauler and Suso from their own lifetimes, and in that of Ruusbroec from shortly after his death. The condemnation also blocked the translation of his vernacular work into Latin, which was an important precondition in the medieval world for the dissemination of ideas beyond the immediate sphere of their provenance. But as a consequence of the diffusion of Eckhartian ideas either through fragments of his own work, circulating anonymously or under another's name, or through the work of those close to him, we do find that certain of his characteristic words and themes, such as the birth of God in the soul, the spark of the soul and the idea of detachment, enjoyed a long life right down into the Post-Reformation period. Such images are removed from their original context, however, and become little more than gestures in the articulation of a strongly felt, internal and individualistic piety. With the sole exception of Nicholas of Cusa, therefore, Eckhart had to await the modern period with its sophisticated resources in order to find interpreters who could do more adequate justice to the full range of his thought.

NOTES TO CHAPTER 10

1. See L. Cognet, *La Spiritualité moderne*, Aubier 1966, p. 190. It appears that Ignatius himself read widely among the mystics of the Rhineland school.
2. e.g. Strasburg, Cologne, Erfurt, Basle. See Quint (1932) for details of the geographical spread of the manuscript tradition.
3. A good deal of the material contained in this chapter is summarized from my own *God Within* (1988), pp. 73–98.
4. The sermons by Eckhart which are included in Surius' translation of Tauler are W 1, 2, 6 (attributed to Eccardus junior), 36, 42 (incomplete), 47 and 40 (of which Quint doubts the authenticity). I have been personally unable to find W 4 in the Surius edition published in Paris in 1623, which Cognet includes in his list of such sermons (p. 117).
5. See A. Haas in A. Raitt, ed., *Christian Spirituality: High Middle Ages and Reformation* (London, Routledge, 1987), p. 153.

6. It would be unfair to regard Tauler beside Eckhart as an inferior speculative theologian. Tauler's exploration of the human condition is indeed rich, and we find in him elements which anticipate the 'dark night of the soul' of the Spanish Counter-Reformation school. He has a deep pastoral sense and does not lack Eckhart's inventiveness either, which is expressed in his memorable application of everyday imagery to a whole variety of spiritual truths. See my own *God Within* (1988), pp. 96–8 and *The Rhineland Mystics — an anthology* (London, SPCK; New York, Crossroad 1989), pp. 63–87.

7. This visit to the 'saintly' Eckhart is described in *The Life of the Servant*, ch. XXI (ET, J. M. Clark, London 1952), p. 65.

8. Suso actually uses the neuter form (*daz wilde*), perhaps in order to stress the facelessness of the Free Spirit heresy which grounded its antinominianism (moral lawlessness) on the extinguishing of self.

9. In Chapter VI of *The Life of the Servant* Suso describes how the 'blessed Meister Eckhart' came down to him from Paradise in a vision and answered certain of his questions (Clark, pp. 30f.). Edmund Colledge (Colledge and McGinn, pp. 18f.) has argued that the Eckhart referred to is in fact 'Eckhart the Younger', a Dominican from Saxony who died in or after 1337. Edmund Colledge refers to a tradition within the Dominican Order to this effect, basing his argument on the *Monumenta ordinis fratrum praedicatorum historica* 4 (1889), p. 258. Despite reference by the editor to earlier works which give biographical details concerning Eckhart the Younger, the tradition that it was this Eckhart who appeared to Suso seems to be a nineteenth-century invention, and would seem to be an attempt at 'rückwirkende Orthodoxierung'.

10. In his valuable study *De Receptie van Meister Eckhart in de Nederlanden gedurende de Middeleeuwen* (Leiden 1978), R. A. Ubbink shows that three sermons in particular were known in the Low Countries: W 8, 84 and 87, although none were well translated or are likely to have been properly understood. More popular was the pragmatic *Book of Twelve Virtues* which, though actually an adaptation of Eckhart's *Talks of Instruction*, circulated under the name of Godfried van Wevel.

11. See my *God Within*, p. 129.

12. Geert Grote also attacked Eckhart as a heretic. See G. Epiney-Burgard, 'La critique d'Eckhart par Ruusbroec et son disciple

Jean de Leeuwen' in Flasch (1984), pp. 177–85, especially
n. 28, p. 184.
13. W. von Hinten, *Der Franckforter* (Munich 1982), pp. 152f.
14. See my *God Within*, pp. 113f.
15. W. von Hinten, *Der Franckforter*, pp. 71f.
16. ibid., p. 105.
17. See my *God Within*, pp. 111f.
18. See Stephen Ozment, *Mysticism and Dissent: Religious Ideology and Social Protest in the Sixteenth Century*, New Haven and London 1973.
19. See my *Rhineland Mystics*, p. 117.
20. H. S. Denifle, *Das Buch von geistlicher Armuth*, Munich 1877.
21. ibid., p. 1.
22. ibid., p. 68.
23. See Cognet (1968), p. 115, n. 27. Cognet mentions W 3 also, adding that it is of doubtful authenticity.
24. Letter to Spalatin of 14 December 1516 (*Weimar Ausgabe*, Briefe I, nr. 30, 58). For Luther and the mystics in general, see Heiko Obermann's article 'Luther and Mysticism' in his *The Dawn of the Reformation* (Edinburgh 1986), pp. 126–54 and Alois Haas, 'Luther und die Mystik' in Haas (1989), pp. 264–85.
25. See *Weimar Ausgabe* IX, 103, 41 (Marginal Notes on Tauler's Sermons, 1516). See also Johannes Ficker, 'Zu den Bemerkungen Luthers in Taulers Sermones' (Augsburg 1508), in *Theologische Studien und Kritiken* 107 (1936), pp. 46–64.
26. See Stephen Ozment, *Homo spiritualis*, Leiden 1969.
27. See Robin Waterfield, *Jacob Boehme: Essential Readings* (Wellingborough 1989), pp. 20–31.
28. Scheffler also seems to have had access to the Rhineland material through a compendium on mystical theology, the *Clavis ero theologia mystica*, by Maximilian Sandeus. See Josef Schmidt's excellent introduction to *Angelus Silesius*, Classics of Western Spirituality series (New York, Paulist Press; London, SPCK, 1986), with translations by Maria Shrady, especially pp. 17–33.
29. Book I, 7. Translation by Shrady in *Angelus Silesius*, p. 39.
30. Book I, 25. Shrady, p. 40.
31. Book I, 61. My translation.
32. Book 4, 137. Shrady, p. 95.

33. Book 5, 126. My translation.
34. Book I, 10. My translation. See Benno von Wiese, 'Die Antithetik in den Alexandrinern des Angelus Silesius' in *Euphorion* XXIX (1929), pp. 503–22.
35. See J. Hopkins, *A Concise Introduction to the Philosophy of Nicholas of Cusa* (Minneapolis 1978) and the same author's translation and commentary on the *De Visione Dei*, entitled *Nicholas of Cusa's Dialectical Mysticism* (Minneapolis 1985). See also P. M. Watts, *Nicolaus Cusanus: a Fifteenth Century Vision of Man*, Leiden 1982.
36. R. Klibansky, ed., *De docta ignorantia* (Latin and German), Hamburg 1977. There is a translation by J. Hopkins, Minneapolis 1981.
37. See the article by Alois Haas, 'Deum mistice videre . . . in caligine coincidencie: zum Verhältnis Nikolaus' von Kues zur Mystik' (Vorträge der Aeneas-Silvius-Stiftung an der Universität Basel XXIV) (Basle 1987).
38. See Degenhardt (1967), pp. 64–8.
39. See Haas (1987), pp. 9ff.
40. See Degenhardt (1967), pp. 175ff.
41. For an account of this episode, see Degenhardt (1967), pp. 50–63.
42. See the article by A. Winklhofer on the influence of Tauler in Spain in E. Filthaut, ed., *Johannes Tauler: ein deutscher Mystiker* (Essen 1961), pp. 400ff. See also J. Orcibal, *S. Jean de la Croix et les mystiques rhéno-flamands*, Brussels and Paris, 1966.
43. See J. Orcibal, *La rencontre du Carmel Thérésien avec les mystiques du Nord* (Paris 1959).
44. See R. Lovatt, 'Henry Suso and the Medieval Mystical Tradition in England' in M. Glasscoe, ed., *The Medieval Mystical Tradition in England* (Exeter 1982), pp. 47–62.
45. J. Bazire and E. Colledge, eds, *The Chastizing of God's Children and the Treatise of Perfection of the Sons of God* (Oxford 1957).

EPILOGUE

We began this book by noting how Eckhart appears to have presented a different face at different times to the various people and groups interested in him. This results largely, we have argued, from Eckhart's seeming position on the margins of the Church, our past ignorance regarding the intellectual and social world which formed him and, not least, his own preferred style of rhetorical prose which can so easily persuade the undiscerning reader that Eckhart is saying things which are actually alien to his meaning. And we have attempted at every stage to reconstruct Eckhart's original meaning, mindful of his social context, his intellectual sources and his own spiritual dynamic. But the question arises as to why we, who live some seven centuries after Eckhart, are so interested in this figure from the medieval past? What is there about him which appeals to the religious mind of the present? For, above all in the English-speaking world, there seems to be a real sense in which Eckhart is a mystic for this age.

Let us begin by noting those aspects of Eckhart which would not seem to recommend themselves to modern sensibilities. Firstly, he is a scholastic theologian who is within that medieval tradition which believed it was possible to penetrate to the very heart of faith through reason; we do not find in him that demarcation of zones of competence which we find in Thomas Aquinas, and which seems foundational in the modern world. Secondly, Eckhart takes for granted an Aristotelian model of cognition, or epistemology, which is quite alien to us, and which he has in common with other German Dominicans of his day (although Eckhart's view of the dynamic nature of human essence – essence literally as 'knowing' – does accord well with modern forms of self-understanding). Thirdly, the philosophical foundation of Eckhart's thought is strongly Neoplatonic in character. This means that he constantly privileges the invisible and intelligent world above the material universe. In his own words the 'body is more truly in the soul than the soul is in the body'. This means that Eckhart is not a mystic who draws fully upon the Christian tradition of incarnation, whereby precisely the body and physical reality are taken up into the divine mysteries. His interest in creation moreover is purely that it is that which we should get away from! Created things have localized and diminished being, and they cause us to 'activate ourselves' through knowledge at a reduced level. If we wish to be truly *real*, in Eckhart's view, and true to our own highest powers, then we must transcend all creatures and all the images which they cause within us. True being is indeterminate and imageless being. This position contrasts quite starkly with our own frame of mind, which is much more heavily weighted towards a materialist view of reality. We are greatly aware of the centrality of ecological questions in Christian ethics and of the social demands of the gospel, with its appeal for justice and peace. Such social values are rarely to be found in Eckhart's work (nor should we expect too much of this form of awareness in a medieval thinker), although they are certainly implicit in his belief in the dignity of the human being and certain of his comments on works.

But what of those aspects of Eckhart's work which do resonate positively with much modern thinking? Here we might point instantly to his preference for a form of internal religion. Inner space is very much a modern conception (as the Rilkean *Weltinnenraum*, the Freudian unconscious or just 'inscape'), and it is one which is abundantly present in Eckhart, though always with a spiritual connotation. For, developing from this sense of interiority is Eckhart's theme of the 'spark', a transcendent potential within the human mind. This is a generous and thoroughly modern idea in that it locates the divine image within every human being. We all possess the 'spark', according to Eckhart, in that Christ took on universal human nature. Here we are reminded of Karl Rahner's Transcendental Thomism, which has been so influential in recent years and which seeks to locate our intrinsic orientation to God in the very processes of consciousness itself.

Second, and perhaps most importantly, Eckhart's preference for speculation expressed in an abstract and philosophical vocabulary still intrigues us today. It has fascinated some of the finest modern minds, thinkers such as Martin Heidegger, Jacques Derrida, Stanislas Breton and Ernst Bloch,[1] who have found in the vernacular writings of Eckhart certain themes of significant importance to current debate. But Eckhart's imagery and language has captured the minds of numerous non-specialists too. Many are touched by his striking conceptual formulations, who have difficulty with the doctrinal positions and spiritual language of traditional Christianity. No one can doubt that Christianity is facing a crisis of communication in its ancient strongholds, and the role of Eckhartian spirituality in this context is potentially an immensely positive one, for behind his teaching on 'detachment' is an authentic insight into the centrality of radical humility, and behind his 'birth of God in the soul' is his vision of a God who incarnates and is active within us through the sovereign self-communication of grace.

Third, we find in Eckhart a positive identification of the ethical and ontological, as Dietmar Mieth's work has shown. This means that right action in the world is to be identified with right being for and in God, and thus the pernicious disjunction between mysticism (private, inner) and social action (public, external), which has affected so much modern thinking, is overcome.

Ultimately, therefore, what we find in Eckhart is a powerful presentation of the Christian faith in terms which are as fresh as they are challenging. Even if the world has changed since he preached in the cloisters and churches of fourteenth-century Rhineland, his unique voice still serves to remind us of the sacred truths and realities which are the horizons of our being.

NOTES TO EPILOGUE

1. See W. Fues, 'Unio inquantum spes: Meister Eckhart bei Ernst
   Bloch', in Haas and Stirnimann (1980), pp. 109–66, Caputo
   (1978), Breton (1985), and R. Silverman, *Derrida and
   Deconstruction* (London, Routledge, 1989). For a contribution
   on Eckhart and the concept of negative discourse in contemporary literary theory, see Marius Buning, 'Samuel Beckett's
   Negative Way: Intimations of the *Via Negativa* in his Late
   Plays' in David Jasper, ed., *European Literature and Theology
   in the Twentieth Century: Ends of Time* (London 1990), pp.
   129–42.

APPENDIX I:
ESTABLISHING THE TEXTS OF
ECKHART'S GERMAN SERMONS

Establishing the authenticity, the original content and the transmission of Eckhart's sermons has presented his researchers with particular problems. This results from two factors. The first is the fact that we are dealing primarily with texts in the form of *reportationes*, which were never scrutinized by Eckhart himself,[1] and the second is that on account of the condemnation the body of Eckhart's sermons never underwent compilation in or immediately after his own day, as was the case with Tauler and other of the leading medieval preachers.[2] His German sermons constitute therefore a *corpus disjectum*. This leads in turn to the difficulties mentioned above as well as to a major problem in our evaluation of Eckhart's thought, namely the lack of a chronological perspective in the evolution of his ideas on the basis of our ignorance of the chronology of the texts in which they are contained.

Prior to the appearance of the edition by Franz Pfeiffer in 1857, the only sermons by Meister Eckhart which were available were those included in different (and rare) editions of Tauler's work. The appendix to the Basle edition of Tauler's sermons included over fifty of Eckhart's sermons.[3] Pfeiffer's work was therefore a landmark in Eckhart studies. But, although massively influential, it fell far short of modern standards of textual criticism. The German works of Eckhart existed in numerous manuscripts scattered all over Europe, and – on account of the condemnation – many of his sermons either appeared under another's name or had no attribution. In addition, the versions of the sermons, which were in any case only *reportationes* were in different Middle High German dialects. Pfeiffer was able to make use of only forty-five manuscripts and, although he never produced a second volume in which he promised he would give a full account of the critical methodology he had applied, his decision as to what was Eckhart's work and what belonged to another hand was necessarily an arbitrary one. In his final edition Pfeiffer also attempted to normalize the different dialects of his manuscript sources by producing the whole in Alemannic (in the belief that Eckhart's birth-place was Strasburg, where this dialect had been spoken).[4]

When, in 1932, J. Quint published an overview of the manuscript tradition with respect to Eckhart's German works, he claimed to have found some two thousand errors in Pfeiffer's edition.[5] The Stuttgart edition began with an extensive search for Eckhartian material by Quint and his colleagues through libraries in Germany, Austria, Czechoslovakia and the Netherlands, which produced over two hundred and twenty manuscripts. As regards the problem of authenticity, Quint decided to apply a series of criteria. He judged those sermons to be best-attested which included material which appeared in the surviving lists of condemned articles. Although this method was not without its problems (e.g. the condemned articles had all been translated into Latin, and occasionally Eckhart had expressed reservations regarding some of the articles he was accused of having taught), it was deemed to be better than any other. These sermons were then followed by those which show a clear affinity with Meister Eckhart's Latin works. Only then did the editors have recourse to internal evidence with respect to other sermons, and to stylistic criteria for authenticity. Having established the authenticity of the sermons as far as possible however, Quint admitted that the construction of a text which would be identical to what Eckhart had actually taught was an impossibility. Due to the diversity of the manuscript tradition, and to the status of the texts as *reportationes*, any final version could at best be only an approximation to the words of the Meister himself.[6] Finally, Quint followed Pfeiffer in producing an Alemannic version of the sermons which had actually survived in different dialects. Quint knew that Eckhart had in fact come from Thuringia, and not the Alemannic-speaking area of

Strasburg, and he chose to do this in order to produce a text in the most standard form of Middle High German, and thereby to make it accessible to the greatest number of people.[7]

Quint's editorial work is universally regarded as herculean, but the danger of imbalance inherent in his editorial criteria, which give priority to the condemned articles, is evident. Recent editorial work has centred in particular upon the *Paradisus animae intelligentis* sermons, thirteen of which are still to be edited.[8] It is hoped in the long term to establish an Eckhartian corpus on broader criteria than those used by Quint, as new manuscripts become available for those sermons which, according to Quint, lacked a sufficient transmissional basis for inclusion in the critical edition.[9] There are now some one hundred and fifty sermons which can be attributed to Eckhart, of which perhaps one hundred are certainly his. The first three volumes of the Stuttgart edition contain 86 sermons, and Georg Steer (Eichstätt) is preparing a fourth.[10]

NOTES TO APPENDIX I

1. See G. Steer's remarks on this in V. Honemann and N. F. Palmer, eds (1988), pp. 400ff., although it has been argued that Eckhart did in fact have more editorial control than has been supposed. See P. G. Völker, 'Die Uberlieferungsform mittelalterlicher deutscher Predigten' in *Zeitschrift für deutsches Altertum und deutsche Literatur* 92 (1963), pp. 212–27, and K. Ruh, 'Geistliche Prosa' in W. Erzgräber, ed., *Europäisches Mittelalter* (Wiesbaden 1978), p. 580.
2. See Ruh, *Kleine Schriften* II (Berlin 1984), pp. 296–317.
3. See Cognet (1968), pp. 115f.
4. Degenhardt (1967), pp. 197ff.
5. Quint (1932), p. xix.
6. ibid., p. xxxvii.
7. Degenhardt (1967), pp. 297ff.
8. See Löser (1986), p. 209, n. 13.
9. ibid., p. 207.
10. See the overview of Eckhart's work in Haas (1989), pp. 156–8.

APPENDIX II:
ECKHART AS BIBLICAL EXEGETE

Medieval scholastic theologians are sometimes regarded as having conducted a non- or unbiblical form of theology. This reputation is undeserved in so far as the commentary on Scripture played a fundamental part in their academic formation, and the foremost theologians have left substantial tomes dedicated to scriptural exegesis. Unlike their modern counterparts however, the medieval theologians understood the Bible according to a highly allegorical system of interpretation. The principle of multiple meanings in Scripture was bequeathed by Origen to the Christian Middle Ages, where it became the established four-fold system of interpretation whereby the text possesses a literal, allegorical, tropological and anagogical meaning.[1]

Meister Eckhart reflects the medieval concern with the central place of Scripture in theology in his extensive biblical commentaries. But, although we do find in Eckhart's work reference to the traditional terms of the four-fold scheme (i.e. *mystice exponere, sensus tropologicus*), we find in practice that Eckhart applies only two levels of meaning: the literal sense and a figurative one (what he calls *parabola*). To read a text *parabolice* is simply to apply to it a level of non-literal meaning, without further sub-division. K. Weiss has argued that we find in Eckhart an Augustinian dual system of a literal and non-literal meaning, for which latter Eckhart employs a number of terms.[2]

In his prologue to the *Liber Parabolarum Genesis* (*In Gen.* 2, n. 1; see EE, pp. 92f.) Eckhart states that the non-literal level of meaning contains *divina, moralia* and *naturalia*, which is to say information pertaining to divine matters as well as those of morality and natural science. Here Eckhart is reflecting the influence of the Jewish philosopher, Moses Maimonides.[3] The sense of the unity of natural and divine law is characteristic of Eckhart's unifying method in general, however, and finds expression also in his harmonization of Aristotle, Moses and Christ, according to which Aristotle taught natural or philosophical truth, Moses moral truth and Christ himself *is* truth in such a way that he contains the other two.

Eckhart places great value on the process of biblical exegesis, and the Book of Commentaries holds an equal place with the Book of Propositions and Book of Questions in his *Tripartite Work*. He even states that 'Christ, the Truth' is the 'hidden marrow' of the scriptures (*In Gen.* 3; EE, p. 94). But it is important to note that Eckhart always interprets that 'Truth' in the light of the philosophical and theological principles already worked out in the other two books. And it is this fact, perhaps, which accounts for Eckhart's preference for a dual system of biblical interpretation, whereby he reserves for himself a greater flexibility and freedom to explore his own ideas through a scriptural medium than would otherwise be the case.

NOTES TO APPENDIX II

1. These are well summed up by Andrew Louth in his article in 'Allegorical Interpretation' in R. J. Coggins and J. L. Houlden, eds, in *Dictionary of Biblical Interpretation* (London, SCM, 1990), pp. 12–14.
2. See K. Weiss, 'Meister Eckharts biblische Hermeneutik' in *La Mystique Rhénane*, pp. 99f.; see also Tobin (1986), pp. 23–9.
3. See Koch (1973), pp. 349–66, and H. Liebeschütz, 'Meister Eckhart und Moses Maimonides' in *Archiv für Kulturgeschichte* 54 (1972), pp. 64–96.

APPENDIX III:
A REGISTER OF ECKHART'S GERMAN SERMONS

W	DW	DP	PF	B	FOX	EV	CS	CL	SCH
1		57	1	1					
2		58	2	2					
3			3	3					
4		59	4	4	17				
5	65		5						
6	1	1	6	13	32			i	
7	76	35	7		23				p.131
8	2	2	8	24	20			ii	p.3
9	86	28	9		34	1,2			
10	25	38	10	17	16	2,11		iii	
11	26	49	11						p.55
12	27	50	12		22				
13a	5a							xxii	
13b	5b	6	13	5	14				
14a	16a								
14b	16b		14					iv	
15		44	15						
16	29	29	74	21	25				
17	28	31	81	20					
18	30	43	66		2		p.58		p.181
19	71	37	19						p.122
20	44		20						
21	17		21					v	
22	53		22	1					
23	47		23	7					
24a	13							xxiii	
24b	13a		24						
25	3		25	9				vi	
26	57					2, 45			
27	34		27						
28	78		28						

W	DW	DP	PF	B	FOX	EV	CS	CL	SCH
29	**38**		**29**			**1,29 & 2,27**			
30	45		30						
31	**37**		**31**						
32a	20a		32					vii	
32b	**20b**								
33		35	33						
34	55		34						
35	**19**		**35**					viii	
36	18		36					ix	
37			37						
38	36a		38						
39	36b								
40	4	4	40	19	29			x	
41	**70**	**53**	**41**						
42	69	40	42	15				xi	
43	41	46	43			2,12			
44	58								
45	**60**	**45**	**45**		27				
46	54b		46						
47	46		47						
48	31	47							
49	77								
50	14							xxv	
51	15				11			xxi	
52	**32**	**30**		**14**					
53	22	23	88					xviii	
54	23								
55	62	48	55						
56		26	56	27	3			xii	
57	12	13	96					xx	
58	26	27	58			2,13			
59	39	25	59		33		p.53		
60	48	34	60						
61			61						
62	**82**	**54**	**62**						
63	40		63						
64	81		64		26				
65	6	7	65	18				xiii	
66	10	11	83					xvi	

W	DW	DP	PF	B	FOX	EV	CS	CL	SCH
67	9	10	84					xvii	
68	11	12	90	12				xix	
69	68	36	69	6	9				
70	67				28				
71	59								
72	7	8	72		31			xiv	
73	73	33	73						
74	74		86						
75			75						
76	61					2,50			
77	63								
78	64					2,1			
79	43	52	79						
80	42	39	80	7	8				
81	33					2,38			
82	8	9	82	16	4			xv	
83	51	24	102	11					
84	84					2,42			
85	85				19	2,43			
86	56					2,32			
87	52	32	87	28	15				p.214
88	75		85		5				
89	49		89		24	2,14			
90			103						
91	79	41	91	10	10				
92	24		94		6				
93	50		95						
94	80	55	97						
95	72	56	98						
96	83	42	99		12				
97	21	22	100		13			xxi	

The above register is adapted from that provided by Richard
Woods in his *Eckhart's Way*, with the additional denotation by
bold face of all those sermons in English translation which are
contained in the *Paradisus animae* collection. The German sermons
included in the two volumes edited by B. McGinn (translated by
E. Colledge and F. Tobin respectively) follow the DW numbering,
as will the German sermons in my own *Meister Eckhart: Selected
German Works* which is under preparation for the Penguin
Classics series.

SELECT BIBLIOGRAPHY

This bibliography contains only the most important works on Eckhart. More complete bibliographies can be found in Degenhardt (1967), Schaller (1968 and 1969), O'Meara (1978), Fues (1981) and Sturlese (1987).

TEXTS

Meister Eckhart: Die deutschen und lateinischen Werke, hrsg., im Auftrage der deutschen Forschungsgemeinschaft. Stuttgart and Berlin, Kohlhammer Verlag, 1936ff.

Jostes, F., ed., *Meister Eckhart und seine Jünger: ungedruckte zur Geschichte der deutschen Mystik*. Freiburg, Switzerland, 1895 (repr. De Gruyter 1972).

McGinn, B., *The Mystical Thought of Meister Eckhart: The Man from Whom God Hid Nothing*. New York, Crossroad Publishing Company, 2003.

Pfeiffer, F., ed., *Meister Eckhart* (Deutsche Mystiker des Mittelalters Bd. 2). Leipzig 1987 (repr. Scientia Verlag Aalen 1962).

Seelhorst, Jörg, *Autoreferentialität und Transformation: zur Funktion mystischen Sprechens bei Mechthild von Magdeburg, Meister Eckhart und Heinrich Seuse*. Tübingen, 2003.

HISTORICAL DOCUMENTS

Daniels, A., ed., 'Eine lateinische Rechtfertigungsschrift des Meister Eckharts' in *Beiträge zur Geschichte der Philosophie des Mittelalters* 23, 5, Münster 1923.

Kaepelli, Th., ed., 'Kurze Mitteilungen über mittelalterliche Dominikanerschriftsteller' in *Archivum fratrum Praedicatorum* 10 (1940), pp. 293–4.

Kaepelli, Th., ed., 'Praedicator monoculus. Sermons parisiens de la fin du XIIIe siècle' in *Archivum fratrum Praedicatorum* 27 (1957), pp. 120–67.

Kaepelli, Th., ed., 'Eine Kölner Handschrift mit lateinischen Eckhart-Exzerpten' in *Archivum fratrum Praedicatorum* 31 (1961), pp. 204–12.

Laurent, M. H., 'Autour du procès de Maître Eckhart: Les documents des Archives Vaticanes' in *Divus Thomas* ser. III, 13 (1936), pp. 331–48, 430–47.

Pelster, F., ed., 'Ein Gutachten aus dem Eckehart-Prozess in Avignon' in *Beiträge zur Geschichte der Philosophie des Mittelalters* suppl. vol. III, 2 (Münster 1935), pp. 1099–1124 (Festschrift for M. Grabmann, vol. 2).

Théry, G., ed., 'Edition critique des pièces relatives au procès d'Eckhart continues dans le manuscrit 33b de la bibliothèque de Soest' in *Archives d'histoire doctrinale et littéraire du moyen âge* 1 (1926), pp. 129–268.

ENGLISH TRANSLATIONS

Blakney, R. B., *Meister Eckhart*. New York, Harper and Row, 1941.

Clark, J. M., *Meister Eckhart: an Introduction to the Study of his Works with an Anthology of his Sermons*. Edinburgh, Nelson, 1957.

Clark, J. M. and Skinner, J. V., *Treatises and Sermons of Meister Eckhart*. New York, Harper and Row, 1958.

Colledge, E. and McGinn, B., *Meister Eckhart: the Essential Sermons, Commentaries, Treatises and Defence*. New York, Paulist Press, 1981.

Davies, O., *The Rhineland Mystics: an anthology*. London, SPCK, 1989; New York, Crossroad, 1990.

Davies, O., *Meister Eckhart: Selected Writings*. Harmondsworth, Penguin Classics, 1994.

Evans, C. de B., *Meister Eckhart by Franz Pfeiffer*. 2 vols., London 1924 and 1931.

Fleming, U., *Meister Eckhart: the Man from whom God nothing hid*. London, Fount, 1988 (based on C. de B. Evans's translation).

Fox, M., *Breakthrough: Meister Eckhart's Creation Spirituality in New Translation*. New York, Image Books, 1980.

Maurer, A., *Master Eckhart: Parisian Questions and Prologues*. Toronto, Pontifical Institute of Medieval Studies, 1974.

McGinn, B. with Tobin, F. and Borgstadt, E., *Meister Eckhart: Teacher and Preacher.* Classics of Western Spirituality. London, SPCK; New York, Paulist Press, 1986.
Walshe, M. O'C., *The Complete Mystical Works of Meister Eckhart.* New York, Crossroad Publishing Company, 2010 (third edn with a foreword by B. McGinn).

The most authoritative translation of the German sermons and treatises is that by M. O'C. Walshe, while A. Maurer and B. McGinn provide good translations of the Latin prologues, Parisian questions and biblical commentaries.

SECONDARY LITERATURE

Books

Albert, K., *Meister Eckharts These vom Sein: Untersuchungen zur Metaphysik des Opus Tripartitum.* Saarbrücken 1976.
Breton, S., *Deux mystiques de l'excès.* Paris 1985.
Brunner, F., *Maître Eckhart.* Paris 1969.
Caputo, J., *The Mystical Element in Heidegger's Thought.* Ohio 1978.
Cognet, L., *Introduction aux mystiques rhéno-flamands.* Paris 1968.
Davies, O., *God Within: The Mystical Tradition of Northern Europe.* London, Darton, Longman and Todd; New York, Paulist Press, 1988.
Degenhardt, I., *Studien zum Wandel des Eckhartbildes.* Leiden 1967.
Fischer, H., *Meister Eckhart.* Freiburg and Munich, Verlag Karl Alber, 1974.
Flasch, K., ed., *Von Meister Dietrich zu Meister Eckhart.* Hamburg 1984.
Fues, W. M., *Mystik als Erkenntnis? Kritische Studien zur Meister-Eckhart-Forschung.* Bonn 1981 (with thematic bibliography).
Haas, A. M., *Sermo mysticus: Studien zu Theologie und Sprache der deutschen Mystik.* Freiburg, Switzerland, 1979.
Haas, A. M. and Stirnimann, H., *Das 'Einig Ein'.* Freiburg, Switzerland, 1980.

Haas, A. M., *Geistliches Mittelalter.* Freiburg, Switzerland, 1984.

Haas, A. M., *Gott leiden, Gott lieben.* Frankfurt am Main, Insel Verlag, 1989a.

Haas, A. M., *Deum mistice videre . . . in caligine coincidencie: Zum Verhältnis Nikolaus' von Kues zur Mystik.* Basel and Frankfurt am Main, 1989b.

Kelley, C. F., *Meister Eckhart on Divine Knowledge.* New Haven, Yale University Press, 1977.

Koch, J., *Kleine Schriften* I. Rome 1973.

La mystique rhénane: colloque de Strasbourg. Paris 1963.

Langer, O., *Mystische Erfahrung und spirituelle Theologie.* Munich 1987.

Largier, N., *Bibliographie zu Meister Eckhart.* Freiburg, Switzerland, 1989.

Libera, A. de, *Le problème de l'être chez Maître Eckhart: logique et métaphysique de l'analogie.* Geneva-Lausanne-Neuchâtel 1980.

Libera, A. de, *Introduction à la mystique rhénane.* Paris, O.E.I.L., 1984.

Lossky, V., *Théologies négative et connaissance de Dieu chez Maître Eckhart.* Paris 1960.

McDonnell, E., *The Beguines and Beghards in Medieval Culture.* New York 1969.

McGinn, B., *The Mystical Thought of Meister Eckhart: The Man from Whom God Hid Nothing.* New York, Crossroad Publishing Company, 2001.

Mieth, D., *Die Einheit von Vita activa und Vita contemplativa in den deutschen Predigten und Traktaten Meister Eckharts und bei Johannes Tauler.* Regensburg 1969.

Milem, B. *The Unspoken Word: Negative Theology in Meister Eckhart's German Sermons.* Washington, DC, Catholic University of America Press, 2002.

Mojsisch, B., *Meister Eckhart. Analogie, Univozität und Einheit.* Hamburg 1983.

Quint, J., *Die Überlieferung der deutschen Predigten Meister Eckharts.* Bonn 1932.

Ruh, K., ed., *Altdeutsche und altniederländische Mystik.* Darmstadt 1964.

Ruh, K., *Meister Eckhart: Theologe, Prediger, Mystiker.* Munich 1985 (1989²).

Schürmann, R., *Meister Eckhart: Mystic and Philosopher.* Bloomington and London 1978.

Seppanen, L., *Meister Eckeharts Konzeption der Sprachbedeutung.* Tübingen 1985.

Soudek, E., *Meister Eckhart.* Stuttgart, Metzler, 1973.

Smith, C., *Meister Eckhart: The Way of Paradox.* London, Darton, Longman and Todd, 1988.

Steer, G. and Sturlese, L. (eds), *Lectura Eckhardi: Predigten Meister Eckharts von Fachgelehrten gelesen und gedeutet.* Stuttgart, 1998.

Tobin, F., *Meister Eckhart: Thought and Language.* Philadelphia, University of Pennsylvania Press, 1986.

Trusen, W., *Der Prozess gegen Meister Eckhart.* Paderborn, Schöningh, 1988.

Tugwell, S., *Albert and Thomas: Selected Writings.* New York, Paulist Press, 1988.

Woods, R., *Eckhart's Way.* Delaware, Michael Glazier, 1986; London, Darton, Longman and Todd, 1987.

Zum Brunn, E. and Libera, A. de, *Métaphysique de verbe et théologie negative.* Paris 1984.

Articles

Albrecht, E., 'Zur Herkunft Meister Eckharts' in *Amtsblatt der Evangelisch-Lutherischen Kirche in Thüringen* Jg. 31, nr. 3, 10 (February 1978).

Brunner, F., 'L'analogie chez Maître Eckhart' in *Freiburger Zeitschrift für Philosophie und Theologie* 16 (1969), pp. 333–49.

Colledge, E. and Marler, J. C., ' "Poverty of the will": Ruusbroec, Eckhart and "The Mirror of Simple Souls" ' in Mommaers, P. and de Paepe, N., eds, *Jan van Ruusbroec: the sources, content and sequels of his mysticism* (Louvain 1984), pp. 14–47.

Davies, O., 'Why were Meister Eckhart's propositions condemned?' in *New Blackfriars* 71 (October 1990), pp. 433–45.

Davies, O., 'Hildegard of Bingen, Mechthild of Magdeburg and the young Meister Eckhart' in *Mediävistik* 4 (1991).

Flasch, K., 'Die Intention Meister Eckharts' in Röttges, Scheer and Simon, eds, *Festschrift für Bruno Liebrucks* (Meisenheim, Glan, 1974), pp. 292–318.

Flasch, K., 'Kennt die mittelalterliche Philosophie die Konstitutive Funktion des menschlichen Denkens?' in *Kant-Studien* 63 (1972), pp. 182–206.

Haas, A. M., 'Die Problematik von Sprache und Erfahrung in der deutschen Mystik' in *Grundfragen der Mystik* (Einsiedeln 1974), pp. 73–104.

Haas, A. M., 'Schools of Late Medieval Mysticism' in Raitt, J., ed., *Christian Spirituality: High Middle Ages and Reformation* (London, Routledge, 1987), pp. 140–75.

Löser, F., 'Als ich mê gesprochen hân' in *Zeitschrift für deutsches Altertum und deutsche Literatur* 115 (1986), pp. 206–27.

McGinn, B., 'Meister Eckhart's condemnation reconsidered' in *The Thomist* 44 (1980), pp. 390–414.

McGinn, B., 'Meister Eckhart on God as Absolute Unity' in O'Meara, D., ed., *Neoplatonism and Christian Thought* (Albany, State University of New York Press, 1982), pp. 128–39.

O'Meara, Th. F. et al., 'An Eckhart Bibliography' in *The Thomist* 42 (1978), pp. 313–36.

Quint, J., 'Die Sprache Meister Eckharts als Ausdruck seiner mystischen Geisteswelt' in *Deutsche Vierteljahrsschrift für Literaturwissenschaft und Geistesgeschichte* 6 (1928), pp. 671–701.

Schaller, T., 'Die Meister-Eckhart Forschung von der Jahrhundertwende bis zur Gegenwart' in *Freiburger Zeitschrift für philosophie und Theologie* 15 (1968), pp. 262–316, 403–26.

Schaller, T., 'Zur Eckhart-Deutung der letzten 30 Jahre' in *Freiburger Zeitschrift für Philosophie und Theologie* 16 (1969), pp. 22–39.

Steer, G., 'Germanistische Scholastikforschung: ein Bericht' in *Theologie und Philosophie* 45 (1970), pp. 204–26; 46 (1971), pp. 195–222; 48 (1973), pp. 65–106.

Steer, G., 'Der Prozess Meister Eckharts und die Folgen' in *Literaturwissenschaftliches Jahrbuch* 27 (1986), pp. 47–64.

Steer, G., 'Meister Eckhart – Predigten in Handschriften des 14. Jahrhunderts' in Honemann, V. and Palmer, N., eds, *Deutsche Handschriften 1100–1400, Oxforder Colloquium 1985* (Tübingen 1988), pp. 399–407.

Stötzel, G., 'Zum Nominalstil Meister Eckharts' in *Wirkendes Wort* 16 (1966), pp. 289–309.

Sturlese, L., 'Recenti studi su Eckhart' in *Giornale critico della filosofia italiana* an. LXVI, fasc. II (Florence 1987), pp. 368–77.

INDEX

à Kempis, Thomas *see Imitation of Christ*
abegescheidenheit see Meister Eckhart: detachment
Abelard, Peter 27, 53n, 85
Agnes, Queen of Hungary 26
Alan of Lille 86
Albert, Karl 108
Albert of Milan 27
Albert the Great 17, 36, 86-95, 142, 198, 205
Albrecht, King 44
Alexander III, Pope 197
Alexander of Hales 86, 141
Amalric of Bene 108n
Ambrose 140
Anexagoras 129
Angelus Silesius 227-8
Anna of Ramswag 76
apatheia 161-2
Archbishop of Cologne *see* Henry II of Virneburg
Aristotle 1, 85, 87, 90, 111n, 118, 129-31, 235, 242
Athanasius 140, 162
Athenagoras 161
Augustine 88n, 89, 91, 119, 128-34, 140-2, 199, 242
Averroes 130
Avicenna 91

Barbarossa, Frederick 41, 52
Basil the Great 140, 142
beatific vision 86, 89, 196
Beatrice of Nazareth 72, 221
Beghards 35-6
Beguines 35-40, 54, 59, 69-79, 221
Benedict of Nursia 161; rule of 161
Benedict XI, 35
Benedict XII 196

Benedictus deus see Benedict XII
Berengar of Landora 33, 37, 71
Bernard of Clairvaux 52, 144, 148, 161, 222
Berthold of Neiffen 42
Bloch, Ernst 237
Boccasini, Nicholas 60n
Boehme, Jacob 227
Bonaventure 128, 142, 144
Boniface XIII 35
Book of Spiritual Poverty 224-5
Bowie, Fiona 52n, 69nn
Brautmystik 61, 148
Breton, Stanislaus 237
Brunner, Fernand 103n
Buddhism 1, 19, 195, 212-13
Büttner, Hermann 15, 16

Cagnoli, Barnabas 33
Cajetan, Cardinal 101-2
Cambrai, Bishop of (Guy II) 65, 67
Canisius, Peter 226
Cassian, John 161
Charles the Great 41
Christina Mirabilis 73
Clement of Alexandria 127, 140, 144, 161
Clement IV 38, 70
Clement V 35
Colledge, Edmund 24n, 221n; and Marler, J. C. 66-7
Conrad of Halberstadt 28, 198
Courtly Love *see* Minnesang
Cyprian of Carthage 128
Cyril of Alexandria 140

Damascene, John 144
Dante, Alighieri 60n
de Certeau, Michel 118
Degenhardt, Ingeborg 13, 14

Denifle, Heinrich Seuse 14-16, 76-7, 155n, 224, 229
Derrida, Jacques 237
Diadochus of Photike 128
Dietrich of Apolda 60
Dietrich of Freiberg 17, 89-95, 116n, 130, 132, 205-6
Dinzelbacher, Peter 74n, 76n
Diogenes of Apollonia 129
divinization 140-1
Dominican Order *passim*
Dronke, Peter 52, 57n

Elisabeth of Beggenhofen 74, 76
Elisabeth of Oye 74-6
Eriugena, John Scotus 130, 134, 144
Evagrius of Pontikus 128

Ferchius 38n
Flasch, Kurt 4n, 116n
Flowing Light of the Godhead see Mechthild of Magdeburg
Fox, Matthew 18
Franciscan Order 24, 27, 34n; 38n, 38-40, 44, 70, 128, 142, 224; Francis, St of Assisi 68, 73, 161
Frauenfrage 68-72
Frederick the Fair 35
Frederick II 41
Free Spirit, heresy of 36, 40, 220n
Freud, Sigmund 130

Gallus, Thomas 222
Gertrude the Great 215
Gilbert of Poitiers 85
Gilson, Etienne 6, 102n
Godefroid de Fontaine 66
Gonsalvus of Valvoa 24, 54n
grace 141-2
'greenness': in Hildegard 52, 57n, 65; in Eckhart 56-9, 182
Gregory the Great 88n
Gregory of Nyssa 128, 130, 134, 162, 222
Grote, Geert 222n
Grundmann, Herbert 16, 65, 77-8
Guerric of St Quentin, Master 86

Guigo II 161
Guillelmus Petri de Godino 30
Guy II *see* Cambrai, Bishop of

Haas, Alois Maria 4n, 17
Hadewijch of Antwerp (or Brabant) 72, 51n, 148n, 221-2, 222 (Hadewijch II)
Harphius 215
Hegel, Friedrich 12
Heidegger, Martin 237
Helfta, convent of 59-60
Henricus de Cigno 29
Henry of Luxemburg 42
Henry of Nördlingen 60
Henry II of England 52
Henry II of Virneburg 27, 30, 33-45
Heraclitus 130
Hermann de Summo 28
Hermann of Minden 70
Herveus Natalis 32
Hildegard of Bingen 51-9, 54n
Hinduism (Vedantic) 212-13
Hornstein, Xavier 33n
Hugh of Rouen 86
Hugh of St Cher 86
Hugh Ripelin of Strasburg 88, 91
Humbert of the Romans 4
Humbert, William of Paris 65

Ignatius of Antioch 161
Ignatius of Loyola 215n
Imbach, Rudi 109n
Imitation of Christ 223
In agro dominico 30-45, 108n, 118-20, 127n, 196-8, 215, 222
intellect: human 87-95, 134-9; divine 89-95, 110-12, 134-9, 205-7
Irenaeus 127, 140, 143

Jaspers, Karl 193
Jerome 131
John XXII, 1, 26, 28-30, 33-4, 39-45, 53; letter to Henry of 3 June 1324 44, 44n
John of Bohemia 43
John of the Cross 230

John of Zurich (Bishop of
    Strasburg) 37, 38n, 39-40
Juan de los Angeles 230

Kaepelli, Thomas 22n
Karrer, Otto 16, 44
Kelley, C. F. 18
kenosis 211
Kilwardby, Robert 31n
Klibansky, Raymund 109n
Koch, Josef 16, 27, 29, 32n, 103n,
    105, 155n

Langer, Otto 71, 77-8, 78n
Leidensmystik 74-5
Lerner, Robert 36, 37n
Lewis of Bavaria 28, 34, 38n,
    41-5
Libera, Alain de 91
'Lives of Nuns' 73-6
Lombard, Peter 23, 141
Lossky, Vladimir 108n, 118n
Luther, Martin 12-16, 105n,
    224-6

Maimonides, Moses 242
Mainz, Archbishop of 53
Marie of Oignies 69, 73
Maximus the Confessor 129,
    140, 144, 162
Maurer, Armand 119
McDonnell, Ernest 71n
McGinn, Bernard 18, 30n, 107n
Mechthild of Magdeburg 51, 53,
    59-65, 72, 215
Meister Eckhart life: 22-50, con-
    demnation 26-45, retraction
    29, 29n; works: *Beati pauperes
    spiritu* 66-8, 200-1, 222,
    biblical commentaries 25-8,
    Comm. on Exodus 120, 203,
    Comm. on John 105, 111,
    Comm. on Wisdom 103, 119,
    Defence 28-30, 119, *Liber
    benedictus* 26-7, 40, 105, 107,
    111 (lost defence 27), On
    Detachment 164, Parisian
    Questions 110-11, 113, 138,
    205-7, Prologue to Book of

Prop. 107, Talks of Instruction
    24, 24n, 71 and n, 169, 221n,
    Three-Part Work 108-9, 111,
    243, sermons 16, 27, 72,
    126-7, 182, 215, 231, 239-41;
    language 5, 17, 176-94, 196,
    poetic imagery 155-7, 174,
    180-4; **spirituality** 160-76,
    birth of God in soul 145-55,
    163, 174, 237, detachment 62,
    162-76, 181, 216, 237, poverty
    of spirit 65-8, suffering 172-4,
    virtues 166-9, works 67, 171-2;
    thought 99-125, analogy 17,
    100-7, 103n, 105nn, 118n,
    138, being and God 107-10,
    116-18, 155, createdness
    (suppression of) 5, 199-201,
    creation 118-19, 151, dialectic
    5, 116-18, 208-9, divine image
    127-39, God and Godhead *see*
    Trinity, God as intellect 110-
    12, 116-18, ground of the soul
    see spark, *inquantum* 107-9,
    117, 138, 154, 188, mystic or
    theologian 3, 99, negation of
    negation, 109, 113-14, 208,
    nothingness (of creatures) 119-
    20, 174, 211-12, 216, One
    112-15, 138, 168, 203,
    orthodoxy 195-214, pantheism
    (charge of) 14, 108, 138,
    paradox 6, 185-7, 192-3, role
    of knowledge 3, 4, spark of the
    soul 63, 131, 138n, 155, 174,
    198-9, 216, 236, transcendent-
    als 104n, 126 *see also* analogy,
    Trinity 4, 117, 201-5, 212, 223
Mercurian, Everard 215
Michael of Cesena 45
Mieth, Dietmar 17, 237
Minnesang 14-15, 59, 61, 72
Mirror of Simple Souls see Porete,
    Margaret
Mojsisch, Bernard 90n, 206

Neoplatonism 1, 17, 85, 89, 113,
    129-30, 201, 210-11, 235
Newman, Barbara 52

Nicene Creed 105, 154
Nicholas V, anti-pope 44
Nicholas of Cusa (Cusanus) 228-9, 231
Nicholas of Strasburg 26-8, 27n, 31n, 32-4, 33n
Nihilianism see Alexander III
Nonnenvitae see 'Lives of Nuns'

Ochsenbein, Peter 74
Origen 128-9, 140, 144, 242
Ötenbach, convent of 74-5
Otto the First 41
Otto, Rudolf 16

Palamas, Gregory 116n, 140-1
Paradisus animae intelligentis 54 and n, 56n, 241
Petrus de Estate 27
Pfeiffer, Franz 11, 13, 18, 239
Phillip the Chancellor 143
Phillips, Dayton 39
Philo of Alexandria 129
Plato: Timaeus 129, 131
Plotinus 129, 210
Porete, Margaret 36, 51, 65-8
Proclus 89-90, 107n, 109n, 210
Pseudo-Dionysius (Denys) 85, 91, 140

Quint, Josef 16, 54, 184, 189-90, 240-1

Rahner, Karl 236-7
Reinerius Frisco 27
Reynolds, Lyndon 203
Richard of St Victor 144, 161
Romanticism 11-15
Rosenberg, Alfred 15
Ruh, Kurt 3, 26, 32n, 44, 65-7, 77
Ruusbroec, Jan van 143, 148n, 215, 221-2, 227, 230-1

Scheffler, Johannes see Angelus Silesius
Schmidt, Carl 13
Schopenhauer, Arthur 19
Schürmann, Reiner 18
Schwamborn, Gregor 34n, 35

Schwesternbücher see 'Lives of Nuns'
Scotus, Duns 38n
Sentences see Lombard, Peter
Siger of Brabant 23
Smith, Cyprian 17
Southern, Richard 70n
Steer, Georg 241
Stoics 161
Strauch, Phillip 15
Sturlese, Loris 11n, 22n, 89n
Suarez 101-2
Surius, Laurentius 216, 226, 230
Suso, Henry (Seuse, Heinrich) 12-18, 75, 215, 218-21, 230-1
synderesis see Meister Eckhart: spark of the soul

Tauler, John (Johannes) 12, 18, 53 and n, 64n, 75, 215-31, 239
Tempier, Bishop Stephen 31n, 118
Teresa of Avila 230
Tertullian 128, 140
Theologia Deutsch 18, 222-30
Thierry of Chartres 86
Thomas Aquinas 14, 16, 44, 88n, 89, 93, 100-2, 108n, 109n, 128, 130, 142-3, 198, 235
Tobin, Frank 18, 105n, 109n, 187
Trusen, Winfried 27n, 28n, 31, 31n, 33n, 34n, 38, 38n
Tugwell, Simon 24n, 85

Ubbink, R. A. 221n
Ulrich of Strasburg 88-9, 91, 93

van Leeuwen, Jan 222
van Wevel, Godfried 221n
Verdeyen, Paul 36n
Vienne, Council of 36, 37n, 39-40, 70
viriditas see 'greenness'
von Baader, Franz 12
von Balthasar, Hans Urs 4n, 208n

Wadding 38n
Walshe, Maurice O'Connell 18

Weiss, Konrad 242
Wenck, Johannes 229
Wentzlaff-Eggebert, F. W. 77
Wesensmystik 72n, 218, 225
Wikbold von Holte 35
William of Auvergne 86
William of Auxerre 143

William of Nidecke 28
William of Ockham 34, 45
William of St Thierry 143, 161,
    221-2
Winkworth, Susanne 18
Woods, Richard 18

Printed in Great Britain
by Amazon

18275241R00159